WINNING
IN THE
A Lifetime
of Football
TRENCHES

Forrest Gregg and Andrew O'Toole

CLERISY PRESS

Published by Clerisy Press
Distributed by Publishers Group West
First edition, first printing

For further information, contact the publisher at:

CLERISY PRESS
1700 Madison Road
Cincinnati, OH 45206
www.clerisypress.com

Library of Congress Cataloging-in-Publication Data:

Gregg, Forrest, 1933-
Winning in the trenches: a lifetime of football / by Forrest Gregg and Andrew O'Toole.
p. cm.
ISBN-13: 978-1-57860-363-3 ISBN-10: 1-57860-363-3
1. Gregg, Forrest, 1933- 2. Football coaches--United States--Biography.
3. Football players--United States--Biography. 4. Green Bay Packers (Football team)
5. Cleveland Browns (Football team : 1946-1995)
I. O'Toole, Andrew. II. Title.
GV939.G745A3 2009
796.332092--dc22
[B]
2009025304

EDITED BY JACK HEFFRON AND DONNA POEHNER

COVER AND INTERIOR DESIGNED BY STEPHEN SULLIVAN

COVER IMAGE COURTESY OF GETTY IMAGES/ROBERT RIGER
THE FOLLOWING PHOTOS COURTESY OF VERN BIEVER: PAGES 13, 19, 98, 120, 134-35
PAGES 76-77, COURTESY OF PAUL HORNUNG
PAGE 152, COURTESY OF THE DALLAS COWBOYS
PAGES 170 AND 187, COURTESY OF THE CLEVELAND BROWNS
PAGE 184, COURTESY OF THE PRO FOOTBALL HALL OF FAME
ALL OTHER PHOTOS ARE TAKEN FROM THE PERSONAL COLLECTION OF FORREST GREGG.

Printed in the United States of America

To the three most important people in my life—

Barbara, Forrest Jr., and Karen—

With love

CONTENTS

Acknowledgments   vi

Introduction   *From East Texas to Canton*   8

1   **WINNING...IS THE ONLY THING**   12

2   **A PLACE CALLED BIRTHRIGHT**   20

3   **COLLEGE DAYS AT SMU**   44

4   **GOD, FAMILY, AND THE GREEN BAY PACKERS**   58

5   **RUNNING FOR DAYLIGHT**   90

6   **THE LONG GOODBYE**   136

7   **STARTING ANEW**   158

8   **REDEMPTION**   194

9   **A PACKER AGAIN**   244

10   **MIRACLE ON MOCKINGBIRD**   270

11   **IT'S JUST NOT THE SAME**   302

Appendix   316

ACKNOWLEDGMENTS

I n the back of this book there is a list of achievements and awards Forrest Gregg has accumulated during the course of his remarkable football career. This accounting is necessary because Forrest isn't one to tout his own accomplishments. Oh, you'll learn of teammates, coaches, and championships in these pages, but since Forrest isn't one to pat himself on the back, I will.

Perhaps the greatest testament to Forrest Gregg as a football player came from his coach, the legendary Vince Lombardi, who once proclaimed Forrest to be, "the finest player I ever coached." High praise, indeed, but he is so much more than a football legend. Most importantly, Forrest Gregg is one of the finest gentlemen to ever step foot on a National Football League field. His rise from very humble beginnings in Depression-era East Texas to one of the NFL's most respected citizens is an inspiration.

I hope readers of this book will find as much enjoyment in getting to know Forrest Gregg as I have.

———

Forrest and I first met while I was writing a biography of Paul Brown. The conversation took place on the telephone, and toward the end of our talk

ACKNOWLEDGMENTS

Forrest mentioned that a few friends had been suggesting that he write his life story. Some months later, after the Brown manuscript was off to the publisher, Forrest and I were brought together by one of his SMU players, Greg Ziegler. I'd like to thank Greg for the significant role he played in making this book a reality. He's been a fountain of information for me and a source of encouragement for Forrest.

Perhaps the most enjoyable aspect of this project was having the opportunity to meet Barbara, Forrest's wife of forty-nine years. Barbara provided me with a deeper understanding of Forrest and offered an intriguing point of view of her husband's life and career. Thanks for everything, Barbara.

A number of others were helpful in putting this book together.

Forrest's teammates and friends—Paul Hornung and Willie Davis

With the Cleveland Browns—Dino Lucarelli and Bob Markowitz

With the Cincinnati Bengals—Jack Brennan, PJ Combs, and Jan Sutton

With Southern Methodist University—Brad Sutton

———

And always, thanks and love to my bride, Mickie. It's a beautiful thing, this life we have.

— *Andrew O'Toole*

INTRODUCTION

From East Texas to Canton

When people see me today they notice the big diamond-studded ring I wear on my right hand.

"What's that ring?" they ask.

"It's from Super Bowl II."

Invariably they respond with, "You were in the first two Super Bowls. Where's the ring for the first one?"

"It's in a safe deposit box," I tell them.

The jewelry may be safely locked up, but the memories still flash in my mind. I was fortunate to play for six NFL championship teams, and that ring from the second Super Bowl holds special significance because it was our third consecutive title in Green Bay, something no other team had previously achieved. But it's the first title—and our victory over the New York Giants in 1961 to win the title—I savor most. I had been in the league for five years at that point, long enough to realize that every player doesn't get the opportunity to play in a championship game. I couldn't know at the time that we would be back to battle for the league title four more times before the decade ended.

It's the luck of the draw when a player is drafted into the NFL out of college. What would have happened to me if I had signed with the

Canadian Football League? Or what if I were drafted by the Los Angeles Rams, which is where I hoped to go? My career would have been far different. I was fortunate that the Green Bay Packers selected me—out of SMU in 1956.

At the time, of course, I wasn't sure if I'd gotten all that lucky. The Packers had been mired in mediocrity for decades. And I wasn't sure where Green Bay was located. Still, I was thankful that a professional football team wanted me and thought I was good enough to play at that level.

Still, the Green Bay Packers?

But fortune smiles on us in funny ways. The Packers were building the nucleus of one of pro football's great dynasties. Bart Starr, Jim Taylor, Paul Hornung, Bill Forester, Ray Nitschke, Jerry Kramer, Dan Curry… so many of us came into the league within a year or two of one another. We grew up together, learned together, and won together.

Indeed, my life has been blessed. Throughout my childhood I lived and worked on a farm where money was scarce and food hard to come by. Heck, I never even laid eyes on a football game until the ninth grade, when I suited up for my first high school contest. I've accomplished much through hard work and diligence, but nothing I've achieved would have come about without the help of others. Our actions, the events we live, and the people who touch us—these are the things that define us. And as I sit down ready to commit my memories to paper, the names and faces rush before me.

I was recruited to Southern Methodist University by Sleepy Morgan, a fella from Sulphur Springs, Texas. I remember Sleepy telling me once, "Don't ever forget where you came from. Don't ever forget the people who helped get you there." And I haven't forgotten. Not Birthright or Sulphur Springs—two dusty Texas towns that helped form me. Nor did I forget Bill Chapman, who hired me to work in his cleaners while I was in high school. He gave me a job, told me how to do it, and he didn't look over my shoulder while I did it. I thought there was something to be gained by that philosophy and never forgot it. I have to admit, however, I might not always have stuck to that approach as a coach.

A generous fella named Wade Scott owned a restaurant in Sulphur Springs. He recognized someone who was in need of help. There were many times when I went to his restaurant, and Mr. Scott would let me slide on the bill. When I worked a little extra I would pay on my tab, whatever I could afford. At one point Mr. Scott waved off my attempt to pay, saying, "You don't owe me anything. Save your money and enjoy your life."

My high school basketball coach, Travis Bruce, pushed his players to their physical limits, telling us, "If you want to win basketball games, you have to be in shape." It was a lesson that stayed with me. You never know the cost of success until someone points it out. Coach Bruce taught me that anything worth having comes at a high cost.

Sleepy Morgan, Wade Scott, Bill Chapman, and Travis Bruce: Before I took one step out of Texas, my core set of values had been formed thanks to those four men.

Several years into my pro career I was introduced to another man who emphasized high standards and commanded excellence. In 1959 the Green Bay Packers were in search of a coach. Enter Vince Lombardi, a little-known offensive assistant with the New York Giants. The first time I saw his warm, engaging smile, I was taken by his charming personality. The first time he hollered at me on the practice field, I recognized his demand for effort and an absolute commitment to one's craft. We had the talent before he arrived, but it was Vince Lombardi who made us champions.

My career has taken me all over the football map—all over America and even across the border to Canada. With me every step of the way was my wife, Barbara, giving support and providing a loving home for me and our children, Forrest Jr. and Karen. They were all with me on a hot

August day in 1977 as I was inducted into the Pro Football Hall of Fame. Indeed, it was a long, eventful road that carried me from East Texas to Canton, Ohio.

I didn't know if anyone would be interested in reading my story. Hell, I didn't know if I even wanted to tell it. I never have been one to live in the past. You can only sit around for so long saying "remember when." And I'm not writing this story to throw anyone under the bus or to pat myself on the back. I have trouble talking poorly about a player because, in a lot of cases, all he has is his good name. I don't want to smear someone's good name. They might say some bad things about me, but I don't really care. They can't diminish what I've accomplished in my life. For a lot of guys, when their career is over, all they have left is their name and memories.

And in the end I guess that's all any of us has.

1

WINNING...IS THE ONLY THING

YES, HE REALLY SAID IT.

Actually, he said it a number of times.

"Winning isn't everything, it's the only thing."

A lot has been written and said about Vince Lombardi over the years. A bit of it is urban legend, and some of it is true. But then again there are degrees of truth. Over the years Vince caught a lot of grief for the statement about winning. "It sends the wrong message to children," some said. Others believed the statement showed a twisted sense of values. Those critics, however, were taking the words out of context. The men sitting in the Green Bay Packers locker room knew exactly what he meant.

The 1960 season had been a wonderful experience for us. We'd gone from winning just one game in 1958 to playing in the championship game two years later. Still, we fell short of our goal. Playing for the NFL championship was great, but losing to the Philadelphia Eagles just made us

Taking a rest during a game in the 1960s.

hungrier. The loss stung, and the disappointment was difficult for a young team. Throughout the coming season, though, Vince continually reminded us that we were good enough. We just needed to learn how to win.

"You guys didn't realize you could win that game," he told us in the Franklin Field locker room. He repeated that statement a number of times during the '61 season, and it motivated us. Though he was a master tactician and had a magnificent football mind, Vince Lombardi's greatest attribute, perhaps, was his brilliant ability to motivate.

And then we came out and lost the first game of the season to the Lions in Milwaukee.

Let's just say Coach Lombardi was not happy with us. We'd had a chance to get off to a good start, continuing our success from the previous season, and we blew it. And when you lose that first one, you're playing catch-up. Vince didn't like playing catch-up. So, as we prepared for the next game, he kept on us all week long and never let up.

Once Detroit was behind us, we went on a roll. In the fifth game of the season we met the Browns in Cleveland. We went into the half with a big lead, and normally at the break the coaches talked to us about the corrections and adjustments we needed to make. Quite often Vince raised his voice and was vocal about our various transgressions during the first half of play. In the game against Cleveland, however, he didn't yell. We all understood that the Browns were a very good football team, one capable of coming back on us. Despite the big lead, we never relaxed or let up in the second half. We displayed maturity as a team and took, I believe, one more step toward becoming champions that day in beating the Browns.

After Cleveland we won seven of our last nine games. We clinched the Western Conference on December 3 in a tightly contested 20–17 victory over the New York Giants. Late in the contest, Jesse Whittenton stole the ball from Alex Webster. We recovered the ball on New York's 30-yard line and proceeded to move the ball down the field. The drive was capped when Jimmy Taylor scored his second touchdown of the day. It was the game clincher for us. At the final gun, fans swarmed County Stadium's field. After every game I always made a point of saying hello to the guys I knew on the opposing team. On this day, however, I never had the chance. Some guy jumped on my back. I guess he was happy because we won, but he unnerved me, so I threw him off. He tried again, but I outdistanced him and headed for the dressing room.

Our toughest opponent all year may have been Uncle Sam. Paul Hornung, Ray Nitschke, and Boyd Dowler were all activated into the Army Reserves. Boyd and Ray both received weekend passes and did not miss any games. Paul, however, missed two games, and it looked as if we wouldn't have him for the championship game either. Vince, though, desperately wanted our star halfback to play, and he went straight to the top. He phoned President Kennedy, who Vince had endorsed in the 1960 Wisconsin primary. The President took the call and was sympathetic to our plight. The U.S. military could spare Hornung for one Sunday, President Kennedy reasoned. The football fans of this country deserved the best two teams on the field that day. So we had Paul for the championship, and what a game he played.

———

A year earlier, as we were preparing for the 1960 championship game, a winter storm hit Green Bay. Because of the snow and ice that covered the city, Vince moved our practice inside so we could have a beneficial workout. On the day of the championship, the temperature in Philadelphia was rather frosty. I believe that Vince attributed our defeat to the Eagles to not practicing in the cold, and he vowed not to let the elements beat us again. From that point on, I don't care how much snow and ice covered the field, we went outside.

And then, as we were preparing for the Giants in '61, Green Bay was again blanketed in snow. This time Vince had the city's snowplows clear our practice field. We always hit the seven-man sled on our two heavy practice days, and the week of the championship, that thing was frozen to the ground. Still, Vince put us on the sled.

As we approached the sled, the linemen looked at each other, unsure what to do. "We'll never get this baby out of here," someone said. We had to break the ice loose by hitting it repeatedly to get it going. Once we started the drill, however, the field was so slick that we kept slipping and falling on our knees.

"You guys are just feeling sorry for yourselves!" Vince yelled at us.

That week made a marked impression on me. Sometime later I was thinking back on that experience when I made the statement, "If the mind is willing, the body can do it."

Come December 31, game day, the temperature was twenty-one degrees—cold, but bearable because we had worked out in much worse conditions. The field was a little crusty, but not frozen solid. Following the game, Bill Forester made an apt observation: "The Giants were more concerned about the weather. They came with tennis shoes and gloves and scarves. We just came to play."

Bringing tennis shoes was pretty common at the time, mostly because of a game between the Giants and the Bears in, I think, 1956. The field that day was frozen, and at halftime the Giants changed into tennis shoes. After the switch, the Giants had better footing than the Bears. The Giants came back in the second half and won the game, and after that, teams copied the Giants' success. When we traveled late in the season to the East or the Midwest, our equipment man would always issue the warning, "Don't forget to pack your tennis shoes." A lot of the same coaches and players were still with the Giants in 1961, and I think they remembered that Chicago game.

I'm not sure what kind of shoes Paul Hornung wore that day, but whatever he had on his feet did the trick. Paul did a little bit of everything. He scored a touchdown, kicked 4 extra points, and booted 3 field goals. His 19 points that day tied a playoff record. It wasn't a one-man show, however. As Bill Forester said, we jumped on them with both feet. We scored 24 points in the second half en route to a 37–0 win. I remember at one point during out preparations for the game Vince told us, "In the New York papers they're calling us the 'Cheese Champions.'" I personally never saw such a quote, but Lombardi did the job of getting us riled.

Recently I watched a complete network broadcast DVD of the '61 championship. So many things struck me as I sat there watching the television. The commercials, the halftime entertainment...it was a much simpler time then. The announcers called my name three or four times, which was a pretty good day for an offensive lineman. I remember at the time of the game I felt pretty good about my performance. Rewatching the game years later, however, I gained a new appreciation for the effort the Packers made as a group. *That* Green Bay Packer team was one helluva football team.

We were all quite pleased with the payday that came with the championship, and I knew I'd soon be fitted for a ring. But just knowing I was a champion—I was overwhelmed and overjoyed by the feeling. As a team we had no celebration or party to speak of, just a lot of back slaps and bear hugs in the dressing room. Following the game we all went our separate ways. I went home and later in the evening Barbara and I enjoyed a nice, quiet dinner. The next day we packed our things and flew home to Dallas.

———

After the game, as we sat in our locker room on that New Year's Eve in 1961, I thought about a store in my hometown of Birthright, Texas. The store was owned by a fella named Jess Orr, and it served as a grocery, but was more of a gathering place for the townspeople. Inside Jess Orr's store a radio played all the time and through that radio we received the news of the world: war bulletins, sporting events. I vividly recall listening to the Joe Louis-Billy Conn fight in Jess Orr's. It seemed like the whole town was huddled around the radio that night. There was also a lot of baseball broadcast from the radio. The Brooklyn Dodgers struck a nerve with me for some reason, and I always rooted for them. Maybe it was because they were usually the underdog. My mother's brother, Tex Shirley, pitched for the St. Louis Browns, and I remember sitting in Jess Orr's listening to Tex pitch in the 1944 World Series. During the off season Uncle Tex lived right down the road from the store.

While savoring the afterglow of our victory over the Giants, my mind took me back to Birthright, and I wondered if my old neighbors were sitting around Jess Orr's listening to my teammates and I win the world championship.

My competitive spirit
helped me succeed on
and off the field.

2

A PLACE CALLED BIRTHRIGHT

IT WASN'T UNTIL I HAD CHILDREN OF MY OWN THAT I realized how special my own childhood was. We had freedom to just take off and go. My brothers and I would get on our ponies and ride through the countryside. Unfortunately, I don't suppose there's any way to relive that time in America.

As far as I remember, I think I was told that I was born at home.

The date was October 18, 1933. My given name is Alvis Forrest Gregg. Alvis was for my maternal grandfather and Forrest for my paternal grandfather. The latter was named for the notorious Confederate general Nathan Bedford Forrest. Following the country custom of the time, I would be known by my middle name. In fact, the only time I went by Alvis was when I was in the Army: *Gregg, Alvis 55547892*

I was the third child and the third boy of David and Due Josephine Gregg. In time my parents had eleven children, five boys and six girls.

Our home for the first ten years of my life was in the middle of the little Texas town of Birthright.

Birthright was located ten miles north of the county seat, Sulphur Springs. While Sulphur Springs probably had a population of six thousand at the time, Birthright was around 250–500 people...probably less than that if you want to know the truth of it. I don't know for certain; I'd have to sit down and count up everybody I knew. Our small community had a blacksmith shop, a grist mill, a cotton gin, a schoolhouse, a church, and three grocery stores. The town itself was named for the Birthright family, and though he wasn't a blood relative, my daddy was a member of the Birthrights. His parents lived in the Birthright area, but they moved from Texas to California when my daddy was nine or ten years old. Daddy stayed behind and was "adopted" by the Birthrights. I think it always bothered him that his parents left him, but like many men of his time, he was stoic and kept his emotions in check. With his mother and father gone out West, he became a member of the Birthrights. Whenever Daddy referred to Mrs. Birthright, he always called her "Momma."

After Mr. and Mrs. Birthright died, their sons David and Roland took over the farm. When they passed away, my father inherited the property, which consisted of a couple hundred acres and an interesting old house that was built just before or during the Civil War. It was an old, rambling board building with a number of rooms: a living room, kitchen, dining room, and, for our ever-growing family, six bedrooms. Our modest house was right in the middle of town. We grew cotton, corn, feed for cattle (we had dairy cows as well as beef cattle). The cotton was planted in rows, and one of my responsibilities was to thin it out; otherwise, the plants would grow too close together and some would die. I'd wait until the plant bloomed and formed in the field and then I'd pick the cotton.

There were hard times, and though I don't really remember the Depression, I recall my parents talking about it and telling us how tough

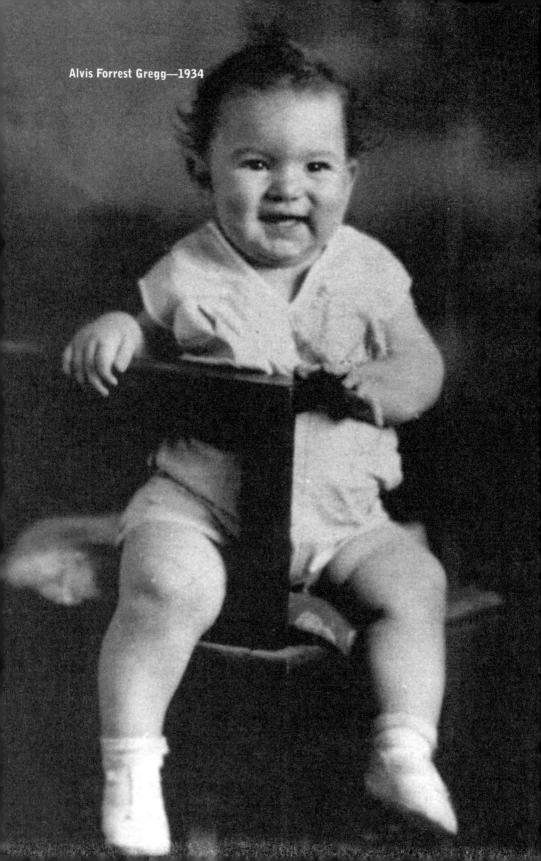

Alvis Forrest Gregg—1934

it was—about how so many people were going hungry. They talked about the breadlines and soup kitchens, and the many shelters that had been erected to house families who had lost their homes. Because we had the farm we always had something to eat. Still, we didn't have a lot of money to spend. But then again, I don't know if anyone did.

On a farm there really is no time off. You'd pray for rain and when the rain did come, we'd get a brief respite from the fields. My mother, though, never had a day off. With all those kids and a home to tend, you can imagine how she spent her day. She was the disciplinarian in our family while my father was kind of quiet. He was more focused on teaching us how to milk cows, pull cotton, and work in the fields. The only sport my father liked was boxing. He was a man more interested in earning a living than in watching sports. I remember someone once suggested that our school should field a football team. My father had seen a football game somewhere, probably Sulphur Springs, and he thought the game was too rough for men to play. He emphasized education and made certain that we attended school. But college, at the time, was not something anyone much considered.

My daddy was too young for the First World War, and when men were called up for World War II, as a farmer he was exempt from the draft. Near the close of the war, his classification was altered and we thought he might be drafted. Thankfully, the war came to an end before his number was called.

I was close to my siblings, especially my older brothers, David and William. On a farm you worked together and played together. It wasn't until we started attending school that my brothers and I began to branch out and meet new kids. David was five years older than me, and William was three years older. The three of us all had our own Shetland ponies, which we would ride all over the countryside. We had friends with ponies of their own, and sometimes we'd go riding together. Someone would say they'd seen a watermelon patch, so late in the afternoon we might make a raid. Stealing watermelons wasn't stealing, it was just eatin.'

Sometimes we would ride to my grandparents' home, which was five or six miles away. Or we might hear that someone had a new horse, or maybe somebody bought a new car, and we would head off. During the war we'd learn that, say, Lloyd Harris was home on leave and off we'd go to see Lloyd. I recall once when three or four guys were home on leave at the same time. Every night after supper we paid a visit to one of the soldiers. We'd sit in the middle of a dirt road and listen to his experiences, the things that he'd seen while he was gone. I remember a lot of young boys who went off to war never to return home.

One schoolhouse, Birthright School, held all grades of students. As a small rural school, it wasn't like the ones where most kids go today. It was a lot looser. I remember one day my brother Bill and I brought our dog to school. We left him out to roam when we went into the building. This other boy, Virgil Fouts, brought his dog to school the same day. Well, all the kids wanted to see a dog fight. So, at recess we brought those two dogs together. I'm not sure if this is widely known, but if you rub the noses of two dogs together, they'll fight. And, boy they got after it. There was a lot of barking and growling and a little bit of biting. I don't know if either dog won, but I do stop and think to myself now, who in the world would bring their dog to school?

There were several boys in particular who my brothers and I ran around with. Jess Orr had three boys around our age. Jack was the oldest, then Flea, and Jake N was my age. Jess had some property near his store, and he built a baseball diamond on the lot. The older men in the community would play on the field, and all the kids went down to watch the games.

The only sports we had at Birthright School were softball and basketball. There were outdoor courts for basketball, a couple of goals, and a black backboard. While I was in grade school I had to sit on the sidelines and watch the older boys play. All that watching sparked my imagination and inspired dreams of when I finally would be given the chance to play. My opportunity arrived when I reached the sixth grade, and the sports were basketball and softball. I also remember Jess Orr buying some boxing gloves. That was right up our alley. Boys like to fight and we were no exception. The bigger boys would spar one another, while the kids my age just went in there and started windmilling. We didn't learn much about the science of pugilism, but it was sport; it was competition.

When I was ten years old we moved from Birthright to a small community called Miller Grove, in the southwest part of Hopkins County. The towns were very similar except Miller Grove didn't have a cotton gin. We weren't making a lot of money on the Birthright farm, and Daddy thought we needed a bigger place to support the family. While in grade school at Miller Grove, I would watch the varsity basketball team practice every day during morning recess along with three of my buddies—LaRond Trevillion, Bill Wren, and Don Garner. We watched every move those boys made, every nuance of their game. And when we started playing grade school ball, the four of us made up four fifths of the team. We took everything we learned watching the varsity boys and put it into play ourselves.

While living in Birthright, we attended the Holiness Church. If I had to describe it, I'd say the congregation was Pentecostal. And then, after we moved, we went to the Nazarene Church in Sulphur Springs. Around that time my father started preaching. There were a lot of little communities about the size of Birthright, maybe a little bit smaller, and Daddy would travel and preach. There were two things you didn't argue with my father about: religion and politics.

My oldest brother, David, was in the eleventh grade at Miller Grove when somebody at Sulphur Springs heard about his athletic ability. David played baseball and basketball, but we never played football in those smaller schools. If there was a good athlete out in the country at one of those schools, a bigger school would recruit him, get him a job, and sign him up for their district. It was a common practice. The coach from Sulphur Springs talked to my parents and explained that David might have the chance to get an athletic scholarship and go to college. Mother and Daddy agreed to it and allowed David to transfer to Sulphur Springs. He played football, baseball, and basketball and eventually received a scholarship to Paris Junior College, and from there he received a scholarship to the University of Houston. He played all three sports at Houston and received an education.

I attended Miller Grove for my freshman year of high school, but I watched what happened with David and hoped it would happen for me. We were living in an area where we could attend any of three school districts—Sulphur Springs, Emory, or Miller Grove. I had been in the same school district for some time and had made a lot of friends, but Miller Grove didn't have a football team. It was a tough decision to make, but I knew if I transferred I could possibly get a college education. So, when I registered for the next school year, I thought about David. I had my younger sisters, Ruth and Ann, with me, and while I signed up for Sulphur Springs, I signed them up for Miller Grove. The bus to Miller Grove ran right by our house, but the bus to Sulphur Springs was a little more than a mile away. I knew in the winter months they wouldn't be able to make that trek. I also knew when I got home I was going to catch hell one way or another—and I did.

When I signed up for Sulphur Springs, I failed to notify them that I had already completed the ninth grade once, and I registered for the ninth grade a second time. I had a job that summer, working all day bailing hay. It was a pretty good job, paying four dollars a day—not bad when you could get three dollars a day picking cotton. One day while I was in the field bailing hay, I started feeling sick. The only nearby doctor was in Sulphur Springs, and getting to him took some ingenuity. There was a

My junior year at Sulphur Springs High School

fella who came by our farm every day to collect our milk, which he took to a Carnation plant in Sulphur Springs. If you needed a ride, you could usually catch one with the milk truck. Sometimes he'd let you ride up front depending on if he was in a hurry or not. Mostly, though, I rode in the back and helped take those cans off and on the truck. I didn't mind one bit, not for a ride into town.

Well, I hitched a ride with the milkman and went to see Dr. Stevens. He examined me and then took some swabs of my throat. He then handed me some medicine and said, "No running, jumping, playing ball, and no strenuous work."

I couldn't believe what he'd prescribed. My father had also been feeling poorly at the time. I looked at the doctor and said, "You're talking about my daddy, right?"

"I'm talking about you."

"What's wrong with me?" I asked

I had rheumatic fever, and my tonsils needed to be removed. "And then we've got to see if we can clear this thing up," he said.

It couldn't clear up fast enough as far as I was concerned. I really missed that four dollars a day. We certainly needed it with the big family, and I really wanted to play football. The man I was working for came by the house a number of times to check on me. I must have been a pretty good hand for him because he wanted to know when I'd be ready to work again. And though I helped around the farm milking cows, I couldn't work on the hay bailer.

Then the new school year began. I was itching to live my dream. All I thought about was sports. But I still couldn't play. On the first day of class, the football coach, Clinton White, stopped me in the hallway.

"Gregg," he said, "why don't you want to play football?"

"It's not that I don't want to play," I told him, and then I explained the illness and medical restrictions.

He got on the phone and called the doctor right away!

"We want this boy released to play football," the coach demanded.

Dr. Stevens patiently listened and then said, "Have him come down here this afternoon. I'll check him out again, but I don't think he's quite ready."

I skipped my afternoon classes and went to the doctor's office.

"You don't have a fever anymore," he told me following an examination, "but we'll still have to wait a little while before you can play football."

A "little while" lasted most of the season. There were three games left on the freshmen schedule when I finally was granted permission to play ball. You talk about a happy camper…I was a happy camper. I went straight to the coach's office and told him I'd been released to play.

"Good," he said. "We're going to Paris today. I want you to go to the field house and check out your equipment. Next week you'll be able to practice."

When I got to the field house the varsity was on the field working out. I watched for a few moments, and then I headed into the dressing room. The equipment manager, Richard Pruitt, was there. "Do you know how to put this stuff on?" he asked me.

"No," I told him. "I've never had it on in my life."

I was the only player in the locker room, and Mr. Pruitt quickly showed me how to put on the pads. Maybe I wasn't paying close enough attention to his instructions, but I looked in the mirror holding my hip pads. There was a pad that protected your sternum and two hip pads, which buckled on. I looked at those things and thought, "Where does this thing go?" With what I thought was great logic, I slipped the pad on. Rather than cover my hips, I unknowingly turned the pad front to back, believing I should be protecting that area.

Mr. Pruitt came by and said, "Boy, where did you come from?"

"Miller Grove," I said.

"I thought so," he laughed. "They don't know how to wear hip pads out there in Miller Grove."

I then went out on the field and thought I'd get a feel for running around while wearing all the equipment. I was going to watch the varsity practice, and then the next week I'd be ready to work out with the freshmen. I sat on the bench and crossed my legs casually. After a little while I started hearing laughter. All the varsity kids were laughing at me. Finally one of the coaches came by and said, "We're getting ready to do some drills, why don't you join us?"

I didn't know what they were doing, and I still to this day don't know. But I did find out that when you put those pads on, people want to hit you, and you've got to protect yourself.

I worked out all the next week with the freshmen, and then we went down to Mt. Pleasant for a game. We were ahead late when Coach Tucker asked me, "Do you want to go in there?"

Without hesitation, I replied, "Yes, sir."

He told me to go in on defense, but I asked, "What am I supposed to do?"

This was not only the first game I ever played, it was the first game I'd ever seen. I didn't know which way was up.

"There will be some guy in front of you," Coach Tucker explained, "and there'll be a guy behind him with the football. Maneuver the guy in front of you out of the way and tackle that guy with the football."

This was my introduction to football.

We won the game—I do remember that. But beyond that fact everything was a blur, everything moving too fast for me. I might have jumped on a pile late, maybe made a tackle or two. What happened after the game is a little clearer, though.

Our dressing room was on a stage in the Mt. Pleasant gym. We walked in following the game, and I heard someone say, "My money's gone!" Turns out everyone who had money with them had been robbed. I know I had thirty cents in my pocket for lunch the next day and it was gone. That night I stayed at Billy Dan Sapaugh's house and the next morning, following breakfast, Mrs. Sapaugh asked me if my money had been stolen.

"Yes, ma'am," I said.

"Well," she said, "here's a quarter for your lunch."

I thanked her then, and I thanked her very much—it was something I never did forget.

————

There were a lot of kids in our family, and we were having a rough go of it. To help make ends meet, we'd pick cotton for other people. Our whole family would go into Millers Grove, where a lot of kids knew me, and somebody would pick us up in a truck and take us to a field where we'd pick cotton all day. A lot of time we'd stop at the grocery store in Miller Grove. I never will forget this one ol' boy. He was two or three grades ahead of me. We all got out of the truck at the store and he started counting us—sort of as a joke. I eased up to him and said, "Don't you do that again."

He looked at me and said, "What are you talking about?"

"*Don't you do that again,*" I said.

And he never did. I was so mad I think smoke was coming out of my ears. We were a big family and that's the way it was. It wasn't anything for anybody to make fun of.

Many days I walked that mile and a half to catch the bus to school. Sometimes, though, I rode my horse to the bus stop. There was a fella with a pasture who told me I could put the horse in his barn. "But I don't want him eating my grass," he said.

That sounded reasonable enough to me. "Okay," I told him. But sometimes I would get there just as the bus was preparing to leave. After a few days of arriving a little late, the bus driver warned me, "If you don't start getting here earlier, I'm going to leave without you."

There were occasions when I'd be running late so I had to take the saddle off, throw it behind a tree, and turn that horse to pasture. One day that guy was waiting for me when I got off the bus.

"Boy, I told you not to let this horse out to pasture," he said. "I've got to save this grass for winter when I turn my cows out there."

From then on I kept my horse in the barn.

There wasn't a bus that took me to the games, however, and a lot of times I would hitchhike five or six miles. Those games were always at night, but I always made it home safely.

By the time I got the chance to play, the season was nearly over. There was only one more freshman game remaining, but I had the opportunity to play in a few B games. One of those B games sticks out in my memory. The game was against Honey Grove, and it was cold. I didn't think it was much fun playing football in cold weather. (Little did I know what my future in football would hold.) Though my on-field experience was limited that year, I did get a feel for playing. I knew that I had a long way too go, but being around my teammates helped me think about football.

For most of the summer before my sophomore year I worked on the hay bailer. In late August we started football practice with a three-week camp. For those three weeks we lived in the gym. Some boys had cots to sleep on. I had a blanket and slept on the floor. Even if I could afford a cot, I wouldn't have known where to find one.

One night the coach turned out the lights and said, "Shut your mouths and go to sleep. Stop your talking and giggling."

We stopped for about a minute and then everyone started talking again. The coach came back and yelled, "If I hear one peep out of you guys, I'm going to have you running the bleachers all night."

He turned off the light and started walking down the hall when somebody said, "Peep!" Bill Seabaugh, my line coach, and Travis Bruce came into the room. Boy, they rolled us out of our beds and put us to running those bleachers. I thought they were going to run us all night. When everyone's tongue was hanging out he said, "I bet when we turn the lights out this time, you guys will go to sleep."

There wasn't even a peep that time.

————

Before leaving for camp my daddy told me, "You can go there and stay ten days, but then you've got to come home and pick cotton."

We had a scrimmage on a Saturday, and the day after the game I told my coaches that my father expected me home to work the fields. I returned to the farm and worked for three days before our opening game against Paris. Coach Bruce asked my daddy if I could come back for the game. I was allowed to return, but I didn't know if I'd lost my spot. Still, they were sure glad to see me. I was handed a playbook and told to study.

Friday night came and we met our opponent, Paris High, coached by Emmett Berry. Starring on that team was Coach Berry's son, Raymond. I think of that contest as the first real football game I played in. It was the first time I knew what was happening on the field.

Still, we lost the game and I went home for the weekend and picked cotton. The first day of school was Monday, and after classes I got to experience my first chewing out by a coach. I wasn't alone, though; the coaching staff decided we weren't schooled in fundamentals. They had us undertake a drill called "head-on tackling."

The defensive guy stood on one side of the line of scrimmage, while the offensive man, with a ball in his hand and no blockers, was on the other. We went through several rounds, and on the last round I tackled this fella, W.R. Fielding, and got my arm caught between his body and the ground. I knew something was wrong immediately, but I didn't know what. Looking down at my arm I saw it was crooked. This was panic time. "My arm is broken!" I called out.

Coach Bruce took my arm and pulled it out straight. "That ain't too bad," he told me. He and Coach Seabaugh then took me to Dr. Stevens. I received a shot in the arm, and though Coach Bruce helped some, the arm still wasn't straight. "I have to set this," Dr. Steven's told me. "I'm going to put a cast on, and you'll have it on for six weeks."

When we were through at Doc Stevens' office, the coaches took me home. They figured it was their responsibility to tell my mother and father what happened. My daddy had just started milking when we arrived. It was one of the few times I saw my father really angry.

"Thank you for bringing him home," he said, "but I don't know how he can milk with one hand."

"Well," Coach Bruce said, "he'll be good as new in six weeks."

"I hope so," was all my daddy said. And that was the last I heard of the incident.

———

About a week later Clinton White approached me at school and said, "We want you to move up to Sulphur Springs."

"That'd be okay with me," I thought. My arm was broken, I couldn't milk, I couldn't do much around the farm.

Apparently they had it all planned out. "We have a room here in the gym, and we'll give you a key to the gym. You can have your lunch in the cafeteria. And there is a restaurant downtown, the Chuck Wagon, which is owned by the father of another player. You can have your other two meals there."

I had a little money saved from my hay-bailing job. First, though, I needed permission from, and the blessing of, my parents. My mother and father gave the proposition some thought, and they both realized this was a good opportunity for me. I moved into the gym and stayed there until spring, just before the end of the school year.

It was a brave new world for me. The working toilets in the gym were the first I'd ever seen. For a time I didn't have a bed, but I made do by sleeping on the wrestling mat. I did my homework by spreading my books and papers out on the basketball court. Sometimes I'd be in bed when one of my friends would throw a few rocks against the window to get my attention. We might shoot baskets at ten o'clock at night. There was always someone wanting to spend the night. I had a pullout bed, which could sleep two—one of the beds was a little lower than the other. Sometimes we'd go out at night and walk to the square just to see what was cooking around Sulphur Springs.

One night my buddy Jack Pogue and I broke into the cafeteria. I grabbed a couple cartons of milk and a big jar of peanut butter. For a time afterward, when I hadn't had a good dinner, which was most days, I'd open up that peanut butter. If you're hungry, you'll do whatever is necessary. Most nights when I was in that gym, I went to bed hungry so it wasn't hard to talk me into breaking into the cafeteria.

Word got around about our caper, and a few more friends dropped by the gym one evening. Again we hit the cafeteria, but that was the end of our mischief that night. There was a little candy store behind the high school. We broke in and snatched Milky Way and Three Musketeers bars and potato chips. A fella who lived nearby drove a 7-Up truck, and we got into that truck, grabbed a case of pop, and headed back to the school. After the heist we went to the boys' dressing room and had a feast.

My conscience bothered me afterward. If my parents had found out about it they would have made me come home and attend Miller Grove. Everything I was working for would have been for naught. The next day

I helped the equipment man line the field while the rest of the team practiced. All day long I was looking over my shoulder for the police. I lived in fear for a couple of months.

———

The time on the sideline was helpful. I learned a lot from watching and just being around the game. I finally got that cast off a few weeks later, but the end of the season was fast approaching. I was able to play in a couple of varsity games as well as a few B games. Though I was progressing as a football player, basketball remained my best sport. The school's basketball coach, Travis Bruce, who had been a basketball player at East Texas State, always called me "Greggs." He told me: "Greggs, I don't know what kind of football player you are, or whether you can be a football player or not, but I think you can be a basketball player if that's what you wanted to do."

I was a starter on the team. Heck, if you scored a few points you might get your name in the paper; that wasn't all bad.

———

Eventually the school needed my room for an office, so my bed was moved to the corner of the gym basement. All I had then was a place to hang my clothes and a bed. Then one day near the end of the basketball season, Coach Bruce came up to meet me as I entered school. "Greggs," he said, "Mr. Gibson wants to talk to you." Mr. Gibson was the superintendent of the school. "What in the world have I done now," I wondered.

When we went to Mr. Gibson's office, the first thing he said to me was, "I want you to be nice to these people." I didn't know who or what he was talking about, and I was too scared to ask.

The Sulphur Springs High School basketball team, 1950-51.
That's me on the far left, followed by Paul Buchanan, Leroy Harry, Eroy Harry,
Mack Pogue, Bobby Cromer, Bob Gideon, Junior Burns, and Gerald Donovan.

Mr. Gibson and I drove through downtown around the square and out to College Street. There were a number of large old houses on College Street, and he pulled up in front of one of Sulphur Springs' biggest homes.

We got out of the car, went up the walk and rang the doorbell. A lady stepped out the front door. "Hello, Mr. Gibson," she said. "Is this the boy you were talking about?"

"Yes, ma'am," he answered. "This is him."

I was introduced to this nice, middle-aged lady. Her name was Ruth Ashcroft, and the beautiful home was hers.

"Forrest, I have a garage apartment," Mrs. Ashcroft told me. "My husband is dead, and except for my mother, I live here all alone. I would just feel comfortable knowing someone is out there. Would you like to see it?"

Would I?

"Yes, ma'am," I answered.

Mr. Gibson and I went to the back, and walked up the stairs to the apartment. It was one room with a bed and some furniture. Compared to what I had been living in it was like a mansion to me.

We left the apartment and returned to Mrs. Ashcroft. "Is it all right?" she asked.

"Yes, ma'am, it sure is."

She showed me the door to the kitchen and told me whenever I came home from school I could feel free to come in and get a snack and a Coke. I never did take her up on the generous offer, though. Unless she invited me, I never did go in by myself. I felt like I'd be intruding.

Mrs. Ashcroft was a thoughtful and kind lady. Sometimes she would catch me when I got home from school and ask if was doing anything that night.

I always told her "No." Even if I did have plans, they would take a backseat to Mrs. Ashcroft.

"Well," she'd say, "there's a movie I'd like to go see, but I don't like going by myself. Would you mind going with me?"

"Oh, no, ma'am, I wouldn't mind at all."

So we'd get to the movie and Mrs. Ashcroft found herself a seat, and then she'd say, "There are your friends. Go sit with them and we'll meet in the lobby when the movie is over."

I lived on College Street a little over two years, and she always acted like I was doing *her* a favor.

———

On the front porch of Mrs. Ashcroft's home during my junior of high school.

By my junior year I had become a good football player. My body had begun to develop. I'd grown a little, and gotten a little bit heavier. At six feet, three inches, 185 pounds, I was starting to believe a scholarship was a real possibility.

In the state of Texas at that time there were three classifications for high schools: AA, A, and B. Most of the B schools didn't have football programs. Prior to my junior year, we were in AA with the big schools. But we were moved into A before the start of the season, and now we were competing against schools our own size. We lost only two of our ten games. Unfortunately, one of the defeats went to Mt. Vernon, which prevented us from advancing to the state playoffs.

The following year we put together another good season. We lost one district game, which again kept us out of the playoffs. But I felt that I knew enough about football that I could compete against just about anyone.

After my junior year we got a new head coach at Sulphur Springs— Skinny Davis. Skinny was a graduate of Southern Methodist University, and he wanted me to consider his alma mater when I was selecting a college for myself. "If they contact you," Skinny told me, "you should listen."

It was Sleepy Morgan, the freshman coach at SMU, who approached me first. Sleepy was from Sulphur Springs, and he didn't make any bones about wanting me to play at SMU. "I want you to come visit us," he said. "I'm hoping they offer you a full scholarship."

————

When the football season came to a close, I paid a visit to several schools, including SMU, A&M, Baylor, all from the Southwest Conference, and also East Texas State, which was a smaller school but nevertheless had a good football program and gave scholarships. I enjoyed my visit to SMU. Dale Moore, a player on the football squad who was from Mt. Vernon,

Fall 1951—the Sulphur Springs High School eleven.
I still remember all those guys. Bottom left to right: Lawrence Bramblet,
W.A. Fielding, me, Billy Bob McCool, Jackie Shroud, Doc Groves,
Wayne Bramfield. Middle left to right: Bobby Cromer, Bill Gideon,
Billy Dan Sapaugh. Top: Mack Pogue.

looked after me that weekend. The school and the people impressed me
a great deal. Unfortunately, the head coach, Rusty Russell, only offered
me a partial scholarship. I flat out told the folks at SMU that A&M had
already offered me a full ride (as had East Texas). I sure wasn't going to
take anything less because I couldn't afford anything less. Ol' Sleepy was
very disappointed. It looked like I was definitely going to A&M. Everyone
who penned a note in my yearbook wrote, "Good luck in Aggie land."

On the last day of school we were released at noon. I went straight
from school to my job at B&B Cleaners. I was working up front when I saw
Sleepy Morgan ride up in his slick '51 Pontiac with white sidewall tires. He
pulled that baby right up to the door, got out, and walked into the store.

"We just lost one of our scholarship players, Bill Chedle, to

Oklahoma," Sleepy said. "Coach Russell told me to come down here and offer you a full scholarship to SMU."

There was not a letter of intent in those days. You could commit to as many schools as you wanted, and the one you attended was the college you showed up at in the fall. Still, I thought my word was worth something.

"I'd like to do that, but I already told those folks at A&M that I was coming down there."

Sleepy wasn't going to be deterred. "I know you always wanted to go to SMU. I'm sorry we didn't offer you the full scholarship before you made your choice. But there are a lot of boys who made up their mind at the last minute. Bill Chedle, for example, and we don't think any less of him."

I was torn, and Sleepy could see that. He suggested we take a little ride so we hopped in his car and drove up to the square. Boy, he was slick. Sleepy knew he was getting to me.

"I've been watching you ever since you've been here in Sulphur Springs. I just want you to know that if you don't decide on SMU, you and I will still be friends."

Reluctantly I agreed to visit SMU one more time. And while Sleepy and I were walking around the square, we ran into Billy Dan Sapaugh. He knew Sleepy—heck, everyone in Sulphur Springs knew Sleepy. He had made the big time as a coach.

"I'm going to TCU tomorrow, why don't I drop Forrest by SMU?" Billy Dan suggested.

Sounded like an great idea to Sleepy. "Okay, we'll see you tomorrow."

The next day we drove up to Dallas, and I visited with Coach Russell and Sleepy. Since I didn't want to make Billy Dan go out of his way to pick me up, I told him I'd go to TCU with him.

Sleepy about pounced out of his chair. "Oh no you don't!" he said, "You got no business there. You came to visit SMU, and I'll take care of you the rest of the afternoon."

SMU had a beautiful campus; it still does. While walking around with Sleepy I came upon a big building, Dallas Hall. We walked up the stairs and when we reached the apex I could see downtown Dallas, exactly five miles away. That view was topped only by the beautiful rotunda inside the hall. I was standing there gawking up at the rotunda—it nearly took my breath away—when Sleepy eased up behind me and whispered, "This building sure would hold a lot of hay, wouldn't it?"

If I had any doubt about where I was going, it had been washed away right then.

————

When we arrived home in Sulphur Springs, Billy Dan pulled his car up by Larner's Drug Store. We saw one of our friends, Jack Pogue, on the street.

"SMU's got him!" Sapaugh hollered to Jack.

The word was out, and I hadn't had the chance to call A&M. I went to the cleaners and asked Mr. Chapman what I should do. "By all means you should call them," he told me. "Use my phone right here."

I called A&M and told them of my change of heart.

I was settled on Southern Methodist University.

•

3

COLLEGE DAYS AT SMU

AT THE TIME I ENROLLED AT SMU, FRESHMEN WEREN'T eligible for varsity ball. The frosh played their own schedule. As a football player, my goal was simple—to play as well as I was capable, while improving as the year progressed. If I achieved this goal, then by the time my sophomore year rolled around I would have a leg up. My priority, however, was the classroom. I was there to get a degree. And I learned quickly that college was far different from high school. I was now an adult, and if I wanted to succeed, I needed to act like an adult. Nobody was there to make decisions for me. Adjusting to the classroom workload was difficult. High school teachers generally lecture their students on the importance of schoolwork. In college it's up to the individual, and what you make of it is up to you.

I stayed in a dorm my freshman year. A bunch of freshmen football players lived in the same dorm, and we were all occasionally hazed by upperclassmen. More often than not, the culprits were sophomores who had recently been hazed themselves. They weren't too bad; however, they wanted to remind us that we were the low men on the totem pole. I remember being run through a belt line; we were made to run the gauntlet while they smacked us on the backsides with their belts.

On one occasion we rebelled. All of us freshmen went upstairs and locked ourselves in the dorm attic. The upperclassmen were on the outside pounding on the door and hollering threats at us. We didn't give in until the dorm director, Tom Dean, made us open the door. Surprisingly, they kind of laid off us after that incident.

The freshmen played their home games on campus at Ownby Stadium. Our schedule only consisted of five or six games. We did, though, get to scrimmage against varsity players who hadn't played the previous Saturday. I got a taste of what varsity football would be like in those scrimmages.

One particular varsity player stood out from those scrimmages— Dale Moore. He had been injured and missed the previous game. The coaching staff didn't know if he was healthy enough for the coming contest, so they told Dale to play in the Monday scrimmage against the freshmen. Boy, Dale was mad. He didn't like having to prove that he could play, and that day he ran over us, around us, and through us. I just cringed every time he came near me. If he hadn't had an injury, Dale probably would have played professionally. He was the real deal.

There was also a guy named Lamar Hunt, who was a year ahead of me. Lamar was a wide receiver, but we had Raymond Berry, Doyle Nicks, and Ed Bennett ahead of him on the depth charts. He was competing with these guys for playing time. Raymond didn't start till he was a senior, which shows you how much depth we had at receiver.

Lamar was really a nice person. I got to know him well as a teammate.

One weekend after returning to campus following a visit home, I asked my roommate, Bob Bakely, "What did you do over the weekend?"

"We went swimming at Lamar's."

"Lamar who?" I asked.

"Lamar Hunt," Bob said.

"You mean to tell me Lamar Hunt's family has a swimming pool at their house?"

Bob looked at me like I was crazy. "Don't you know who Lamar Hunt is?"

"No," I said. "I just know him as a teammate and a friend."

"Lamar's father is one of the richest men in the country."

I couldn't believe it. Lamar was just like one of the guys. He dressed in blue jeans and T -shirts...he was just a regular guy.

In a practice we ran a drill called the "Oklahoma drill," which was named for Sooner coach Bud Wilkinson. I was blocking against Raymond, Nicks, Bennett, and Lamar, tackles against ends. Years later when I was a coach, I always said that if I had known Lamar Hunt was going to own a team and I was going to be a head coach, I would have let him win a few of those Oklahoma drills.

Years later, of course, Lamar would be known as the owner of the Kansas City Chiefs, but I think it's important that people understand that Lamar wasn't just an owner of a football team. He had the foresight and the vision to start another league and go up against the NFL. Before starting his own league, he tried to get an NFL franchise in Dallas, but the NFL said they weren't ready to expand. Lamar wasn't easily deterred, however. He started the American Football League and created his own team, the Dallas Texans. Then, lo and behold, the NFL put a team in Dallas. Lamar moved his team to Kansas City a couple years later because Dallas couldn't support two teams.

After I had been in the league a few years, I was selling cars for a man named Ken Grantham in Irving, Texas. Ken had played a little ball at SMU, and he caught me one morning following the '59 season.

"I was talking to Lamar Hunt the other day and your name came up," Ken said. "Lamar told me to tell you to come and play for him. I asked

Posing for a photo with Lamar Hunt (center) and Raymond Berry (right) as we show our Hall of Fame rings.

Lamar, 'What are you going to pay him?' 'Whatever he wants,' Lamar said." Believe me, I thought about it. I thought about it hard. But that was Vince's first year, and I really thought our future was bright.

Years later, Lamar was proud of being in the Hall of Fame. One time Lamar, Raymond, and I were going to attend a banquet in Dallas. A week before the banquet Lamar gave me a call. "Be sure to wear your Hall of Fame ring," he said.

"Sure," I said, "but why."

"I want someone to take a picture of the three of us with our Hall of Fame rings.

———

Shortly after my freshman season, Rusty Russell was fired as the Mustangs' head coach. Replacing Rusty was Woody Woodard, a junior college coach from Kansas. With the coaching change came some new assistants. Tom Dean, our freshman coach (and dorm director), was moved to the varsity staff while Sleepy Morgan shifted to the freshman team. Ironically, I never had the chance to play for the guy who recruited me. I was disappointed, but Sleepy never forgot me: He always took time to visit with me any time he saw me around campus. Sleepy was a super scout who had recruited most of us on the team.

With Woodard, we switched from the single wing and went to the T-formation, which we started practicing in the spring of that year. That was a drastic change for us. Coach Woodard wanted to see where everybody fit in the new system, and at the time I was third team at left tackle. Over the summer I moved up the depth charts when one guy ahead of me didn't make the grades needed to keep his eligibility, and another man on the line left school altogether.

"I'm one player away from being the starting tackle. Is this really me? Is this really me?"

When we started in the fall I was second team. Our coaches played us two deep, sometimes three deep, and thankfully I received quite a bit of playing time.

Before the 1953 college season, the NCAA instituted a rule declaring that players had to play both ways. Substitution was allowed only when someone was injured. As a freshman I played defensive end the whole season. I had played sparingly on offense, and quite frankly I didn't like offense. The thinking behind instituting the two-way rule was that the disparity between the smaller schools and the larger ones would be diminished. The rule change didn't alter the playing field, however. If anything, the differences between large and small schools were exacerbated. At SMU we went two deep, while other universities were able to go four deep.

During my sophomore and junior years, I would sometimes play sixty minutes. Let me tell you, I didn't enjoy it, not one bit. In Dallas, we sometimes played in ninety-degree heat with high humidity. I categorized it as "cruel and unusual punishment." At the end of the game, there wasn't much left in the tank.

I had first been to the Cotton Bowl as a member of the Sulphur Springs football team when the booster club took us to watch SMU play Wake Forrest. And, of course, as a freshman I sat in the stands and watched the varsity each Saturday. But now it was my turn. We practiced there before our first home game against Missouri. That probably took the edge off of any nervousness I might have had. I had dreamed of playing ball in the Cotton Bowl, and when my chance came I was overwhelmed and more than a little bit in awe.

The atmosphere was gripping. The pro game hadn't yet come to Dallas, and we regularly drew 75,000 to our games—considerably more than Wildcat Stadium in Sulphur Springs. Following each Saturday I gained confidence in my ability. Georgia Tech, Missouri, Rice. My first airplane ride came when we traveled to Atlanta for the Georgia Tech game. The plane was a DC-6, four-engine prop. I was sitting next to Raymond Berry on the flight. As we started going down the runway, I thought we were never going to get off the ground. The plane just kept going faster and faster, and I almost lost my stomach once we were airborne. The plane was flying due east. Raymond and I both looked out the window wondering if we would see Paris or Sulphur Springs. We peered out the window intently, and though eventually we saw the outskirts of Paris, we couldn't see Sulphur Springs.

The best game I played all season came against Notre Dame in South Bend. I was up against All-American Art Hunter. On the very first play, I lined up over him. Boy, did he come up off that ball on first down and really pop me. It was the hardest I'd ever been hit, and it was a heckuva wake-up call.

49

"If this is how he wants to play…"

At one point I made two consecutive tackles on the goal line, which kept the Irish out of the end zone.

It's funny the things you remember. Stuck in my mind some fifty-five years later is the image of Notre Dame linemen—almost every one of them had teeth missing in the front. A couple of weeks earlier when we were playing Baylor, there was a guy with a wide plastic bar across the helmet. I didn't have anything on my helmet. We locked up and his bar cut my nose. The next week I had a bar of my own. And then there I was in South Bend, glancing across the line at my toothless opponent, thinking, "I guess that's what I have to look forward to if I don't wear this bar."

We lost our last game of the year at South Bend, leaving us with a 5-5 record. Shortly after the season ended, our public relations man called me into his office.

"I got something for you," he told me. Lester then handed me a letter from Notre Dame saying I had been picked for their all-opponent team. That was pretty significant for me. Just a couple of months earlier I was giving pro football no thought whatsoever. My ambition was to be a high school coach. Playing football was just an entertaining diversion and a means to achieve my goals. Now I began to think that maybe this thing would go a little bit further.

———

Before my junior year I was named preseason All-Conference. And though I don't mean to brag, I had it figured out. Unlike a year earlier, I knew what to expect as the season began.

Our team goal was to win the Southwest Conference and play in the Cotton Bowl. We lost three games—to Georgia Tech, Baylor, and Notre Dame. It was the loss to Baylor, however, that kept us from playing on New

Talking to SMU head coach Woody Woodard after a game against Notre Dame in 1954.

Year's Day. We took a train from Highland Park to Fayetteville and beat the eventual conference champion, Arkansas, on November 13. But by falling short to Baylor the following week, we lost our chance at the Cotton Bowl.

————

The loss to Notre Dame came in the final game of the season. We played them tough, right down to the wire. Ralph Guglielmi was the Irish quarterback, and he ran all over us that day. But what stands out to me from that contest was one innocuous play. I was up against their best—a big tackle named Frank Varrichione. At one point during the third quarter Varrichione jumped off sides, and I hit him ass over tea kettle, as the Birthright colloquialism goes. I still remember it because that's the play people wanted to talk about afterward. The game was on television, and so for a brief moment at least, I was a television star to my friends.

———

It wasn't easy being a student-athlete. Football was time consuming. There was spring practice, fall practice, and then the season itself. Plus I went out for the track team in the spring. SMU was not an easy school; it was very demanding academically. Though I wasn't appreciative of that fact at the time, later in life I was grateful that I needed to work hard for my degree. I enjoyed playing football and sometimes had to remind myself exactly why I was there—to accomplish something in life. SMU made me stretch a little further than I wanted to go in order to get that education, but in the end it was worth every minute of work I put into it.

In each of my three varsity seasons I was named to Notre Dame's all-opponent team. I was proud of the accomplishment because I had a lot of respect for the players and the program. The honor also came in handy later when I teased Hornung. When he would brag about Notre Dame, the tradition, the campus, I would tell him, "Man, I cleaned up on you guys."

———

My senior year was a bit of a disappointment. We had the talent. There was Tiny Goss, Don McIlhenny, John Roach, John Marshall, and myself; all of us were taken in the first three rounds of the NFL draft. Still we had a frustrating season, mostly because our coach lacked motivational skills. He was a good man, but not an inspirational guy. When we were in the locker room getting ready before the Notre Dame game, he read us a poem. He wanted to calm us down before we took the field. A *poem*, can you believe that?

My last game in college was against Texas Christian in Ft. Worth. TCU had a running back named Jim Swink. He wasn't big as running backs go, but Jim had great speed. He was a jitterbug, very hard to get a hold of. We lost the game and Swink was the reason. We'd have him cornered and the next thing you knew, he was someplace else.

When you've played as many games as I have through the years, some contests are just blurs while others stand out. That final game at Texas Christian was one of the memorable ones. For some of my teammates, it would be the last time they played organized ball. I was confident that I would have a chance to play again at the next level. But it would be the last time I would wear the colors of SMU. Lying ahead for me would be many honors, championships, and awards. Nothing, however, equaled the thrill I had, and the pride I felt, representing Southern Methodist University.

———

Professional football had never been a goal of mine. I wanted to get my degree, and I hoped to coach football, probably at the high school level. But as my senior year progressed, several pro teams expressed interest in selecting me in the annual college draft. The Los Angeles Rams had contacted me by sending a letter asking if I would play for them if they drafted me. I was intrigued by the Rams in particular. Perhaps my attraction stemmed from a movie I'd seen—*Crazylegs* with Elroy Hirsh.

The Detroit Lions and the Baltimore Colts each sent similar letters. The Lions had Doak Walker, and that was an attraction to me. Plus I'd seen them play on Thanksgiving Day, but that's as much as I knew about the team.

The Colts had Raymond Berry, who had gone from Paris High School to SMU then to Baltimore. Raymond was just a skinny kid when we were in college. He was a year ahead of me, and I remember standing on the sideline watching him. They kept putting Raymond into the game, and he kept catching the football. He had the best hands of anyone on the team by far. I spoke with Raymond when he returned home after his first year, and he told me what it was like in the NFL and Baltimore. After our talk I began thinking that I would like to be selected by the Colts. They seemed to be an up-and-coming team on the cusp.

I heard nothing from Green Bay, however, until a week before the November 29 draft, when I received a telegram asking the same question as the earlier letters had asked: Would I be willing to play for the Packers, should they select me in the upcoming draft? Since they had waited so long to contact me, I didn't believe the Packers would really draft me. And unlike the three previous letters, I did not respond to Green Bay's telegram.

Teams asking whether or not a young man was willing to play professional football wasn't unusual. Believe me, at the time, there wasn't a great deal of difference between a job in professional football and a "real" job—maybe a couple of grand. There were examples of guys who were drafted by the NFL but never pursued professional football. In some cases they didn't want to leave home, and in other instances some already had a decent job lined up. But I was interested in pro ball. Since I'd also been contacted by the Canadian Football League, I knew there would be an opportunity somewhere for me.

On the day of the draft I went to class as usual. The draft wasn't publicized back then anything like it is today, and I didn't know for sure when it was being held. Following my classes that afternoon I stopped by the athletic department and while there the school's publicity director, Lester Jordan, called me into his office. Something must be up, I thought, because Lester had never invited me into his office before.

"Forrest," he said, "we just got a call from the Green Bay Packers.

They drafted you in the second round."

My initial reaction, I have to admit, was disappointment. I was hoping for the Rams or the Colts, even the Lions, but Green Bay...?

"What should I do?" I asked Lester.

"There's but one thing to do if you want to play professional football. You'll be playing for the Packers. I suggest you call them."

I hesitated. In 1955 you just didn't make long distance calls at the drop of a hat.

Lester must have recognized the concern on my face. "You can use the phone in my office," he told me.

I called Green Bay and was put on the line with a man named Jack Vainisi.

The Packers were glad to have me aboard, he told me, and then said that the Packers had drafted a running back from the University of Miami, Jack Losch, in the first round.

"Thank you," I said, "I appreciate very much the Packers selecting me."

"Now that we drafted you," Jack said, "we need to come to an agreement on a contract."

Not two minutes had passed before I was introduced to the *business* of professional football.

I hung up the phone and searched for a map. I didn't even know where Green Bay was—Michigan or Wisconsin? I wasn't sure which.

It was probably the best thing that could have happened to me. At the moment, though, I wasn't very excited to be a Green Bay Packer. Then I remembered that a couple of guys from SMU had played for the Packers—Bill Forester played linebacker, fullback, and defensive line and Val Joe Walker played defensive back. We Mustangs are kindred spirits.

Suddenly Green Bay wasn't looking so bad.

Following the collegiate draft a man came by the SMU athletic offices. His name was J. I. Albright. I guess you could say J. I. was ahead of his time. He was what we now call a player agent. He wanted to know if we could make a deal for him to represent me. He already had Alabama's quarterback, Bart Starr, as a client.

I was a little confused. Why would I need representation? The only team interested in me was the Green Bay Packers.

"That's not true," J. I. explained. "There are a couple of teams in Canada that would like to sign you."

We talked a bit longer, but I had to go to class. Besides, I wasn't sure if I wanted to get mixed up in all this business. Still, I offered to meet J. I. later in the coach's office. Before seeing J. I. again, I went to see Matty Bell, SMU's athletic director, and told him about my appointment.

"Forrest," Matty said, "I don't know anything about this guy. He might have a great idea, but there's only so much money you can make playing pro football. I would think you could find out how much the market will bear on your own."

That settled it for me. And later, as I started explaining my position to J. I., he cut me off.

"The Montreal Alouettes of the Canadian Football League want you and they're offering eighty-five hundred dollars."

Montreal?

I was impressed; this J.I. had done his job, whatever that was.

"They speak French up there?"

"Yep," J.I. answered.

"Well," I explained, "I've never been any place like that."

I also found out that the Calgary Stampeders put an offer of seventy-five hundred on the table with a five-hundred-dollar, no-strings-attached signing bonus. Calgary, I was told, was like an east Texas oil town, a place I could relate to.

I ended up negotiating with the Packers, and I handled the negotiations myself, on the telephone with Jack Vainisi. He offered seventy-five hundred and a $250 signing bonus if I reported to training camp and was still a member of the team at the end of camp. The money might have been slightly better in Canada, but the NFL was where I wanted to play. It's where I belonged. I'm sure Jack knew how I felt. Our "negotiations" only lasted a few moments before I agreed to the Packers terms.

Green Bay it would be for me.

4

GOD, FAMILY, AND
THE GREEN BAY PACKERS

A FEW PACKER ROOKIES WERE SCHEDULED TO PLAY IN
the 1956 College All-Star Game—Bob Skronski, Cecil Morris, Jack
Losch, Bob Burris, and myself. In those days the annual College All-Star
Game pitted the NFL champions against the best collegiate players from
the previous season. The exhibition contest was played each summer at
Chicago's Soldier Field. We had to report to training camp at Green Bay
so we could work out for a few days and get acquainted with the system
before heading to Chicago to face the Cleveland Browns.

Upon arrival, I was surprised to see that the big leagues weren't necessarily big time. The Packers practiced on a run-down field, East High Stadium. And the dressing room resembled some high school locker rooms I'd
been in back home in Texas. The equipment we were issued was tattered and
worn. I took a look around and thought to myself, "*This* is pro ball?"

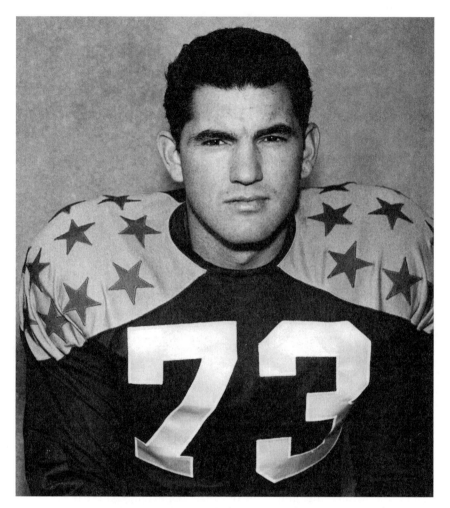

The College All-Star Game against the Cleveland Browns gave me my first taste of the NFL.

We stayed at Northwestern University for a couple of weeks while preparing under the tutelage of our coach, Curly Lambeau, who was, of course, a legendary coach and founding owner of the Packers. It was an educational experience for me. Most of us on the All-Star team were going to play on Sundays, and it was fun meeting guys I'd heard about, or fellows I'd played against. We scrimmaged a great deal in preparation for the

Browns, and that gave me a good indication of what competition in the NFL would be like. The game itself was a lopsided 26-0 victory for Paul Brown's world champion Cleveland squad, but to play against the best, and to hold my own, was pretty satisfying. I returned to Stevens Point ready for professional competition, and confident in my own ability.

While we were at Evanston, Morris and Burris, who both attended Oklahoma, started talking to one another, and they decided they didn't want to play professional football. Jack Vainisi came up to Northwestern University and tried to talk them out of their decision, but neither man changed his mind. And then, when we returned to training camp, Skronski and Losch decided they, too, didn't want to play. We had an inter-squad on Saturday and on Sunday they hoofed it. Jack sent the state police after them. I think they were caught in Indiana. Vainisi spoke with them on the phone and talked Losch and Skronski into returning. That's precisely why teams asked prospects, "If drafted, do you intend on playing professional football?"

———

The Packers' staff didn't seem to know what to do with me. The defensive coaches wanted to play me on the line, while Lou Remkus, the offensive line coach, wanted me on his side of the ball. Throughout the preseason I moved around a bit. Primarily I was used on the offensive line, though I did see some action on defense. When the regular season began, I wasn't a starter, but I was seeing a lot of playing time.

Starter or not, the entire year was a learning process.

Early in the season we were facing the Baltimore Colts, and for me in particular, Big Daddy Lipscomb. Big Daddy never attended college; his only experience prior to the pros was in the Army, where he played a little ball.

Boy, he was tough, and I knew I was in for a rough day. I wasn't sure if I could block Big Daddy or not. So, on the first couple of pass plays I resorted to holding him. Then, about halfway through the first quarter we called a running play. Big Daddy grabbed my arm as I headed back to the huddle following the play.

"Hey, Forrest, lets make a deal."

I was surprised he knew my name.

"What kind of deal?" I asked, though I was skeptical.

"If you don't hold me," Lipscomb said, "I won't kill you."

I was a reasonable man, and that seemed like a reasonable proposition. "That's a deal." And believe me, I didn't hold Big Daddy again.

There were other things I learned that year. Sitting in the locker room before my first preseason game against the Eagles in Milwaukee, the guys on the team were getting taped by our trainer, Bud Jorgensen. Jorgy was wearing white training pants with big pockets. I was watching as players walked up, said something to him, and Jorgy just patted one of his pockets. The player would then reach into the pocket, pull out a bottle of pills, take two or three, put the cap back on, and then go about their business.

As a rookie I had to wait to get taped, but I was watching the peculiar scene play out before me. I looked over to Henry Gremminger.

"Henry, what are those guys getting?" I asked.

"You don't know?"

"No."

"They're getting bennies," he told me.

This was all new to me. "Bennies?"

"Benzedrine," he said. "They give you added zip during the game."

At the time, amphetamines weren't illegal, though the league later outlawed their use. Usage wasn't widespread on the Packers; only a handful of players made it a practice. Though I rarely took bennies, I wasn't completely innocent. One episode in particular stands out in my mind. We were in Bangor, Maine, playing the Giants in preseason. In those days we played in some obscure towns in an effort to spread the popularity of pro football. It was a hot, humid day in Bangor, and one player said to me in the locker room, "I think I'm going to take a bennie tonight; it's awfully hot out there."

That sounded like a good idea to me so I took one also. It was the worst thing I could have done. The effects of the pill made my mouth dry, and I couldn't drink enough water during the game. I actually drank so many fluids that I became waterlogged.

———

The Packers' head coach during my rookie season was Lisle Blackbourne, who was in his third season at the helm in Green Bay. As a coach, Lisle could be very caustic; he was quick to criticize performance. But that's the way it was. If you did something wrong, you expected to get chewed out.

One particular mistake from my rookie year stands out. I had good speed for a lineman, and I was given a spot on the special teams punt coverage. Against the Colts I went down to cover a punt with Lenny Moore receiving the kick. Instead of staying outside in good contain position, I went straight for Lenny thinking I could get him. However, Moore juked me and returned the punt about 40 yards around my side.

After we watched the game film on Tuesday, Lisle called me into his office.

"Do you know what I called you when I saw you cover that punt?" he asked.

"No, coach, I don't," I answered.

"I called you wild ass," Blackbourne told me. "You were a wild man. I hope you learned what that word 'contain' means."

All I could say was, "Yes, sir," and believe me, I never did forget.

On December 10, 1956, two days after we lost to the 49ers in San Francisco, I was drafted into the Army. While the rest of my teammates went on to Los Angeles for the final game of the year, I flew back to Milwaukee where I was inducted into the service. I was put on a bus early the next morning and taken for a physical. I tried to think of every way I could possibly fail that exam—a pulled hamstring, a strained groin—but the doctor told me I was in good health. The following day I was put on another bus; the destination this time was Ft. Leonard Wood in Missouri for basic training. I couldn't afford to lose the paycheck from that final game. The Packers wouldn't budge, though. It didn't matter how badly I needed the money, "Sorry, we can't give it to you," I was told.

In the service they try to break you down. If you don't do what you're told, they threaten you with jail. If jail was worse than the Army, I didn't want anything to do with it. We stood in line for everything in the Army. For chow, for equipment, for anything we needed. It seemed like all we ever did was stand in line.

My second day at Ft. Leonard Wood was when my Army life really began.

"Grab blankets and pillows," someone bellowed at the new draftees, "and follow that guy right there."

I looked over and there was a sharp-looking sergeant carrying a swagger stick just like George C. Scott did in *Patton*.

"Okay, meatheads, follow me," he said. There were four of us, and we followed the sergeant up a flight of stairs in the barracks. On the second floor we followed as he walked along a big red stripe of linoleum. He turned, saw what we were doing, and blew his top.

"Kings and very few queens get a chance to walk on that red stripe," the sergeant barked at us. "If I ever see you walking on that, I'll have you court-martialed."

I wasn't nearly as happy about Army life as this picture suggests.

He then went over to a bunk and halfway turned over the bedding with a sleeping soldier in it. "Private, show these meatheads how to make a bunk!"

The next morning we were all rousted out of bed in a similar fashion. Boy, I was a pro football player, and even though I was a player with little experience or acclaim, I had been treated with respect by people. But the Army respects no one. I knew right then, when my time in the service was up, I was gone.

Following eight weeks of basic training I was assigned, of all things, to clerk/typist school. I finished eight weeks of typist school and since my fingers didn't fit the typewriter too well, I was sent to the fifth Army headquarters in Chicago. I was there one week when an old sergeant approached me.

"Are you in love with staying here in Chicago?" he asked me.

"No," I told him, "not necessarily. What do you have in mind?"

"Would you like to go somewhere and play football?"

I didn't have to be asked twice. "Yes, sir, I sure would," I quickly answered.

"Let me make a call out to Ft. Carson and see if the coach I knew is still there."

A few weeks passed and the sergeant came to me. "I'm cutting your orders today; you'll be leaving for Colorado tomorrow."

He wrote a name on a piece of paper and handed it to me. "Here's the guy you look for when you get to Ft. Carson. You look him up as soon as you get to the base," he said. The name on the paper was Doug Dickey— the same Doug Dickey later became a successful college coach, first as an assistant in Arkansas and later as a head coach at Tennessee and Florida.

After arriving at Ft. Carson, I checked into my barracks and went straight to the gym, where I was told Coach Dickey's office was located. I introduced myself to the coach and after some small talk he asked me, "How long are you in for?" When I told him I'd been drafted, he responded, "You'll be here for the rest of the year most likely."

"Yes, sir," I agreed, "I'm sure." I didn't like the Army life too much, but at least I'd spend the remainder of my days in the service playing ball.

"We're getting ready to start spring practice," he told me, "After you get assigned, I'll make sure you are free in the afternoons to practice."

I was designated to headquarters company and found my duties were mundane clerk work. Sitting at a desk all day didn't agree with me, but you don't complain in the Army. Still, I guess someone sensed I wasn't happy with being stuck inside an office. I didn't gripe, but some people can tell if you're a square peg in a round hole.

I was told that I would be assigned to G-2. After trying to remember what G-2 was, I realized it was intelligence. "They want me to be a spy!" I said.

I reported to Master Sergeant Tom Sheehan, a genuine, dyed-in-the-blood Irishman. My job wasn't anything quite as exciting as spying. I processed security clearances. If someone was assigned overseas into a system that was delicate, we had to make sure the person had never been in jail. We would fingerprint these soldiers; I felt like a lawman. The atmosphere in G-2 was a lot more casual than it was at headquarters; we didn't see nearly as many officers.

The security work lasted for several months, until the start of the football season. At that point I was reassigned to the football team, which made me happier.

———

In the Army, there were guys coming and going all the time; you never knew who was who. Earlier, in the fall, I took a ten-day leave and went home to Texas for a visit. Before I left Ft. Carson I had requested a new pair of shoulder pads to replace the thread-bare set I'd been given. When I returned to Colorado at the end of my leave, I walked into the locker room and sitting two lockers down from me was a big guy—a big guy with a real nice smile. I stepped toward him and this new guy stuck out his hand.

"My name is Willie Davis," he said.

As I shook his hand I noticed that he was wearing my new shoulder pads.

The two of us got to talking, and Willie told me that he'd gone to Grambling and had been drafted by the Cleveland Browns. The Army, however, got a hold of Willie before Paul Brown had the chance. On the base team, Davis and I each played both ways. On offense we were both tackles, and on defense Willie played linebacker while I played tackle. Though he didn't have anything to do with it, through the years, I never let Willie forget that he'd taken my shoulder pads.

We played ten games that season. Hamilton Air Force Base in Ohio, Ft. Sill in Oklahoma, and Ft. Bliss in Texas were some of the teams we faced. The level of competition varied from week to week, though most of the time it resembled college play. There was one team, however, Ft. Bolling Air Force Base in Washington D.C., that might have been competitive against some pro teams. In fact, their roster was filled with a number of men who had pro experience. They were good, I'll tell you that right now.

Once the season began, football was our job seven days a week. We ate together, trained together, and practiced together. Every once in a while we'd have an Army course to take, like map reading, just enough to let us know we were still in the service.

Several days after we played the final game on our schedule, Lt. Dickey called us in for a meeting.

"We got one more game to play, boys, down in Cape Canaveral, Florida," he said.

Coach Dickey explained that we'd been selected to play in an All-

Army Championship, the first Satellite Bowl game. They had just begun to launch the burgeoning space program at Cape Canaveral, where we stayed for a week on an Air Force base. It was like a working vacation for us. They even let us eat out in restaurants a few times instead of feeding us that old Army food.

Our opponent in the December 29 game was Ft. Dix, from New Jersey. On that team were a couple of standout players, including Rosey Grier and Sherman Plunkett, an offensive tackle who later played for New York Jets. Plunkett was huge. He'd just roll over anybody in his way. He was my man that night, and at 290 pounds, he had fifty pounds on me. He was one of the biggest men I ever went against. Still, I held my own in that contest. Our regular quarterback had received his discharge from the service, so Lt. Dickey had to step in behind center. You talk about pressure. Here was our coach, our commanding officer, playing quarterback. The linemen on the team knew better than to let anyone in on Lt. Dickey.

The officers at Ft. Carson had divergent opinions on our football program. Some didn't care for it. They were career soldiers and believed that the service wasn't about fun and games. Others, though, saw victory in football games as a point of pride for Ft. Carson, something that built morale among soldiers on base. These officers especially wanted us to beat Ft. Dix, which we did when Lt. Dickey, playing safety on defense, intercepted a pass late in the game, sealing our victory.

We returned to Colorado and enjoyed a big celebration at the gymnasium. I spent much of my remaining days in the Army lounging pool side. In college I had taken Red Cross lifeguard training and earned my certificate as a lifeguard. So when I was lucky enough to be offered a job as a lifeguard at the base pool, I jumped at the chance.

At the time, when you were drafted into the Army, you were obligated for two years. However, if you had seasonal employment, you got out three months early. And that is what I did. I missed the entire '57 season, and I returned to the Packers in the summer of '58. I saved up twenty-eight days of leave, which allowed me to attend training camp, and though I did not report in time for the beginning of camp, I was present for most of it.

I was discharged from the Army on September 10, 1958, and a lot had improved in Green Bay while I was gone. We had better equipment, a nicer practice field, and our own dressing room. More noticeable, the Packers had a new stadium, and for the 1958 season, a new coach. A year earlier, on September 29, the Packers dedicated their beautiful new home, City Stadium. Lisle Blackbourne resigned after a 3-9 1957 season (which followed a 4-8 '56 record). Taking Blackbourne's spot was Ray "Scooter" McLean. McLean had been an assistant for the Packers several years earlier. He had even served as co-head coach of the team along with Hugh DeVore for the final two games of the 1953 season.

Before the start of the season Scooter made a bold statement. "We're not shooting for just a good season," he said. "We're going for the championship."

Scooter had been a player himself years earlier. He was a good guy, but being a good guy isn't always a good thing in football. Scooter tried to get too close to his players. He'd play cards with them, and it's never a good idea for a coach to owe money to a player, or vice versa. Scooter also was lax on discipline, and his leniency was taken as a weakness. He was too mild-mannered and forgiving to be an effective head coach, and Scooter was taken advantage of by some members of the team.

Are these the reasons we fell short of Scooter's prediction and finished the 1958 season 1-10-1? Not entirely, but the lack of discipline throughout the team did not help. A coach just can't play poker with his players and end up owing them money. That just doesn't sit well.

I learned a lot observing that season. As a coach, you can like your players and respect them, but you must maintain a certain distance from them.

————

At the end of the season, Scooter decided he had had enough. Or the Packers had had enough of Scooter. Did he jump, or was he pushed? I don't know, and now that we're fifty years down the road, it doesn't really matter. The official announcement was that Scooter had resigned as Green Bay's head coach three days after our December 14, season-ending loss to the Rams. But I believe it was a resignation under pressure from management. His was the shortest head coaching tenure in Green Bay Packer history. About six weeks later, on January 28, Vince Lombardi was named as Scooter's successor. Lombardi had been an offensive assistant with the New York Giants for five years. Around the league, Lombardi had developed a fine reputation as an offensive coach, but personally, I didn't know from beans who he was. Not long after the hiring was announced, I was in Dallas at an SMU function where the school announced the hiring of Hayden Fry as the new coach. The event was held at a downtown hotel, and I was standing outside when Tiny Goss walked by. Tiny had attended SMU, and he had played a little ball in the NFL. He was drafted by Cleveland and briefly played for the Browns, but he'd also spent some time in New York with the Giants when Lombardi was an assistant coach.

"Do you know this guy Lombardi?" Tiny asked me.

"No, I don't," I said. "Do you know him?"

His answer was succinct: "Yeah."

"Well, what's he like?" I asked.

"He's a real bastard." Tiny was short and to the point; I didn't feel the need to ask any follow-up questions.

————

Later that summer I rode to training camp with John Symank. John was one of our defensive backs who also lived in Dallas. On the second night of driving we made it as far as Milwaukee. Since we were both veterans, John and I weren't obligated to report for another two days, so we decided to spend the night in Milwaukee before heading on to Green Bay the next morning. After we settled in our hotel room, I suggested to John that we call Dave Hanner, a defensive tackle on the team. Dave was an old veteran who had reported early, and he always knew what was going on around the team. So we got Dave on the phone and asked him how this new guy was running camp.

"Ooo-wee! You wouldn't believe it," Hanner exclaimed.

We asked a few more specific questions, and Dave gave us a little more insight into what was going on up there.

After we hung up the phone, John and I began talking. Maybe we should get up there tonight. After a few minutes of discussion, we both agreed that it was probably for the best. We grabbed our bags and jumped back into John's car.

We arrived very late, signed in, and a camp boy showed us to our dorm. I told the young man, "Since we got here so late, just let us sleep in, and we'll report for the afternoon practice."

At 7:00 a.m. there was a knock on the door. I got out of bed and opened it to see a different camp boy standing there. It was this kid's job to wake up all the players.

"Breakfast is at 7:30, and Coach Lombardi wants to see you," he told us.

John looked at me, and I looked at him. Without saying a word we got dressed and went over to meet the new coach.

———

First impressions can last a lifetime, and I certainly remember vividly the moment Vince Lombardi stuck out his hand and welcomed me to training camp. I can still it see now.

That smile.

Lombardi had a real nice smile, a firm handshake, and as he spoke he looked me directly in the eye. "I want to thank you guys for coming up early because we've got a lot of work to do."

The niceties over, Coach Lombardi then told us what time practice started, and after breakfast John and I took the bus out to the field. Because we were veterans, we didn't have to wear pads for the first practice. But I quickly found out a Lombardi practice was anything but easy. That day was my introduction to grass drills, or what we called "up downs." Conditioning—that is what Lombardi believed in for his players. I'll tell you right now, after about fifty "up downs," I didn't know if I'd survive.

When that aspect of practice concluded someone ventured that surely the worst part was over. We assumed the rest would probably be ordinary as far as football is concerned. But that was just hope. There were two more grueling hours of calisthenics and agility drills.

It quickly became very obvious that this team was going to be very well conditioned. Under Blackbourne and McLean, I had never truly felt like I was in proper football condition. At SMU I always felt like I was in shape. We ran a lot, we hit during practice, ran wind sprints after practice. Training in Dallas, in that ungodly August heat, you had to be in shape. If we weren't in condition, we never would have made it through. So I knew the difference. The first couple years in Green Bay, I never felt like I was in suitable condition to play an entire game. You expected the coaches to get you in condition; I didn't expect to do it myself. In the past when things got tough during practice, veterans would convince the coaches to let up on us. "It's a long season," someone would say. "We've got to take it easy."

Somehow we all instinctively knew that wouldn't work with Lombardi.

He not only whipped us into excellent condition, he also pulled us together as a team. When you suffer through something as a group—in our case the demands of a Lombardi training camp—the misery has a tendency to draw you together. It was a shared experience. We survived and persevered under Lombardi. It bonded us as a team, and that first day you could feel a surge among the players. We were starting anew and everyone had a chance to show what he could do as a football player. Lombardi's obvious intent was not to just play, but to *win*.

————

When the rest of the veterans reported, Lombardi gathered us all together. He laid everything out for us step by step: what we were going to do, how we were going to do it. He spoke about winning, something we hadn't been doing recently in Green Bay, and before Lombardi nobody even *talked* about winning. Scooter had predicted a championship the year before, but those words were hubris. In the locker room we didn't believe him. We knew we weren't ready yet. But when Lombardi spoke, the words sounded different, and he immediately captured our attention.

"I am not remotely interested in just being good," Lombardi declared. "Only three things should matter to you: Your religion, your family, and the Green Bay Packers. In that order."

————

He didn't just talk about winning; Lombardi had a definite plan on how to accomplish that goal. In our first offensive meeting, Lombardi stood in the front of the room, stepped to a blackboard, and drew up a play. What he diagrammed for us was the play that would become known as "the Green Bay sweep."

"Gentlemen," he said, "in order for us to be successful, this is one play that we have to make work. Everything we do is based on the success of this play."

We worked on that play continuously, the nuts and bolts, everything was broken down into minute detail. Each man on the field knew his assignment and what was expected of him.

The play started with a split back formation. In other words, the quarterback was behind center, the halfback was behind the weak-side tackle. (If the tight end is to the right, that's the "strong" side, thus making the left the "weak" side.) The reason the play was so successful is we'd give the same look for a wide variety of plays.

Paul Hornung had been a quarterback at Notre Dame, and he was very accurate with his throws. This allowed us to pass off the sweep, which then gave the defense two things to look out for.

We could run the sweep weak because Hornung was a good blocker. Most of our passes were run from the same formation.

We had an off-tackle play to the strong side in which we double-teamed the defensive end and kicked out on the strong-side linebacker with the guard.

It was important to our offense that we have guards who could pull, who could maneuver in the open field.

The opponent would see the formation. They could look at the formation and say, "here comes the sweep," but maybe it was an off-tackle play. Maybe it was a short trap or a long trap. They might think the sweep, and we'd throw the ball. Or, is the sweep coming strong side or weak side?

We'd bring Boyd Dowler, our end, to a 3-4 split on the weak side, and because Hornung and Taylor were big backs who could both block and run, we could run the play either weak side or strong side.

We also ran our traps from the same formation. In the long trap, we targeted the defensive end. In the short trap, we took out the tackle. The first step for everybody in the backfield was the same as the sweep.

Coach Lombardi's philosophy was simple: "Run to daylight!"

————

A lot of pieces were already in place when Lombardi arrived in Green Bay. We had the nucleus of a good football team. I think the Packers had done a good job of recruiting, scouting, and putting together a talented group of guys. Take a look at our 1958 roster: Paul Hornung, Max McGee, Jim Taylor, Dan Curry, Ray Nitschke, Jerry Kramer, Bart Starr. The core of a championship team was there. What the team needed was discipline and direction, and that is what Lombardi gave us.

One other thing we needed was confidence. We needed to believe we were good enough. Regardless of what position we played, Lombardi's demands and expectations had a lot to do with our own expectations.

I don't care who we were playing—I could be lined up across from Gino Marchetti, who in my opinion was the best defensive linemen I ever played against—Lombardi didn't cut me any slack. He expected me to win most of the battles. And after a while you begin thinking to yourself: "If he believes I can do this, then I must be able to do it. My expectations should match Coach Lombardi's." Pretty soon everybody on the team felt that way.

He talked about conduct. "No one man is greater than the team," he repeated over and over again. *"No one man is greater than the team."*

A few days after camp began, I was going through drills with the offensive line and all of the sudden I heard someone yelling and screaming on another part of the practice field. I looked over and Coach Lombardi was giving it to Max McGee. Max had run a pattern, and on the way back to the huddle he made the mistake of walking rather than jogging. I don't believe I had ever heard a coach, any coach, yell at a wide receiver,

Preparing to block for Paul Hornung, who has taken a handoff from Bart Starr as we execute the famous Packer sweep. The game is against the Browns, sometime in the mid 1960s.

running back, or even a defensive back. They saved their yelling for us poor linemen. But with Lombardi, one thing had become obvious: he was going to treat us all the same. He expected the quarterbacks to be leaders on the field and didn't yell at them in front of the team, but he did talk to them in private about whether they were doing things to suit him or not.

"I paint you all with the same brush," he told us. The rules he laid out weren't just for a few, but for everybody. Vince expected us all to abide by the rules of the game and the rules of the team.

At one of his first meetings with us, Vince told the team, "You can't play for me if you have any kind of prejudice." We took him at his word, and in short order backed up his words with action

Every year we played the Redskins in preseason. We would stay in Greensboro, North Carolina, and in my first two years when we went down there, the black players stayed in another hotel in a separate part of town. Come meal time the black members of our team had to come through the back door to eat at the training table with the rest of us.

When Vince saw this situation, he blew up. He addressed us as a team and promised, "We'll never do this again." And we didn't. In '61 we went to Ft. Benning in Georgia. There we could bunk together, eat together; we were all together as a team. From that point on, if we couldn't come in the front door together as a team, we didn't go.

———

We learned very early in Lombardi's tenure a new way to tell time. You were either fifteen minutes early, or you were late. We called that "Lombardi time."

I was fined once in my entire career. We were in training camp in the summer of '59 at a country club in Pewaukee, outside of Milwaukee. This was before our last preseason game, and there were meetings scheduled that day. You were never late to a meeting, and you certainly never missed a meeting or it might be your last. Well, I took a nap after lunch. I think my roommate had been cut, so I was in the room by myself. The ringing phone in my room woke me up. On the line was Jack Vainisi, who in addition to being player personnel director, had a multitude of other duties.

"You know you're late for a meeting," Jack told me.

"Oh my God!" was my instinctive response. I jumped up, grabbed my playbook, and took off for the meeting room. Lombardi was at the chalkboard diagramming a play that we had just put in the playbook. I tried to sneak in, but he looked up and saw me.

"That'll be ten dollars, Gregg," he said.

That was the last ten dollars he got from me.

Even today I follow Lombardi time. My wife, Barbara, always tells me that socially you don't have to arrive fifteen minutes early, that it's not the thing to do.

Another Lombardi rule: "You will have a coat and tie!"

It was a mandate, and no one ever got fined that I can remember for being out of dress code. Lombardi had sports coats made for us—green with a gold emblem. Vince had everyone measured so the coats fit well and we looked good.

"You are professionals and I want you to look like professionals when we travel," he told us.

On the bus to the stadium, in the hotel lobby, and on the plane…we were the Green Bay Packers and we were professionals.

We were proud to have the sports coats, and it was nice not having to worry about what to wear on road trips. And to get a free sports coat was a pretty good deal.

Lombardi's transition in Green Bay was helped considerably by the addition of Emlen Tunnel to our team. Vince acquired Emlen before the '59 season from the New York Giants. Emlen was a defensive back with the Giants while Lombardi was in New York, and besides being a great player, he became a vital source of information for us about our new coach's way of doing things. Maybe Lombardi brought him in to help us make the transition; maybe not. Either way, it worked.

"He don't like this," Emlen would tell us, or, "He don't like that."

After a few days we got used to Coach Lombardi's screaming and raving, his expectations to get us to put out more. And then one day Emlen called him "Vinny."

None of us had mustered the nerve to call him anything but "Coach Lombardi."

When I heard Emlen say "Vinny" I nearly passed out. "Man, this guy is brave," I thought, "or he knows him really well." It turned out to be both. The rest of us marveled at Emlen, but nobody else took that assumption. It would be "Coach Lombardi" for the rest of us.

He would tell us, "You need to work up a temporary hate for your opponent." A critic heard that and said that Lombardi was "teaching hate." But he pointedly said "temporary." He wanted us to not be nice guys on the field, to be as aggressive as we could be within the rules of the game. He always stressed "within the rules."

Among other changes that Coach Lombardi brought with him was filming practices, scrimmages, most any time there was hitting. We'd break up into offense and defense that night and go over the pictures. Lombardi would just give you hell if you made a mistake.

There were things that he just wouldn't tolerate. One was lack of effort; the second was not getting the job done. The players believed that credit should be given to the other guy; sometimes you're going to get beat on an individual play. Lombardi didn't view things that way…you were *supposed* to win.

Through the years these sessions became legendary among Packer players. Those meetings were like going into a courtroom knowing they got the goods on you. Even if you thought you'd had a good game, Lombardi would find some mistake you made. Most of the time guys would be sweating all over while we waited for the meetings to start. Usually we sat in silence, but occasionally someone would ask, "How did you do?"

"Man, I don't know. I think I did all right."

Even after a good game I would think, "Is there anything he can get me for?" We not only had to get ready for the game, we had to be ready for the film on Monday.

Our first preseason game in '59 was against the Bears in Milwaukee. Chicago beat us on the last play of the game on a screen pass; I think it was to Rick Casares. We were not at all happy that we lost the game, but we felt pretty good about ourselves. In the past the Bears beat us handily, but on this occasion we were able to stay in there right to the end against a pretty good team.

We returned to Green Bay and waited for the film session that Monday. Everything was calm and quiet as we waited for the meeting to begin. When the coach finally entered the room, he was smiling. "My God!" I thought. "He's going to kill us." We were all expecting to have our rear ends chewed out, but instead he told us that we had played a good game. That we'd been beaten on the last play, which he wasn't happy about, but we "played good football against a good team and that shows what you're capable of." He corrected a few things we did wrong, but in a positive manner. That day we found out, depending on the circumstances, a loss could be acceptable.

The regular season began well for us as we came out of the gate with three wins against Chicago, Detroit, and San Francisco. The great start exhilarated us, a young team not accustomed to success. Unfortunately, we couldn't keep the momentum going. Jimmy Taylor carried the load in the first few games, but he suffered severe burns in an accident in his kitchen and missed several contests. (Vince made certain to instruct the rest of us to "keep out of the kitchen.") Following those first three games, we dropped our next four. LaMar McHan started the season behind center, but during the losing streak, Lombardi tried Bart Starr at quarterback. Bart joined the team the same year I did, in '56. In his rookie season he served as a backup to Tobin Rote. While I was gone in '57, they had Babe Parelli and Bart, whose playing time increased. But when he was finally given an opportunity to be the starter, Bart took advantage of it. He learned the offense backward and forward, up and down. The confidence Lombardi placed in Bart made an enormous difference.

From the sideline, Lombardi would yell at us out on the field, things like, "*What the hell is going on out there?*" Any time something went wrong, a fumble, an offside penalty, we would hear from the coach: "*What the hell is going on out there?*" He would pick on us more than the officials, which I guess was a smart thing to do. In a game against the Redskins we were struggling to get a first down. The coach was hollering at us so loudly that Fuzzy Thurston yelled back, "Coach, shut up, we can't even hear in the huddle."

I don't know if Vince heard Fuzzy or not. He never did say, but it relaxed us, and if memory serves me, we went on to score a touchdown.

The final stretch in '59 began with wins over Washington and Detroit before we headed out to the coast for our last two games. At the time, Green Bay always started the season with several homes games, and closed out the year on the coast due to Wisconsin's unpredictably cold December days. With twelve teams and twelve games, it wasn't difficult to schedule, though it did seem to be a competitive disadvantage to close the year on the road every season. We would stay on the coast for those two weeks. In '56 we took a train out to the West Coast following a game in Chicago. It took us two nights and two days, and we ate all our meals on the train. Things had progressed in three years. We now flew to the coast, and we were winning.

We beat both San Francisco and Los Angeles to finish the year at 7-5. It was the first time a Packer team had won both games on the coast. On the flight home we were feeling good about ourselves, our coach, and the city of Green Bay, and I think our fans could see some light at the end of the tunnel. It was a heckuva lot more fun winning than it was losing.

————

Jack Vainisi phoned a few weeks after the '59 season ended and asked me if I knew of a player from Grambling. "His name is Willie Davis and he plays for the Cleveland Browns now," Jack said.

"Yeah, I sure do know him. I know him really well," I said.

"Is he a good football player?" Jack asked me.

My interest was piqued. "Do we have a chance to get him?"

"Yeah," Jack said.

"Well, you better get him right now. He can help us. If you have the chance to trade for him, do it today. If you can't do it today, do it tomorrow."

I didn't know how much my endorsement meant, but I knew Willie was a better defensive end than anybody we had on the Packers. And, a couple of days later it was in the papers that we got Willie Davis. The trade was lopsided in our favor; we got Willie and gave Cleveland A.D. Williams. Years later I asked Paul Brown about the deal. "We had an experienced football team that was also a winning team," he told me. "I just felt like [Davis] was expendable."

Helping teammate Bill Quinlan get ready for a TV commercial in 1962.

Willie coming to Green Bay was not only good for the Packers, it would prove to be good for me. I went up against a great player in practice every day. I had to stay on my toes all the time. Even though practice wasn't always a full scrimmage, it was physical. Willie and I would put in extra time. He would work on his pass moves, and I would practice my pass blocking. We would come out before practice started and do some extra work, anything to make us better individually and as a team.

———

In the winter of '59 I met Barbara Dedek at a friend's party in Dallas. She was cute and had a great personality. I had her number but still hadn't tried to call her when we ran into each other on a street in Dallas. The chance encounter gave me the opening, and I asked Barbara for a date, which she accepted.

We went out and hit it off. At one point she asked what I did for a living.

"I play football," I told her.

Barbara nodded and replied, "Okay," and that was that. Sometime later, after she learned that I was a professional football player, Barbara told me that she thought when I said I played football, I went out in the park and played with my friends.

The '59 football season interrupted our courtship, but we continued to speak on the phone and write letters. When I returned to Dallas at the end of the season, we began dating even more regularly. At the time I proposed in May of 1960, Barbara had no idea where Green Bay was, but she agreed that we should be married there following training camp. That is, provided I made the team. Even though I made the Pro Bowl a few months earlier, there was no guarantee I would make the Packers. In those days, when there were a limited number of teams and roster space was scarce, there was no certainty.

But I began to think that maybe we shouldn't wait, the sooner the better. And so, on the eve of training camp, July 12, 1960, we were married in Barbara's hometown of Marietta, Oklahoma.

Shortly after we said the "I dos," Barbara laid down the law. When we were dating I used to sing country and western songs to her, and she said she liked when I sang. But that ended with the "I dos."

"No more fishing and no more singing to me," she insisted, and I've done my best to comply. As we near our fifth decade of marriage, I have to say that it was the best deal I ever made.

———

Vince Lombardi is rightfully praised for making Green Bay "Title Town USA." But he had a lot of help putting together the Packer roster, especially from Jack Vainisi. Jack scouted in person, and he also oversaw people all over the country who scouted for him. Once the legwork was completed, Jack spent a lot of hours putting that data together. He had the confidence in his scouts who were giving him information. I guess you could call them a football version of bird dogs. He was always asking about guys I played against in college. Jack wanted to quiz me about 'that Hornung.' He was responsible for a number of us being members of the Green Bay Packers including Bart, Jimmy Taylor, Hornung, Nitschke, Jerry Kramer. Heck, Jack played a big role in bringing Vince to Green Bay. He did his homework, asking football men he respected who they would recommend for the open coaching position. After several endorsements for Lombardi, including the stamp of approval of Paul Brown, Jack brought Vince in for an interview. After their talk, Jack was convinced that he'd found the right man, and once Vince was in Green Bay, the two men enjoyed a great partnership.

As we did every season, the Packers played the Lions on Thanksgiving Day, 1960. Detroit beat us that afternoon, handing us our second loss in five days. Our record stood at 5-4 with three games remaining. For us to win the Western Conference, we needed to sweep our final three contests. But before we played another game, the Packer family was jolted by a tragedy that put football into perspective.

When he was young, Jack had rheumatic fever and the illness did some damage to his heart. For the rest of his life, he suffered from heart problems. On November 27, three days after our loss in Detroit, shortly after coming home from mass with his young family, Jack Vainisi suffered a fatal heart attack.

Jack's death was deeply felt by the organization, the team, and Coach Lombardi particularly. The day after Jack died, Vince gathered us together. He struggled to keep his emotions in check as he spoke to us. "We lost a real good friend," was all he could manage to say.

The loss of Jack Vainisi clouded an otherwise successful '60 season.

As we embarked on our annual season-ending trip to the West Coast, the Western Conference title was within our grasp. We managed to shut out the 49ers 13–0, and beat the Rams 35–21 to win the conference championship.

The flight home from California was filled with celebration and speculation. We had been told that the people in Green Bay were so happy that they had planned some kind of party for us when we arrived home.

"I wonder what they're going to do," somebody said aloud. So we all started guessing.

One guy said, "I think they're going to buy us all cars."

All the way home the conjecture continued.

A DC-6B, a four-engine prop plane, carried us home from Los Angeles to Green Bay. As we approached the airport, the pilot came on the intercom, "The people of Green Bay want us to circle the city one time before we come in for a landing. Everybody in town is going to blink their porch lights."

We circled the city and, boy, you looked down there and it seemed like every porch light in Green Bay was on. The view was unbelievable. "I know they're going to give us all cars!" someone said.

The plane landed and we disembarked. There was a stage set up at the airport. Dominick Olejniczak, who was the president of the Packers' board of directors, stood up and congratulated us. The whole town, he said, was behind us. And with that, the big crowd that came to greet us let out a roar.

And they did give us something. It wasn't a car, though. They gave us all blankets. Green Bay Packer blankets.

————

We left for Philadelphia on Christmas Eve and woke up the next morning to a white Christmas. Because the holiday fell on a Sunday, and in those days Christmas was still sacred, the championship was played on

Monday, December 26, at Franklin Field. It was a cold Philadelphia day. The muddy turf was flecked with snow and the footing was poor, a combination not conducive to offensive production. The Eagles were led by their quarterback, Norm Van Brocklin, and wide receiver Tommy McDonald. But the soul of the club was the last of the sixty-minute men, Chuck Bednarik, who played center on offense and linebacker on defense. Bednarik was a big factor in the championship, playing every minute of the contest with the exception of kick-off coverage.

On the opening play from scrimmage, Bill Quinlan intercepted a Van Brocklin pass at the Eagles' 14-yard line. We ran the ball on 3 consecutive plays, but we failed to cross the goal line or get the first down. Lombardi opted not to kick the short field goal, though, and it was a decision that would be second-guessed after the game. He was trying to set the tone for the game; he wanted an early advantage. He knew it was going to take more than 3 points to win the game. "We got here on the run..." was the philosophy, and we tried again on fourth down, but the play was stopped cold.

A similar situation played out on our opening drive of the second half. At the time we were down 10–6, and Vince again decided to go for it on fourth down, and we were stopped. I didn't question either of the decisions. An offensive lineman always thinks he will make the necessary yardage. Later, in the fourth quarter, we briefly took the lead, 13–10, after a Max McGee touchdown. The Eagles, however, scored a touchdown of their own and led 17–13 as we made a final drive for the championship. With eight seconds remaining, we reached the Philadelphia 22-yard line. On the final play, Bart hit Jim Taylor with a pass. The only thing between Jim and the goal line was Chuck Bednarik, who dropped Jim at the eight, and, for good measure, lay on Jim as the clock expired.

You don't remember much about the ones you lose, and it's not because my memory is faulty. We had substantially more first downs and yards gained than the Eagles, but we couldn't cross the goal line. Maybe it was a moral victory for a young team, but it was a loss—one that still stings today.

In the locker room afterward, Coach Lombardi had a few words for us.

"Perhaps you didn't realize that you could have won this game," he said, speaking to our relative youth and lack of experience. "We are men and we will never let this happen again. Now we can start preparing for next year."

5

RUNNING FOR DAYLIGHT

I ALWAYS THOUGHT WE WERE IN THE LEAGUE AT A UNIQUE time. When I first joined the NFL, I'd come home in the offseason and people would ask, "What have you been doing? Are you still in the Army?"

And then television hit. I recall coming home after the '60 championship and nobody even mentioned it, other than my closest friends. Then in '61 the Packers were on television a lot more, thanks to our success the year before. Because they were able to watch the games on TV, friends and neighbors now knew what I was doing. I received more publicity over recovering a punt in the championship against the Giants than I did in four previous seasons combined. All because they said my name on television.

We won the championship in 1961—an indescribable feeling. By the start of 1962's training camp, we had all received our rings, and everyone was wearing his with pride. But we couldn't rest on our laurels—of that Vince Lombardi made certain. Throughout training camp he reminded us how hard it was to repeat.

"You're the motivation for other teams to play well," he told us. "Everybody is coming for you."

As a team we made up our minds: we'd done it once, we could do it again. We were well conditioned, well schooled, and we executed with a passion to win. And beginning in the preseason that's what we did. We won all of our exhibition contests and continued our winning ways throughout the regular season. Our record stood at 10-0 when we traveled to Detroit on Thanksgiving Day. The Lions were always very competitive with us, and that afternoon they had our number.

There was a picture taken that day of Bart being sacked; all four members of the Lions defensive line converged and had a piece of him.

Our offense had the three-step drop and throw, the five step, the seven step, and the bootleg. That was the extent of our passing offense. The play in which the Lions got to Bart was a three-step drop. As an offensive lineman, you set up in front of your defensive counterpart. When he realized the quarterback was dropping back to pass, the defensive lineman would attack the line of scrimmage, and I would chop down on his knees and keep his hands low so the quarterback could see his receivers. The primary receiver on a three-step drop was the tight end or the halfback swinging out of the backfield crossing the line of scrimmage looking inside for the ball.

On that play Starr didn't have anybody to throw the ball to, and everyone had unloaded on their defensive lineman. They got through and just clobbered Bart. They all had a hold of him like they were fighting over the wishbone. I'll tell you this for sure: I think everybody in Detroit had a copy of that picture hanging on their wall.

The Lions put it to us pretty good. They were up 26-0 as we entered the forth quarter, and our 2 touchdowns in the final fifteen minutes weren't enough to make up the deficit. Perhaps it was *Look* magazine, but I'm pretty sure it was *Life*—whichever weekly magazine it was, the plan was to put us on the cover had we beaten the Lions. A nice candid team picture did make it inside the magazine the following week, but we missed out on the chance at being cover boys.

We bounced back from that loss and won our final four regular season games, finishing a Thanksgiving game away from perfection. Our 13-1 record earned us the opportunity to meet the New York Giants at Yankee Stadium for the 1962 league championship.

The temperature at kickoff on December 30 was twenty degrees, and by the end of the game it had dipped to ten. But the cold was only part of it; the gusty winds made the temperature bite all the more and affected playing conditions enormously. The Giants not only played their games at Yankee Stadium, they practiced there also. The excessive use left the playing field in terrible condition. The once green turf had been worn away; the only grass remaining was the small area near each sideline. The wind stirred up the dirt covering the field and swirled the dust around; it was like playing in a sand storm.

The Giants were particularly physical that afternoon, wanting to avenge the loss from the '61 championship game. In particular, they focused much of that aggression on Jimmy Taylor. Sam Huff and Andy Robustelli pounded Jimmy all day. After the game, Huff said he "did everything I could to that sonofabitch." Jim was a tough guy, though. He was battered and bruised, but at the end of the day he was still standing. After he scored a touchdown in the second period he turned to Huff and hollered, "How do I smell from here, Sam?"

It's funny the memories that stay with you through the years. We battled all day, and it was anybody's ball game right up to the end. Hornung was our regular place kicker, but because he had a leg injury, kicking duties fell to Jerry Kramer. The game was won with a couple of late field goals by Jerry. One in particular still sticks out in my mind. He lined up to kick and the wind was blowing like the dickens. Jerry booted that ball, and instead of going end over end, it spun like a top and went straight through the uprights. He kicked that helicopter about 30 yards. I can still see Jerry looking over at Lombardi, his arms held out with both palms up and shrugging as if to say, "Oh well, at least it went through."

I played that game to win it, but I also had another goal in mind. However modest it was, I enjoyed the fame I received from the '61 championship, when my name was mentioned on national television after I recovered a fumble. That mention of my name brought me more attention than everything I accomplished in my first five years combined. As we entered the '62 season I set a few goals for myself, one of which was, if we were fortunate enough to reach the championship game again, I would do everything possible to recover a fumble so my name would be mentioned on TV again.

All day long, on every punt I tore down the field so I would be in position if the return was muffed. In the third quarter the Giants' return man fumbled a punt, and I was there to jump on the ball. It felt like every member of both teams piled on top of me, but I still had the ball securely covered up. All I could see in the scrum were shoulders, elbows, and rear-ends. Then suddenly there was some movement, and I could make out Nitschke.

"Hey, Forrest," he said, "Give me the ball."

Nothing doing

"It's mine, Ray."

Nitschke wasn't to be deterred. "I already have an interception, a fumble recovery, and a bunch of tackles. If you give me this fumble, I'll be the MVP and we'll win the car." (Notice he said "we.")

Ray actually had deflected a pass that was intercepted by Dan Currie. But I figured he did have a good chance of being the game's MVP. I gave him the ball, and he jumped out of the pile holding it aloft. Sure enough, Ray was the game's MVP—but he wouldn't even let me ride in his car.

Jerry's 3 field goals sealed the 16–7 win and gave the Green Bay

Packers another championship. When I returned to Dallas after the season, I ran into a couple of friends. They didn't say, "Hey, Forrest, congratulations on the championship." No, the first thing they said to me was, "What happened on Thanksgiving Day?"

———

Lombardi brought with him to Green Bay many new philosophies and ideas. Some changes were evident immediately, others were seemingly incidental. I remember in his first year Vince had a sign placed in our locker room.

What you see here, what you say here, what you hear here, let it stay here when you leave here.

Vince didn't want the local media to know what was going on in our clubhouse. Green Bay was a small town, and the community didn't need to know every time he yelled at a player. Lombardi was also concerned about gamblers getting inside information from a player. Vince lectured us all the time on gamblers. The way he put it, the gamblers were always trying to gather information. He told us they would ask questions like, "How are you preparing for the game?" and "Who's hurt?" They also wanted to know the team's attitude on the game.

It was around this time, 1962 or '63, that a friend of mine from Dallas called me during the season. Back then, people didn't often make expensive long-distance calls—at least people I knew.

"Hey, Forrest," he said, "How are you doing?"

"I'm doing all right, Tommy. How are you?"

"Good," he replied, before getting to the point. "Who are you guys playing this week?"

I paused for a moment. Everybody who cared knew who we were playing, but I told him anyway.

"Is there anybody hurt on your team?" was the next thing on Tommy's mind.

I politely demurred and pretended not to hear the question.

"Well," Tommy continued, "how's the team feeling about the ball game?"

A bell went off. "Uh-oh," I thought, "that's three key questions that Coach Lombardi warned us about. From that point on, I gave Tommy a stock answer to anything he asked. A short while later we ended the conversation cordially, though Tommy must have sensed my reservations. After that call he stopped phoning altogether.

————

Paul Hornung had a reputation, so did Max McGee, but I can't verify any of the many stories told about those two. All I know for certain is Paul and Max liked to have a good time that occasionally lasted well past curfew. What I can say is that they were both great teammates. And Paul's contribution, in particular, was vital to the Packers' success.

The thing about Hornung—off the field, during the week, we never saw him. He was somewhere doing his thing. On Fridays, though, we'd be sitting around waiting for the meeting to begin. The offensive line all lockered in the same area, and Hornung came over every Friday while we were waiting.

"We're going to need this game, boys," he'd say. "In order for me to help this team and get some yardage, y'all are gonna have to do some blocking up front."

Every Friday he came over. I think he believed he needed to pump up his boys. We'd see him coming, look at one another, and say, "Oh, hell, here he comes."

"How are my boys today? We're going to score a lot of points Sunday."

In mid-April of '63 we were all shocked to learn that Paul had admitted to betting on NFL games. Commissioner Pete Rozelle did the only thing he could to maintain the integrity of the league and suspended Paul indefinitely. Personally, I didn't have any idea that Hornung was gambling. None of us did. And I don't remember Paul ever playing poorly or putting us in a situation where we lost a game. Not to excuse him, but the word I got was that Paul bet on other games, never on the Packers.

Still, we had a good football team going into the 1963 season, even without him. We had Tom Moore and Elijah Pitts at tailback, and both were good ball players. But Paul's absence stung. We also had to play without Bart after the Cardinals whacked him on the sideline and knocked him out of a game as well as the next four. We played well that whole season but two losses to the Bears hurt us. Chicago came to Green Bay to open the year and beat us 10–3. The rematch was in mid-November at Wrigley Field. With John Roach filling in for Bart, the Bears beat us handily the second time, 26–7. If I had been a betting man, I would have put money on the Packers to win that day. Well, I guess that's a poor choice of words, but I was sure we'd take that game in Chicago.

———

We finished with an 11-2-1 record, while the Bears were 11-1-2. You can't help but wonder, what does a player mean to a football team? What does a Hall of Fame player mean to a football team? It's difficult putting into words what not having Paul meant to us. He was an integral piece of the Packers—the champion Packers. He might have made a difference in one of those Bears games, potentially altering the fortunes for both teams.

———

Shortly after our final regular season game, a 21–17 win at San Francisco,

I received a phone call from Doug Dickey, my old coach from Ft. Carson. Doug had recently been named the head coach at the University of Tennessee. He wanted to know if I was through playing football. In retrospect, that seems like a strange question, in that I was in the prime of my career.

"Well, I don't know," I said, "Maybe. What do you have in mind?"

"I want you to come to the University of Tennessee and be my line coach," he said.

I intended to coach when my playing days were through. If I hadn't played pro ball, I probably would have been a high school coach. I knew that coaching was the path I wanted to follow. What I didn't know was the timetable. I had turned thirty the previous October, and I wasn't making a ton of money with the Packers. The monetary difference between a college coach and a pro player wasn't enormous. In the game of football, you never know what's going to happen. Would I have an opportunity this good somewhere down the road?

I went to Knoxville and met with Doug on a couple of occasions and discussed the job. Following the second visit I decided to accept his offer. I announced my decision a couple of days before we played the Browns in the Playoff Bowl, which pitted the runner-up in each conference. The game was ending when Vince came up to me on the sideline.

"Man, I can't wait for next year," he said. "I think we're going to have a great team and season." Then he added, "I don't agree with what you're doing, but as well as you've played for me and the Packers, I can't do anything but wish you the best."

I knew exactly what Vince was doing. The man was a master motivator, and his words left their mark. Still, following our 40–23 win over Cleveland, I returned to Dallas, ready to begin my new career. As training camp neared, the Packers, however, reached out to me. Phil Bengston called and asked, "What would it take to change your mind?" Phil called at the right

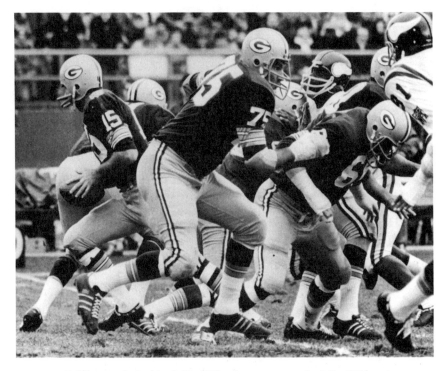

Getting ready to block Carl Eller in a game against the Vikings in the late 1960s.

time. I was already giving my retirement a second thought. Barbara and I had discussed the offer from Tennessee when I took it, and after the Packers called, she and I talked more about it. We had two children now. Forrest Jr. was not quite two years old, and Karen was a newborn.

"You're the one playing ball," Barbara told me. "Whatever you want to do, you do."

Following some deliberation and renegotiation of my contract, I decided to put off coaching for a while and return to Green Bay. The initial decision was an honest one. Though I got a pretty good raise, my "retirement" was not a ploy to wrangle more money from the Packers. I was glad to be back. The coaching career I aspired to would still be there when I retired. Besides, I reasoned, the longer I played the better coach I would become.

We had a couple of injuries during the course of the 1964 season. For part of the year Jerry Kramer and Fuzzy Thurston were hurt, which meant Dan Grim and I filled in at the guard position. I mentioned earlier that I was more comfortable playing tackle. The lay person may not understand the different responsibilities between the two offensive line positions, so let me offer a rudimentary explanation.

With our offense, the guard had to do a lot of pulling. I always thought pass protection was a little bit easier on the inside at guard. Because there are so many bodies in there, the defensive men didn't have any maneuvering room. The man opposite on the defensive line was head-up with you. All you had to do was get a good set and take him on whenever he came to you. At the end position there were guys like Gino Marchetti and Deacon Jones, who could maneuver out in the open field and get around you. Marchetti was strong in the arms and upper body. It was always tough to keep his hands off me so he couldn't grab my jersey and pull me out of position. He was good at that. Deacon just had great speed. He could beat you around the corner if you weren't careful.

Those two fellas, Gino and Deacon, stand out among the many defenders I went up against during my career. Gino was the best all-around football player that I played against. He was a great pass rusher and also excellent against the run. It was a dog fight all day. He didn't talk, and I didn't talk. We might have said hello before the first play, but other than that, no conversation passed between us the rest of the day. The day after we played the Colts and Marchetti, every muscle in my body would be sore. It took everything I had to keep on an even keel with Gino. Sometimes I'd win, and sometimes he'd win, but I know I earned my pay when we played Baltimore.

He had such knowledge; I could tell he studied our offense. The first step I took told him the play, and he would try to counteract it. I used to work in the offseason, thinking about different plays we ran, thinking about how I'd keep Marchetti from making the tackle. It was never going to be easy. It was a battle royale with Gino. It was never dirty. He never slugged me or anything like that. And I was very careful not to hold him, because I felt he was a clean football player, and I wanted to be the same way.

That's not to say I never held. Sometimes I did it on purpose, though, like any lineman—I'll deny that to officials until my dying day. I didn't want to cost my team 10 yards, but occasionally I would hold when things got desperate. In the end the calls probably evened out. There were times I didn't hold and got called, but then again, there were times I did hold and didn't get caught. It wasn't a standard part of my blocking technique, but sometimes my hands were out there, and there was cloth and I'd grab it.

I recall a game against the Baltimore Colts when referee Bill Downs called me for holding Gino.

"Mr. Downs," I said, "what is your interpretation of 'holding?'"

"You've got to keep your hands in to your chest when you're pass blocking," he told me.

To which I replied, "Mr. Downs, why don't you give me your whistle, and I'll call you trying to block Gino Marchetti with your hands to your chest."

He didn't appreciate that, but he didn't throw a flag either.

———

Before every game, like clockwork, Henry Jordan would come over to me in the dressing room and sit down next to my locker.

"Are you nervous?" Henry would ask.

"Yeah," I would admit, "I'm a little nervous."

Next Henry wanted to know who I was playing against. After I told him Henry responded, "*Welllll*, you'll *kill* him. Forrest, you'll beat him on every play."

Henry just oozed confidence, and his words always pumped me up. I would try to do the same for him, but Henry never needed his self-esteem boosted. I'd ask who he had that day, and Henry would tell me.

"How are you going to handle him?"

"Well," Henry answered, "I'm going to open my bag of tricks." Henry always had a bag of tricks he was going to use.

One Sunday afternoon we were getting ready to play Baltimore and here comes Henry.

"Are you nervous?" he asked.

"Yes, I am."

"Who do you have today?"

"Gino Marchetti."

Henry blanched when I said Gino's name. "Oh shit!"

When I really needed my confidence boosted all I got was "Oh shit!"

————

Football is an intense, violent game. To be successful one must not only possess the physical tools, but also the mental buoyancy and drive to prevail. Outside distractions and thoughts were put aside for three hours every Sunday. All my focus was on the man on the opposite side of the line of scrimmage. Barbara's knowledge of football was limited when we married. I remember her asking me at one point, "Why don't you look up in the stands and wave to me like some of your teammates do to their wives?"

"Barbara," I said, "When I'm out there on the field, I'm thinking about the game. I'm not thinking about you." I had enough on my mind going against the likes of Marchetti.

Deacon Jones was right behind Gino. They were the two guys who caused me to lose sleep. He was a great pass rusher and at six feet, five inches, 240-250 pounds Deacon had great speed. He could make that corner and get around you. He also had developed his trademark head slap. He was so quick he could give you that double head slap on a pass rush, Boom! Boom! You better not flinch or that's what you'd get all day long. He was also a great pursuit player. He could catch a running back from behind on any offside play. He had the quickness to beat you inside, if he decided to take the inside rush.

Deacon also was one of the great talkers. He tried to get your mind off business. Of all the defensive linemen I played against, Deacon talked the most, though he might have talked more to the media than he did on the field. And if he thought he was being held, he would let everyone know of the injustice. He would yap at the offender, tell the officials, the whole stadium would hear about it. He was never a guy to hold back. If Deacon had an opinion, he would let you know.

I remember our next-to-last game of 1967. We were playing the Rams in Los Angeles. The most difficult thing about facing Deacon was intersecting him at the proper point when he tried to get around me. Sometimes he'd start inside, then move outside and outrun me to the quarterback. By the fourth quarter of that '67 game, I had been doing a pretty good job on Deacon. He hadn't sacked Bart all day but had put on a rush two or three times. Still, I knew I had to remain alert. On second down I looked across the line and could tell by the way Deacon got in his stance that he was going to try and burn me on the corner. I got a good set as he came at me. He put his head down, and I made contact with him at just the right intersection. I pushed him farther outside and thought, *I got him*. But just as Deacon passed Starr, he reached back with his right arm and knocked the ball out of Bart's hand. I thought I had done everything right, everything I needed to do to keep him off the quarterback, and all I got out of it was a fumble. And when I reached the sideline, Vince was there to greet me with, "*What the hell's going on out there, Gregg*!"

Today I see Deacon at the Hall of Fame ceremonies and he hasn't changed a bit. He's still a great talker and very personable; we always have a good time together. We laugh about that play from 1967 now, but it wasn't too funny at the time.

Sam Huff was another great one. He was a good, tough football player from West Virginia. I played with Sam at the College All-Star game in '56 and we became pretty good friends during that time. I always said Sam was a friendly guy off the field, but he'd take no prisoners on the field. That's how he played the game. There was a TV show back then called "The Violent World of Sam Huff." The producers had Sam miked during a game. We all kidded him about that, about being a "TV star." But when I think of Sam, the '62 championship in particular stands out. He gave us a hard time all afternoon. He did everything he could to keep us from winning that game.

There were many great defensive players that I was never matched up against. For example, I went up against Rosey Grier head to head on just one occasion, in the Satellite Bowl when we were both in the service. Ironically, Rosey was on offense and I was playing defense at the time.

We had a couple of nasty guys on our side too. Ray Nitschke was one of those guys who never stopped; he practiced just like it was a game. During one practice we were kicking field goals, and Ray wanted to put some pressure on Don Chandler. I was in the guard slot and Nitschke came through the middle...he broke through and slugged me! I didn't take kindly to the punch and the two of us got into it. The very next play, here comes Ray and I slugged him. Again we started to fight, but our teammates quickly broke it up. "Save it for Sunday!" Lombardi barked.

———

When our defense was on the field and I was on the bench, I would keep an eye on Willie and the man he was up against. I gave him tips on how the opponent was trying to block him, and Willie did the same for me.

"That guy is trying to set you up and then come inside on you," Willie would tell me. Before long other guys on the team were doing the same thing for one another. We looked out for one another, but that didn't keep me from admiring some of the greats we went up against. I watched Raymond Berry especially, every time we went up against the Colts.

The most memorable game of Raymond's was one I saw on television, though. I watched the '58 championship between the Giants and Colts with Jack and Mack Pogue. The game is famously remembered for Alan Ameche's game-winning overtime touchdown dive. Others remember the heroics of Johnny Unitas during that Baltimore victory, but to me the MVP of that game was Raymond Berry, who made a number of clutch catches, especially on the game-winning drive.

Raymond had great natural talent, but it was his hard work and incredible drive that made him the greatest receiver of my era. Above all else, Raymond was a meticulous student of the game. One of his quirks was carrying a scale with him wherever he traveled. Raymond knew exactly what his best playing weight should be so he regularly monitored himself. Whenever the Colts came to Green Bay, I always knew where to find Raymond so I could say hello. Like clockwork, he came out and walked the field to find the soft spots, to see if there were any frozen spots—anything for an advantage.

Raymond had a teammate who was difficult not to admire, even from the other side of the field. I saw Johnny Unitas play a number of great games, but none was as impressive as the 56–0 shellacking he and the Colts gave us in 1958. Man, Unitas was hot that day. Everything he threw was on the mark, and our defense couldn't do anything to stop him. I got a better appreciation for John when I played my first Pro Bowl following the '59 season. We were running plays in practice against our defense at about half speed. Unitas dropped back to pass and threw the ball over my head. I'd never heard anything like it—the football whistled as it went past. Boy, he had a whip.

————

Two consecutive years of runner-up bowls did not please Coach Lombardi. We beat the Browns following the '63 season, and the next year we lost to the St. Louis Cardinals. Training camp had always been tough under Lombardi, but nothing compared to the summer of 1965. Vince let us know in no uncertain terms that he was "sick of being second."

We struggled all season to keep our heads above water offensively. Some people said that we were becoming predictable. Our offensive game plan hadn't changed significantly since Lombardi arrived. That's not to say we didn't make any adjustments, but I don't remember anything in particular that we did differently. Fuzzy was injured, so I started the year at left guard, and later Jerry was hurt so I had to fill in for him. Still, we kept our heads above water. We started the season strong, winning our first six games before we split our next four. On November 28, we fell to the last-place Rams, 21–10, and the loss rankled Vince. On Tuesday morning he was still angry over our sloppy play. Just before the team meeting was about to begin, Coach asked all of his assistants to leave the room. He waited a moment until it was just him and us, and then he started raving. Vince was really giving us what for, and in the midst of his tirade he roared, "There's not anyone here that wants to win but me."

Boy, I saw red when I heard that. The next thing I knew I was on my feet.

"By God, Coach," I shouted. "Excuse me for cussin', but I want to win. It tears my guts out to lose."

Nothing but silence filled the room. I found myself standing there, and for a moment I wondered, *"What am I doing?"* But he had pressed a nerve. *"If he cuts me or kills me, so be it."*

It seemed like time had stopped as I stood there, but then Lombardi barked, "Is there anybody else that feels that way?"

First there was one voice. I think it was Willie Davis that said, "I do." And then there was another and another. Before you knew it the whole room was saying "Hell yeah!"

I'm sure that's what Coach was after. He was trying to see if our team had any fight left in it.

The reason I said, "excuse me for cussin'" was because a few weeks earlier I was giving a referee a hard time, cursing a little bit. The ref had called something I thought was wrong, and I started giving him some lip. Of course, the referee was far enough away that he couldn't hear me. But that didn't stop Coach Lombardi from jumping on me. He grabbed me by the arm and said, "Gregg, quit cussing. That shows a lack of vocabulary."

———

The next week we went out and beat the Vikings 24–19 at Metropolitan Stadium. It was a game we should have won easily, but the contest was not decided until late, when we blocked a Minnesota field goal attempt. Henry Gremminger recovered the ball and returned it deep into Viking territory and we converted for the winning score. As he came off the field, Vince laid into a big metal trash can with his foot. He kicked the can so hard that it was nearly bent in half from the impact. In the locker room he was so angry I thought he would pop.

"You guys didn't deserve to win," he bellowed at us. "You were lucky."

We all looked at one another. Lucky, hell, we were all happy we won. What was he so mad about? Our equipment manager, Dad Brasher, said he was going to ask the league to install plastic trash cans so Vince wouldn't hurt his feet in case there were future eruptions.

First place in the Western Conference was in the balance when we traveled to Baltimore the following week, on December 12. Our record stood at 9-3, while the Colts were 8-3-1.

The weather in Green Bay was pretty bad so Vince decided we would leave for Baltimore three days early. He set the team up in a Rockville, Maryland, resort, which was a bus ride from Baltimore. Coach Lombardi wanted us to get away from everything and put our full concentration on the game. We arrived three days early, and it became something of a miniature training camp. The first day it was nothing but meetings and practice. All of our meals were served at the resort *and* we had a curfew.

Evidently there was quite a bit of grumbling among the guys. They wanted a place to go and relax, maybe have a couple of beers. Following dinner on the second day, Nitschke stood up and said, "Coach, I've got something to say to you."

"What's that?" the coach asked.

"Well, you brought us out here in the middle of nowhere. We have meetings in the morning, practice in the afternoon, and more meetings before dinner. We even have a curfew! To top it off we don't even have a place to get a beer. I think it would be nice if you'd get us a couple of beers."

For a moment the entire room filled with nervous silence. The tension was palpable. How would Lombardi react to that request? Appearing in the Runner-up Bowl was getting old. Vince wanted us back in the championship game, and he'd been riding us hard.

Vince looked at Ray. Ray looked at Vince. After a long pause Vince finally said, "I think that's a pretty good idea."

The whole room erupted in laughter at Vince's words. He pushed us hard, but in the end he had a sense of humor. And the next night he got us some beer.

Sunday morning we bussed over to Baltimore. We arrived at Memorial Stadium early and took a walk around the field before going to the dressing room. The weather was so foggy we couldn't see the upper deck from field level. We couldn't even see the press box. Paul Hornung scored 5 touchdowns that afternoon in probably the greatest game he ever played. There was 1 touchdown that stands out in my mind's eye to this day. Paul came out of the backfield and ran up the left hash mark where Bart hit him with a swing pass. Paul caught the ball and continued up the hash mark where a couple of Colt defensive backs were within range of tackling him. How Paul outran them, I'll never know. He just took off and outran a fella that was faster than him. I lost sight of Paul in the fog right before he crossed the goal line. That touchdown pretty much sewed up the contest for us. He was the Golden Boy on a foggy Baltimore day, leading us to a 42–27 victory.

As an offensive lineman you're always happy when a teammate scores. It's not as if we lived vicariously through their exploits, but we got a sense of satisfaction knowing we played a part in their success. And that day in Baltimore was particularly memorable because of Hornung's performance. Both Paul and Jimmy Taylor were always quick to give us credit when they had a good game. That acknowledgment, however insignificant it may have been to outsiders, meant a lot to us lineman and made us work a little harder for those guys.

All we needed was a victory the following week in San Francisco to clinch the division. Unfortunately, we could only muster a 24–24 tie with the 49ers, which put us in a dead heat with the Colts at the conclusion of the regular season. Thanks to winning a coin flip, the playoff for the Western Conference was played at Lambeau Field. City Stadium had been renamed in honor of legendary Packer coach Curly Lambeau, who had died in 1965. I always say there's one game a player will remember as the most physical of his career. The '65 playoff against the Colts was mine. The Colts were without the injured Johnny Unitas or his backup, Gary Cuozzo. Instead, behind center, Baltimore had Tom Matte, who played the game with a wristband that had the Colts offensive plays written on it. Though he wasn't Johnny U, Matte proved difficult for us to defense. Our guys weren't used to stopping an offense with a running quarterback. Matte threw some from the pocket, but it was just enough to keep the defense honest.

Early in the game we fumbled, and the Colts scooped up the ball. Bart chased the defender and made the tackle but was hurt in the process. For the rest of the game Zeke Bartkowski filled in for Starr and performed admirably. Late in the game Don Chandler lined up for a kick that would push the game into overtime. There was a strong cross-wind, and the ball went over the crossbar inside the post. Once it went through, however, the ball was blown quickly to the side. That's how we saw it anyway. The Colts didn't see things that way.

In the offseason Willie Davis was asked if the kick was good. "I thought it was good. The referee thought it was good. I know all our players thought it was good. It must have been good because I'm wearing this ring."

Some guys have nervous stomachs. Boyd Dowler threw up before every game. Bill Quinlan did also, especially before big games. I never got so nervous that I threw up, but when we kicked that field goal, the clock ran out, and they sent us all to the sidelines, I did. We won the toss and drove straight down and got in field-goal range. Don Chandler came in, booted the ball through the uprights, and won the game for us. We were conference champions.

———

The morning of the league championship game, I woke up to see that Green Bay was in the midst of an incredible snowfall. By the time I arrived at the stadium a couple of hours later, the groundskeepers had the tarpaulin off the field and were getting ready to paint the lines. A helicopter was hovering above the field, trying to blow the snow off. The maneuver wasn't very effective, however, because it was a wet snow. The solution was to put brushes on the front of a jeep to clear the snow off the field.

Our opponents were the defending NFL champs, the Cleveland Browns. The Browns spent the night before the game in Appleton, and the snow delayed their team bus. When I got to the field there were only two or three Browns at the stadium. Some guys like to come early and hang around the dressing room, or they come in to get taped. Personally, I never was that way. But Dick Modzelewski, a Brown who had played under Vince in New York, was on the field.

"Modzelewski!" Lombardi hollered when he saw Dick. "Where's your team?"

"I don't know, Coach," Dick said. "I'm here, but I can't take you all on by myself."

The Browns eventually arrived at City Stadium, but they were so late the Cleveland players had to hustle to get dressed in time for kickoff.

It was one of those days where the defense didn't let us down. There are two years that stand out where I believe our defense was exceptional: 1962 and 1965. We reached that championship in '65 mainly because of our defense. It was no different in the championship game. They knew what they had to do to beat Cleveland, and that was to stop Jim Brown. Brown was not only a great running back, but he was also a great receiver out of the backfield. We were fortunate that the field was wet and sloppy. The snow was melting after the temperature warmed up a little, making the field slippery. And though they never completely stopped him, our defense kept Brown in check all day. The league's leading rusher was held to 50 yards.

The Browns had the early lead at 9–7, but we came back strong. Offensively we had Fuzzy and Jerry back, and Hornung and Taylor both played really well. Between the two of them, they ran for 201 yards. In the third quarter, Bart led us on 90-yard drive, which culminated with a 13-yard touchdown run by Hornung. We came out on top of a hard-played game 23–12. Winning was such a relief for us. All year we struggled to keep our heads above water, and then to be in the championship game and to win it....

Toward the end of the game, with the outcome settled, Vince began pulling out his starters so the home crowd could give us a hand. It was out of character for Lombardi, but I think maybe he felt the same way we did—relieved to be champions again.

———

We were a close team, a very close team. There were no factions among us, no cultural divides, no racial animosity. Horning, Dowler, Starr, Taylor—all those great players and yet there never seemed to be any jealousy on the team. Not about publicity or anything else. We all got our little piece of the pie. We enjoyed each other, on the practice field, in the locker room, and most of all, on Sundays. Of course, winning makes everyone more compatible. As tough as it could be playing for Vince Lombardi, we still had a lot of fun together.

At training camp we always made the rookies sing—that was the tradition. It was an amusing break from the monotony in the midst of a grueling camp. Vince even appointed two or three veterans and called them the "entertainment committee" to keep things rolling. It was their job to get the rookies singing every night at dinner. It was also their responsibility to make sure the entertainment was good. "The old man don't like your singing; you guys have to do better than this," they'd tell the rookies.

Talking to Willie Davis, Barbara, and sportswriter Lee Remmel at the annual Packers awards banquet in Milwaukee, in 1967 or '68.

If things didn't improve, Vince might chew us out over that. *"This singing has got to pick up!"* When Boyd Dowler was a rookie I got so sick of hearing "Glory, Glory Colorado." That was all he would ever sing—his school's fight song. Boyd would get booed and heckled, but he never came off that song. "Glory, Glory, Colorado!" I knew that song inside out.

Lombardi liked those rookie shows. The rookies would do a skit. One year a group of them pretended to be the team's assistant coaches, who were all as scared of Lombardi as the players were. At the end of the show there was always a song, something to do with training camp. Sometimes a veteran would be imitated. Every year though, somebody always impersonated Vince. That was always the big question: "Who's going to play Lombardi?"

Of all the guys who played him, the best was Elijah Pitts. Elijah had all of Vince's mannerisms down. He was an exception in that whoever played Lombardi on Rookie Night was usually cut. That's why all the veterans wanted to know who was going to play him. As camp started winding down, we'd start picking out the guy we thought would play Lombardi and then get cut. By the time we got to the Rookie Show there was not a lot of talent left. We never brought many rookies to camp to begin with. Most of them were ball players not actors. The whole thing was an inside joke. If someone on the outside saw the show, they wouldn't crack a smile, but we all got the jokes.

Fuzzy was kind of a clown, and Lombardi always said a team needs a guy like Fuzzy Thurston…he's a character and he always comes up with something to keep the team loose. If the team was down, Fuzzy was always uplifting. He liked to make up songs. I remember one that was sung to the tune "He's Got the Whole World In His Hands."

He's got Max McGee in his hands
He's got Max McGee in his hands

Then Fuzzy would add other players, maybe Willie or Hornung or Nitschke. Vince always wanted Fuzzy to sing that song.

———

The country was changing during the sixties, but you couldn't tell by the Green Bay Packers' locker room. We were busy in our own world at that time. With the championships, we had our own thing going. We weren't involved in the politics of the time. The only changes I noticed were longer hair and the music in the dressing room. I didn't have any idea who Bob Dylan was; I had to ask some of the younger players. I did know who Johnny Cash was, though. I liked Johnny, Merle Haggard, Buck Owens, and, of course, Hank Williams. There was a priest we knew at St. Norbert's who would sometimes bring in acts to the college. I found

Forrest Jr., Karen, and Daddy at Karen's first birthday party.

out Johnny Cash was coming to town and I called him up and asked if it was possible to get a couple of tickets to the show. He said "Sure, would you like to go backstage and meet him?"

Boy, I guess!

We went to the show and afterward we met Johnny backstage. He was kind of quiet, letting June Carter do most of the talking.

A year or two later the team was in Milwaukee for a game when I went down for a pregame meal. Johnny was there in the Pfister Hotel holding a press conference. Standing off to the side was some little guy who looked like he was in charge. I walked over and told the guy who I was and told him that I was a big fan of Johnny's. He took me aside, and following the press conference I got to meet Johnny again…and this time I made sure to get a photo.

Willie Davis lived eighty miles down the road from me when we were growing up. It's one of those funny things: we were that close but still living worlds apart. Birthright was an all-white town, and between my hometown and Sulphur Springs was a small community, Cainey. Driving through the area I would see black families out farming their land. Jim Crow was the law of Texas, and while I was attending Sulphur Springs, the black kids in the vicinity went to Douglas High. When we had an away game, Douglas would play at home. There were a couple of occasions when I was able to watch the Douglas kids play, and in time I got to know and became friendly with a few of their players.

I was still living in a segregated world when I was enrolled at SMU. My first opportunity to play alongside a black man didn't come until the East-West Shrine Game in December of '55. During my college career we only played a handful of integrated teams, including Kansas, Missouri, and Notre Dame. Competing against black kids might have bothered some of my teammates, but no one made an issue of it that I was aware. In fact the entire Southwest Conference remained all white until 1964 when Warren McVea broke the color barrier at the University of Houston. Segregation and Jim Crow laws were a part of our life. Our country was a drastically different place sixty, fifty, even forty years ago. But within the Packer family there was no racial animosity or discord. We were a team, in the dressing room, on the field, even away from the stadium.

Football teams live and work together for six or sometimes seven months a year. In the course of a long season, players practice together, sit through meetings together, travel together, and play together. Our situation in Green Bay was unique, however. We did all the things that every other club did, but given that we were playing in the smallest community in the NFL, we ran into one another all over town. The Packer players became part of the fabric of Green Bay. I might be filling my gas tank when a teammate pulled into the filling station. Or I'd be sitting in the barber's chair when a Packer walked in to the shop. Maybe we'd be shopping for groceries when a teammate would bump into our cart.

It wasn't just the intimacy of Green Bay that brought us together. As mentioned earlier, we also shared the common bond of suffering under the rule of Vince Lombardi. We worked hard physically, maybe harder than any other team during that era.

Sometimes we'd go out after a game, ten or twelve couples.

Early in my career the team would take the train to Chicago. We'd leave in the morning and eat together on the train. Traveling by rail was more intimate than flying, but every road trip allowed for camaraderie. We had a regular ritual: upon arriving in a city on Saturday we'd jump in a bus and go directly to the stadium for a brief practice. From there we'd go to the hotel for a team meal and meeting. And with the Packers we traveled to two home games every year—in Milwaukee, where we usually stayed at the Pfister Hotel downtown.

Yes, the Packers were a close-knit group, but personally I was wary of getting too close to teammates. In pro football, players come and go. In training camp, especially, teammates can be gone before you know it. Men you locker next to can be cut, waived, or traded; a teammate one day might be an opponent the next. It was inevitable that the core group of Packers who played together for those many years developed relationships that continue to this day. I know one thing—winning cures a lot of ills in a clubhouse. It's always easier for guys to like each other, to help each other, and pull for one another, on a successful team.

———

Our two best teams, I believe, were the '62 and '66 Packers. In 1966 we were relatively healthy, and we finished the season with a 12-2 record. We lost to Minnesota, when Fran Tarkenton ran our legs off, and to the 49ers in San Francisco. We clinched the Western Conference in Baltimore, and on the flight home everybody was singing.

"We got the best team in the world,

"We got the best coach in the world....

When Vince heard us sing "coach" he stood up and sang a line of his own.

"We've got the best *players* in the world."

The celebration ended as soon as our plane landed in Green Bay. We wound up the season in Los Angeles with a 27–23 win over the Rams before we shifted our focus to the league championship game and our opponent, the Dallas Cowboys. Lombardi decided that we should leave Wisconsin and prepare for the game in a warmer climate. It was the first time the Cowboys had reached the title game, and he wanted to keep us away from the Dallas media as we got ready to play. Splitting the difference somewhat, he decided on Tulsa, believing the weather there would be decent. We arrived in the city late on Monday, and by the time we were ready to practice on Tuesday, Tulsa had been blanketed in snow. We assumed they were going to close practice, but the media showed up, as did a number of people from the city and from Tulsa University. The field was covered with snow and ice, and people were out there with shovels trying to clear the playing surface. They had their top coats on, shoveling the snow so we could practice. Anybody who came to see us work out was invited to lend a hand. We asked one another, "Why'd we leave Green Bay? It's no colder there than it is here in Tulsa."

Under all that ice and snow was mud and slop. Wouldn't you know that turned out to be one of our best practices all year. We sloshed through the mud with meticulous precision. But Wednesday we moved indoors to the Tulsa Exposition Center, a big building with plenty of room. However, the ceilings were very low and we couldn't practice kicks or punts without the ball dinging off the tin roof, making a horrible racket. Vince didn't like that, not one bit. The following day he said to heck with it, let's go on to Dallas.

On Friday and Saturday we worked out at Dal-High Stadium, a high school field in Dallas. Finally Sunday came, and the seventy-five thousand fans that filled the Cotton Bowl saw a helluva game. This was the first of many great Cowboy teams. Offensively, they were led by quarterback Don Meredith and receiver Bob Hayes, the world's fastest man. On the other side of the ball, Dallas was using the "flex" defense, a scheme they were just beginning to master. Bob Lilly, the Cowboys great defensive tackle, was the juice that made the machine run. I remember back in '61 when we were getting ready to play Dallas, and Bob was a rookie that season. My old college coach, Sleepy Morgan, came to practice and drove me back to the team hotel.

"Who you got tomorrow?" Sleepy asked.

"Bob Lilly, and man I'm nervous," I told him.

That was the wrong answer for Coach Sleepy. "Why are you nervous? He's TCU. You're SMU. He's a rookie. You're a veteran."

"Coach Sleepy," I told him, "it don't work like that. Some of these young guys are pretty good football players."

I had every reason to be nervous against Bob Lilly, the rookie, and five years later Bob and the Cowboys had grown a lot as a team. We knew we were going to have a tough game, and we weren't wrong. The championship went right down to the wire. We were up by a touchdown and the Cowboys were driving. They reached our 2-yard line and overtime looked like a certainty. The way things had been going, we wanted nothing to do with overtime. Dallas was moving the ball at will, and we were struggling on offense.

And then Jim Boeke, a Cowboy tackle, was called for illegal motion, which pushed the Cowboys back 5 yards and forced them to throw. On the next play Dave Robinson pressured Meredith and made him throw the ball quicker than he wanted. Our safety, Tom Brown, intercepted the pass, which sealed the victory for us.

An old friend had invited Barbara and me out to dinner after the game. Mack Pogue was a high school teammate of mine. We played football, basketball, and baseball together, and we continued to stay in touch through the years. Well, we all went out to eat, and I think I was the only guy in the whole restaurant who was happy. You'd think that he would have been happy for me, his old teammate, but Mack was blown away that Dallas had lost. That showed me that people sure do stick by their teams.

––––––––

Winning the NFL championship didn't end the season that year. For the first time the NFL champ was scheduled to meet the American Football League champ. I hadn't given the other league a lot of thought through the years. Sometimes I watched an AFL game on TV, but because we played all of our games on Sundays back then there wasn't a lot of opportunity. There were a lot of AFL players who I had played against or who'd been in our training camp, and I was interested to see how they developed. Ben Davidson was one of those guys. He was a defensive end with us for a couple of years, and it was interesting to see how Big Ben was fairing with the Oakland Raiders. We knew he physically was able to dominate, and when he got in that other league he did dominate.

My old SMU teammate, Lamar Hunt, played a vital role in the making of the AFL. So, from that point of view, I was intrigued by the other league. Just the fact that the AFL existed gave us leverage and helped us make more money. Some guys would get cut from the National League and go play over there. But it was primarily the escalating salaries for rookies and the bidding for their services that drove the two leagues to a merger agreement. Beginning with the 1970 season the NFL and the AFL would play under the same umbrella. Until then the champions of both leagues would meet in what

Waiting for my introduction before the first Super Bowl. That's Vince Lombardi on the left and Fuzzy Thurston running off on the right.

was being billed as the AFL-NFL championship, the first of which pitted the Green Bay Packers against the Kansas City Chiefs in Los Angeles.

Ordinarily when we played on the coast the Packers stayed in Santa Barbara. Just a couple of weeks earlier we had stayed there when we closed out the regular season against the Rams. There was no significance in that other than the town had a nice place for us to practice and a hotel with good meeting rooms where we could have privacy and nobody would bother us.

There was a great deal of pressure for the NFL to prevail in that initial meeting. Lombardi felt it, and so did we. The Packers had played in a few championships over the years, but none of us had ever seen so much media in one place. Everybody on both teams was getting more press than they had in their whole career. Writers and broadcasters from all over the country were there, and they talked with everyone, and I mean everyone.

Kansas City's defensive lineman, Jerry Mays, had attended SMU, and he told the press that I had been his hero when he suited up for the Mustangs, so much so that when he was in college he took my number—75. When he came to Kansas City he still wore it. But Jerry Mays wasn't the Chief that garnered our attention. The biggest talker was Fred Williamson, a defensive back. Williamson called himself "the Hammer" because of the forearm chops he liked to deliver to the heads of opposing receivers. "Two hammers to Dowler and one to (Carrol) Dale should be enough," Williamson boasted to the press.

We heard the Hammer talking. We *all* heard him talking, but we kept our mouths shut until game time.

For our part, no one on the Packers said anything that could potentially rile the Chiefs. Fuzzy put things in perspective. He was asked by a reporter, "Are you over-confident?"

"I'm playing against a guy we've never played against before. He's six feet, seven inches and he weighs three hundred pounds, and you think I'm going to take it lightly?"

Fuzzy summed up the way we all felt. As a team we did not take the Chiefs lightly. Even if we were so inclined, Coach Lombardi wouldn't let us. We were facing the unknown. I'm sure it was the same for the Chiefs. We were the Green Bay Packers, the NFL champions! That's probably all they ever heard. But we had no idea how good they were. We could watch them on film and watch them play and evaluate the competition, but we also didn't know how good the teams they were playing were. Up until this point there hadn't been a game between the leagues. That's what made it so intriguing and also made us concentrate much more.

I think we were two pretty well-matched teams. Certainly we had the advantage in experience. We'd been there before and had felt the pressure and knew what it was like to play in a championship game. And it was obvious that this first game between the NFL and AFL wasn't going to be just any old game.

About halfway through, our offense made it close to the Kansas City goal line, though the Chiefs were using some defensive fronts we had never seen before. We had worked on them during our preparation for the game, but we weren't as comfortable with them as we were with the basic 4-3 that everybody used at the time. They put some new fronts on us, and we weren't solid on every play. As we approached the line of scrimmage before a play, I looked at the Chiefs front and thought, "Where do we go from here?"

I looked over at Jerry Kramer. He shrugged his shoulders, turned his hands up and said, "I'll take number 58 and you take the guy whose hero you are."

From across the line Jerry Mays said, "You really know how to hurt a guy."

The star of the game was Max McGee, an unlikely hero. By 1966 Max was an old veteran who had seemingly seen his better days. He'd lost his starting position at end, but he still punted for us, and he was always ready to step in when needed. Boyd Dowler was injured against the Cowboys in the NFL championship game, and his status for the Chiefs was uncertain until game time. I had no idea what Max was up to the night before the game. I didn't learn about his exploits until later, but when Boyd was unable to go, Max stepped in with one of football's most memorable performances. Heck, Max forgot to bring his helmet with him to the field. He had to borrow someone else's before trotting into the game.

The game wasn't very old when Max made an incredible one-handed catch and raced past the Hammer to score the first touchdown in the AFL-NFL championship. By the end of the day, McGee caught 7 passes and scored 2 touchdowns, not bad for a fellow who was out until the wee small hours of the morning. Still, the game was tight, and we were slugging it out toe-to-toe until Willie Wood's second-half interception. A 14-10 halftime lead expanded to a 35-10 final score.

In the late part of the game the Hammer was knocked out when Donny Anderson caught him with a knee to the head. And though we weren't trying to intentionally hurt him, when the Hammer didn't get up, everyone on our sideline cheered. You hate to see a guy knocked out—we weren't blood thirsty—but everyone on the Packers' sideline thought, "There's more to this game than just talk."

I don't remember the exact words Vince said in the locker room afterward, but he sure was happy we won—extremely happy. He walked around the room wearing that big warm smile. There was also an unmistakable look of relief on his face. We were carrying the banner for the entire league, and thank goodness we didn't drop it.

———

The 1967 season was a long hard struggle for the Green Bay Packers. Jimmy Taylor was gone. He had played out his option in '66 and became a free agent. Hornung, too, was no longer a Packer. He was left unprotected in the expansion draft and was selected by the New Orleans Saints. But we had some younger fellas to fill in. Jim Grabowski and Donny Anderson had been drafted the year before, and we still had Elijah Pitts. Elijah, however, was injured during the year and we were forced to pick up Chuck Mercein and Ben Wilson.

Even without Paul and Jimmy, the Packers were the oldest team in the league, averaging almost five years of pro experience per man. But that experience is what kept our heads above water all season. We were getting by on instinct and know-how. Our record at the end of the year was 9-4-1, which I thought was pretty good considering all the changes we endured. Some of the big names were gone, but the young guys played a big role in our success. Travis Williams was one of those guys who gave us a big boost. We called Travis the "Road Runner," and for good reason; he returned 4 kickoffs for touchdowns during the season.

In the next-to-last game of the year, we played the Rams in Los Angeles and lost, 27–24. On Monday Vince just tore us apart, telling us, "You're the worst football team I've ever seen."

The next day during our morning meeting before practice he said, "You know, I've looked at that game again. We played those fellas pretty well. In fact, we should have won that game."

We all looked at one another, thinking, "*Well, that's what we thought.*"

I don't know, maybe he wanted to build us up after tearing us down so far. He needed to give us some hope of winning. We didn't hold up our end of the bargain. A loss to Pittsburgh forced us into a playoff with the Rams for the conference championship.

The rematch was held in Milwaukee on December 23. At the time the Rams were an up-and-coming team with a great defensive line, led by Deacon Jones, who talked all week long to reporters about how the Rams were going to beat us offensively, defensively, and on special teams. Every way possible, the Rams were going to put it to us. In addition, Deacon said, the Packers were old and gray, while the Rams had youth on their side. The way we concluded the regular season, losing to Los Angeles and Pittsburgh, many experts agreed with Deacon, believing that the younger and seemingly hungrier Rams would beat us. But Deacon's words just served to inspire us, myself in particular. I knew who he was talking about getting old…*me!*

The gods smiled on us. It was a cold day in Milwaukee, and I knew Los Angeles would have a tough time playing in frigid weather. George Allen, the Rams head coach, came out for pre-games in a dress shirt and tie without a coat. I'm sure he wanted to show his players that they could handle this cold. But Allen went inside after the warmups, and when he came back out, he had so many clothes on you couldn't recognize him.

George was no fool.

We played one of our best games of the year and beat the Rams pretty handily, 28–7. We played good, solid football and beat a good team. What stands out from that game, though, was a more revelatory moment.

Before the contest, the referee warned each team that during the course of the game there would be "television" timeouts.

We looked at one another. "Television timeouts?"

Sure enough we found out exactly what a TV timeout was. We'd just gotten started on a drive and—boom—all of a sudden the game was stopped.

"Who called the timeout?" We all started bitching about this television timeout when the referee started in on us.

"As much as television is paying you all to play this game, you shouldn't complain about a TV timeout."

It was the first time I thought about how the game was being altered by television. Sure, over the previous decade more people recognized me simply because of our annual Thanksgiving Day game with the Lions as well as our seemingly annual appearance in the championship. But this was different. Television was beginning to affect the game itself, the natural flow of the contest.

———

One week after defeating the Rams, we met the Cowboys to determine the NFL's champion. Lambeau Field held about fifty thousand people at the time, I believe, yet I swear there had to be at least five-hundred thousand people at the 1967 NFL championship. Everybody in Green Bay says they were there. It's either, "My father took me," or "My uncle got me in" or some similar story. I don't know exactly who was present, but the place was packed and those who were there had their snow mobile suits on or their orange deer hunting jackets. Looking up into the stands all you could see was the steam coming from their mouths.

I woke up that morning not having any idea what the weather was like outside. There were a bunch of Packers living in apartments on the west side of town, and often we would catch rides with one another to the stadium. Shortly after I got out of bed my phone rang. It was Jim Grabowski, who was going to drive me to the game. However, he wanted to know if I could drive.

"My car won't start," he told me.

"Your car won't start? What's wrong with it?" I asked.

"Do you know what the temperature is?"

I looked out the window and saw a clear sunny day with no additional snow on the ground.

"It's fifteen below," Jim told me, completing his weather update.

Thankfully, I was able to start my car, and when we reached Lambeau Field you could really feel the cold seeping into your bones. "My oh my," I thought, "this is going to be interesting."

We had just finished warming up, and I was running by the Cowboys, who were winding up pre-game preparations also. I saw Cowboys quarterback Don Meredith, who grew up fifteen miles from me in Texas.

I hollered, "Don, it never gets this cold in Mt. Vernon, does it?"

"No," he said, "and it doesn't in Sulphur Springs either."

————

Gale Gillingham was in his second year with us and was worried to death before the game about playing against Bob Lilly. He had a right to be worried because Bob Lilly was a great football player.

"Gale, you're going to be okay," I told him. "You're not a starting left guard without having earned your position."

"Man, I hope so. The one thing I don't want to do is let this team down. I don't want it to be my fault if we don't win."

During the game he was doing okay, and then early in the second half we went to the sideline and Gale said to me, "Bob Lilly's got on soccer shoes."

"He's what?" I asked.

"He's got on soccer shoes," Gale repeated.

Well, Bob Lilly wasn't dumb. The field was frozen, and the rubber cleats really helped with his footing. Gale was really worried.

"I don't know what I'm going to do," Gale said.

"Gilly, you just do what you've got to do. Go ahead and wear the shoes you're wearing and you'll be fine." And he did a good job against Lilly. Bob told me later that he thought Gale Gillingham was the best guard he'd ever played against.

———

I don't think most fans realize just how hard it is to handle a football in such extreme cold. Each team had a couple of fumbles during the game, and being able to catch a pass and hold onto the ball was nearly impossible. While we were on the field during a drive, there was no way to stay warm. The cold just penetrated. On the sideline I put on a cape and anything else I could find. We had heaters, but none of us wanted to spend the whole day standing around the heaters. We didn't want the Cowboys to see us hovering around a heater because they might start thinking, "Hey, we got 'em now."

Except for Ken Bowman, our center, everyone on the offensive line wore gloves. They were those old cotton gloves that didn't give the hands much protection. It was just enough to stave off some of the shock, and blunt the wind a little bit. During one timeout, we huddled on the field. Our tight end, Marv Fleming, was trying everything to keep warm. He even tried putting his hands under my arms to get a little body heat on them.

For all the hype about the weather surrounding the "Ice Bowl," it's easy to forget that it was a great game. We got an early 14–0 lead, but the Cowboys never quit. They fought back all day, and on the first play of the fourth quarter, Lance Rentzel scored on a 50-yard touchdown pass from Cowboys halfback Dan Reeves, which gave Dallas a 17–14 lead, which was the score when we got the ball with 4:50 showing on the clock. It was do or die, but we'd been in situations like that before. Admittedly, though, not under these circumstances, and we hadn't done much offensively in the fourth quarter.

We were 60 yards away from the end zone, and in the huddle we looked at each other, every man knowing that this was it. Either we score or it's all over.

And then we put together a pretty good drive. Donny Anderson caught a couple of passes and Chuck Mercein made a great catch on a flair pass out to the left. He ran it down to about the 11-yard line. From there we could have kicked a field goal and tied the score, but Vince wasn't sure how well Don Chandler could kick with the bad footing.

Instead of trying the field goal, we ran 3 plays and got the ball down to the 1-yard line.

In our playbook we had several goal line plays where we had our guards pulling. But the field had gotten so slippery, you couldn't stand up. The backs were having trouble getting their footing. So I went to the sideline after the third-down play and told Vince that the guards were having trouble standing up when we tried to pull.

I went back on the field leaving Bart behind with Vince. When he came back to the huddle, Bart said, "We're going to run a quarterback sneak, and we're going to block a 31 wedge."

We broke the huddle and walked to the line of scrimmage. I wasn't even cold. I felt pure exuberance. This was it, there was nothing left—all or nothing. Everybody was scratching like a bunch of chickens trying to get a place for our footing where we could halfway dig in. I looked across at the Cowboys defense and they were in a normal goal-line alignment. The tackles were in the gap, the middle linebacker was stacked behind the center, and the defensive ends were tight on the offensive tackles.

We planned a double team between Ken Bowman and Jerry Kramer, with everybody else taking the next inside gap and pushing the line of scrimmage as much as possible. Each man's goal: Don't let anybody get around you so they can get a hand on the quarterback. Ken and Jerry doubled Dallas tackle Jethro Pugh. My role was to secure the next inside hole. I slanted down in the hole as tight, and as quick, as I could. I got my body between Willie Townes and the ball carrier and was able to cut him down. He fell over the top of me and wound up behind the play. Jerry really got his legs moving. I could see out of the corner of my eye that he was pushing the line and everybody else was on the ground. The next thing I knew, Bart was in the end zone with the football in his hand. That was it. It was over.

We won the game. We deserved to win and were the champions once again. The Cowboys, though, played very well, and it was a struggle down to the last snap of the ball. Through the years I've often wondered, why didn't we kick a field goal and push the game into overtime? But then I think neither the Cowboys nor the Packer players—nor Landry and Lombardi for that matter—wanted to stay on that field a minute longer. There was no shaking of hands with the opponent after the game. Everybody headed straight for the locker room where an exhausted and frozen bunch of Packers pounded one another on the back. We were all so happy—we were downright giddy. Happy that we beat the Cowboys, certainly; ecstatic because we knew our next practice wouldn't be in sub-zero Wisconsin. Soon we would be in Florida preparing for the AFL champions, the Oakland Raiders.

———

The rumors were out there. Before we faced the Raiders we heard talk that Vince might be stepping down as our head coach. It was in the back of every Packer's mind as we prepared for Oakland. Still, I think we were all in denial. At one team meeting during the week, I think it was the night before the game, after we put together the game plan, Vince kind of laid it out for us without really saying anything at all. Reading between the lines, we could see that he was telling us he was going to quit coaching and maybe step into another position with the team. I left that meeting feeling very melancholy. We all did. And each man walked out of that room with a burning desire to win the game for our coach.

Vince was concerned that we might be in for a letdown after the stirring win against the Cowboys. But he had no reason to worry. A year earlier we weren't sure about the Chiefs because we had nothing to compare them to; the AFL was a great unknown to us. But after beating them we knew we could take Oakland. And it wasn't as if we were overconfident. With the definite prospect of this being Vince's last game, we certainly didn't want to lose.

The second AFL-NFL championship wasn't the most memorable game, especially with it being played in the shadow of the Ice Bowl, but we played with enthusiasm and a great deal of effort. The Raiders weren't pushovers. They were a strong club, but they just didn't have our level of experience. Don Chandler kicked 4 field goals, and Herb Adderly returned an interception for a touchdown as we went on to a 33–14 victory.

———

Three championships in three years, five in seven years. There is no disputing that the Green Bay Packers were a great team. We had great players who lived up to their expectations, many of whom have been named to the Pro Football Hall of Fame. I've been asked before, with so many extraordinary players, wouldn't the Packers have been successful under any coach? How much did Vince Lombardi have to do with the team's success? My answer is quick and to the point—he had everything to do with it, with the championships. He's the reason most of us have had the privilege of being enshrined in Canton.

When Lombardi came to Green Bay there were only twelve teams in the league. Every team had great players, but we had one thing that no other club had and that was the guidance and leadership of Coach Lombardi. Still, playing for Vince Lombardi wasn't for everyone. There were guys who came and then quickly went because they couldn't handle the pressure that came with playing for Lombardi. Some didn't want to perform under such circumstances, while others just couldn't. The pressure didn't come during the games. In fact, Sunday's were a relief.

It was the practices that were so difficult. Some people think Vince was cruel, but he was dealing with grown men playing a kid's game. It was fun, but it was serious. It was a business. Believe me: he didn't skip over me when it came to criticism. And in 1959, that first season with Vince, it was a shock to our system. Those of us who were there for the long haul understood what it was all about.

Take Gary Knafelc for example. Gary was a receiver for us when I arrived in 1956. Lisle Blackbourne, my first coach in pro football, used to criticize Gary all the time about his blocking. He wasn't a knock 'em dead blocker. Gary liked to catch the ball.

In '59 he became our starting tight end under Lombardi. Once a reporter asked him, "Gary, what's the difference between your ability to block in the past years and your ability to block now?

The answer to that question was easy for Gary. "Hey," he told the writer, "I'm a lot more afraid of that guy on the bench than that guy in front of me."

Everybody on the Packers had their own personal relationship with Vince. I felt that he liked and appreciated me as a player, but we weren't

A couple of photos of the growing Gregg family. That's me with Karen and Forrest Jr. at the team's picture day (right), and (below) that's the four of us at home in 1969.

the best of buddies. I don't believe you can have that relationship with a coach while you're playing for him. While Vince was still coaching the Packers, I really only had one opportunity to spend time with him away from the practice field and the locker room. I don't remember the exact year, but I had been in the league a few years, and he had been our coach for a while. There was some sort of NFL meeting held in Dallas during the offseason, and all the players who lived in the area were invited to attend. I had the chance to sit at the same table with Vince for about an hour and a half, and even then we weren't alone.

He was warm and personable, and he wanted to know about my family. Vince always asked about family, about the kids. It was just one evening. It was only ninety minutes, but I cherish the memory, and I've always been grateful for spending those few moments with Vince away from the football field. Sometime ago I tried to explain to a writer that I didn't fear Vince. The fear in my mind was that it would be taken away from me, that I wouldn't be a part of the Green Bay Packers and be coached by that special man.

———

After the final gun had sounded at Super Bowl II, we gathered on the field, soaking up the moment when Jerry Kramer looked at me and said, "You grab one leg and I'll grab the other," and then we hoisted the old man up and carried him off the field.

Indeed, there was glory, but there was also sadness. It was a moment, one of those moments that is frozen in my mind. Another championship shared and earned with Coach Lombardi.

Jerry Kramer (right) and I decided to give Vince Lombardi a ride after we won Super Bowl II. It was his final game as coach of the team.

6

THE LONG GOODBYE

THE MAN GIVEN THE UNENVIABLE TASK OF REPLACING
Lombardi was Phil Bengston. The official announcement declaring Phil
the sixth head coach in Packer history came on January 15, 1968. He had
served as our defensive coordinator the entire time Vince was in Green
Bay, and he was a good one. Phil had great success at the position, and
he put together one of the finest defenses in the league. Right up front
Phil told us he wasn't like Vince. Though Phil was a quiet guy, I can't say
that he was easygoing. In fact, he was demanding. He was tough, but not
nearly as vocal as Vince.

When I arrived at training camp in August, there was talk of a
players' strike in the air. A number of veterans, myself included, reported
on time despite the labor unrest. We were all politely turned away by the
Packers general manager.

"I'm very unhappy about this," Lombardi told the press. "I didn't put thirty years in this business to come to this. I always hope, but I've never seen the owners so united. They made a very generous offer to the players."

The Packers opened their camp with rookies and free agents while the veterans scheduled their own practices. We worked out at a high school on the west side of town. Not one soul I ever played with or against liked "up-downs." Still, the first thing we did each day was calisthenics, including "up-downs." We worked on plays and did everything we normally would have done had the coaches been there. Each man knew the practice schedule inside out. We didn't miss a whole lot, just somebody yelling at us.

I was very appreciative of the Players Association's efforts on our behalf. In 1960 we negotiated a pension plan, which was a big step forward for us. When it came to the union, Vince skirted all around the perimeter. He didn't want anything that would upset or damage the league. His main concern was the sanctity of the NFL. But I believe in the back of his mind, he wanted us to get something for our efforts. He never instructed us not to join, but then again he didn't encourage us.

"Think about what you're doing and make a decision on what you believe is best for you," he told us.

In the summer of '68, when the Players Association threatened to strike, I wasn't comfortable with the situation at all. The fact that we weren't reporting to training camp on time was disconcerting. But we were fighting for a bigger piece of the pie. When it was all said and done, though, we wanted to make sure there *was* a season...and a paycheck, because we had to play to get paid.

————

Throughout my playing days, I never had an agent represent me. In fact, at the time I was in the league very few players had agents. As my career was coming to a close, however, things were starting to move in that direction.

When the AFL came into existence and established itself, we suddenly had some leverage. We heard about Joe Namath's big contract with the New York Jets. The St. Louis Cardinals had selected Namath twelfth overall in the 1964 draft, while the Jets picked him third. The bidding between the two clubs reached an astounding four-hundred thousand dollars. Nobody could believe that number. Personally, I was making what I considered to be good money with the Packers, and I didn't seriously consider the AFL, but then again no one was offering me four-hundred thousand dollars.

Namath was an anomaly. As a rule, salaries weren't publicized during my playing days. We didn't even know what the men in our own locker room were making. In fact, management specifically instructed us not to share salary information with one another. They feared that if we learned the man playing next to us was making more money, we would be resentful. This belief, however faulty, kept us in line for years.

Without an agent, I was left to negotiate my own contract. We were given one-year contracts with a one-year option. The process began with Jack Vainisi, and after Jack died, Pat Peppler filled the position. Jack or Pat would make an offer, I'd counter, and then when it got down to the nitty gritty, they'd call in the big dog.

It was the same routine every year. I would sit across from Vince in his office.

"Forrest," Vince would begin, "you're a great football player, and I wish I could pay you what you're really worth to this football team. We're trying to compete, and Green Bay doesn't have the money to spend that a lot of teams do. Now we've got this new league to deal with, and I just can't pay you what you're worth."

He was so damn sincere. "*I just can't pay you what you're worth.*" And I fell for it every time. More or less Vince was telling me, "That's just the way it is." It didn't stop me from asking for more, but asking and getting were two different things.

"Here's what I can do," he would continue, and he would come up with something that was better than what was on the table—something in the range of what I wanted. I'd give a little, he'd give a little, and we would come to an agreement.

It was a simpler time, that's for certain.

————

The lockout only lasted a few days before veterans were allowed to report to camp. The transition was probably easier with Phil, someone we knew, someone from within the system. He continued what the Packers had been doing under Lombardi. The training camp schedule was nearly identical to the one we'd used for the previous decade. The camp wasn't as difficult physically as those run by Lombardi—it couldn't possibly be. Some players liked it for that reason, while others wanted a harder regimen. And Phil didn't chew us out like Vince did. After a while I think we started to miss it.

In his new role as the Packers general manager, Vince never interfered with his successor running the team, to my knowledge. I'm sure he was there if Phil ever wanted advice, but other than that, Vince stayed in the background. Still, I saw him a lot that year. He was there for us. And if we wanted to talk with him, we could go to his office and visit. I went to him for advice a couple of times. He used to come out to practice every once in a while, but he wasn't there too much. He didn't want to be "underfoot." He would never have done that.

There was a photo of him in the newspaper that summer, sitting on a tackling dummy. He was wearing a white shirt, a coat and tie, and he wore a wistful expression on his face. At that point there was no question in my mind that he would be coaching again. I just knew down deep he wouldn't be happy on the sidelines. His love of the game was coaching.

Our personnel in 1968 were pretty much the same as it was the previous season. We were all, however, a year older. Some were contemplating retirement, including me, but I kept those thoughts to myself. Still, on the field we fell precipitously from the year before and everybody was looking for answers. We were still a pretty good football team. A field goal here or there, maybe a fumble here or there, and the season may have turned out quite different for us. But we finished with a 6-7-2 record. Every player was giving his best and honest effort, but there was something missing, and I think that something was Vince Lombardi. If Vince had been coaching us, I don't necessarily think we would have won our conference, but we wouldn't have finished below .500.

On December 7 we were playing our final home game of the season against the Colts. It was apparent by that point that our championship run was over. With the Colts well ahead of us in the fourth quarter, Dominick Olejniczak, the Packer's team president, got on the public address system and spoke to the crowd.

"I wish all you fans would stand up and give a cheer for these players who gave us so many great memories, and gave so much of themselves," Olejniczak said.

The fans at Lambeau stood and gave us a great ovation. I have to say, at the end of a frustrating season, it made us feel pretty good.

———

From the moment Vince took the position as the Packers general manager, I believed he took the job so he could wean himself away from Green Bay. We all thought he would eventually go to New York. With two teams in the city—the Jets and the Giants—we figured sooner or later an opportunity would come open. Vince was a big city boy; he had grown up in Brooklyn. But before one of the New York clubs was in the market for a coach, the Washington Redskins approached Vince with an offer. Washington owner Edward Bennett Williams put a lot on the table—coach, general manager, plus some equity in the team. I'm sure that the final incentive helped sway Vince to take the job. I know he liked Green Bay and felt affection for his players, but it was time for him to move on. Vince always loved a challenge, and Washington hadn't had a winner in decades. Turning that team around was a challenge he couldn't resist.

————

Following the 1969 season there were several stories in the press that lumped my name with some other Packers expected to retire. It was an assumption on the part of a few reporters, because I never told anyone I planned to end my career. I'm sure my age had something to do with the speculation, but even at thirty-six (going on thirty-seven), I wasn't finished. When Vince left for Washington he asked me if I'd like to join him as a coach. The offer piqued my interest, but I was still tied to the Packers contractually.

And then Green Bay offered me an opportunity I couldn't pass up.

Going back to my short-lived retirement in 1964, the Packers understood that I hoped to enter the coaching profession when my playing days were through. Phil Bengston wanted me back in 1970 as a player, but then he sweetened the offer to player/coach. I jumped at the opportunity; you can't buy that kind of experience.

My duties as a coach required a year-round commitment. Rather than return to Dallas for the offseason, Barbara, Forrest Jr., Karen, and I remained in Green Bay. The coaching staff began preparations for the draft not long after Vince left for Washington. When spring arrived and colleges began their spring practices, I went on the road. My territory consisted of Ohio, Michigan, Indiana, and Kentucky. The players we were interested in were finishing their junior years, preparing for their senior season. I already had an idea who I wanted because our scouts had graded the best prospects. The coaching staff then put in our opinions.

The remainder of the offseason was filled with a variety of tasks. We studied film constantly, whether it was scouting other teams or looking at individual players from around the league. We graded each player on every team; therefore, if a man was placed on waivers, we already had a book on him. Or if a trade proposal arose, we would already have an evaluation on the player in question, and we would be ready to pull the trigger.

The transition from player to player/coach wasn't nearly as awkward as it might seem. Many of my buddies were gone from the team by then. All my old line mates—Fuzzy, Jerry, Bob Skoronski—had retired. Bart was still there as was Zeke Bartkowski, but there weren't too many old Packers still around. The guys I was coaching were relatively new.

Still, my new role required some adjustments. One day linebacker Dave Robinson and I were sitting together at meal time and he asked, "When we get out there and have a scrimmage, if I hit you, am I hitting a coach or am I hitting another player?"

"When you see me with a coaching cap on, that's a symbol of authority," I told him. "But when I have a helmet on, I'm fair game."

Wearing two hats certainly kept me busy.

Sunday—We played our games.

Monday—The coaches met, reviewed and graded film from the previous day. Then we would begin working on the game plan for our next opponent.

Tuesday—We worked out and practiced.

Wednesday—The game plan was put in.

On Wednesday, Thursday, Friday, and a little on Saturday, the coaches continued to work on the game plan. The life of a coach is hard on the family. The hours are long, and the evenings run late. Our late nights were Monday and Tuesday; we would stay till midnight those days.

We'd bring our lunch and on the nights that ran late, we would go home for dinner and then head back to work. In Green Bay that wasn't hard to do, being such a small town.

Unless there was a coach's meeting, on Wednesdays Phil Bengston let me off after practice for some family time. On Saturday, if the team played in Green Bay, I'd take Forrest Jr. to practice with me. As an NFL coach, you make time for your family whenever possible.

I was a coach the entire week, and I was working out at my position along with the rest of the Packers. It wasn't an easy situation, but it was fulfilling. The competitive desire to take the field still burned inside, and I had long hoped to enter the coaching profession…this was my chance.

———

During the season I made headlines thanks to a consecutive game streak. Through the years I never thought about it. My sole objective was to be prepared and line up each week. I wanted to play the game, not run up a "streak." And then in the fall of 1970, somebody added up the number of consecutive weeks I had played. The number was in the 180s.

I was extraordinarily fortunate to avoid a serious injury throughout my career. I did hurt my knee during the '65 season. I was playing left guard at the time, and though I was able to run a little bit, the coaches decided not to start me on the line when we played the Lions in Detroit. However, I was used on the field goal team

I didn't know until my playing career was over, but the injury I suffered from was a detached knee ligament. After I quit playing, my knee started bothering me so I went to a doctor who scoped my knee.

"When did you get that detached knee ligament?" he asked me.

"I never did," I told him

"Yes, you did," the doctor said, "there's barely anything connecting the ligament with your muscle."

I explained that I had injured the knee years before, and the team doctor told me I had a "strained ligament."

The good doctor looked me in the eye and said, "Well, they lied to you."

That '65 game in Detroit was the closest I'd come to being out of the lineup until the 1970 season. On November 9, I broke my right ring finger while playing the Colts in Milwaukee. Bubba Smith and I were in a little tussle, and I got my finger caught in his facemask. On the sidelines they taped my pinky, ring, and middle finger together to give it some support.

I returned to Green Bay and an X-ray confirmed what I feared: the finger was broken.

"What can we do?" I asked the doc.

"We can put a pin in it, but that means you'll be out for the rest of the year."

That option didn't sound too good.

"What else?" I said.

"We can brace it and put a cast on that hand to protect it. Then you can play, if you can stand the pain."

I didn't understand exactly what "stand the pain" meant until the doctor tried to reset the finger by manipulating it. He gave me a shot and sent me back to work. I was coaching, and the staff was busy preparing for the next game. The pain killer lasted for three or four hours. Boy, by the time I made it home, the pain was terrible. A return visit to the doctor got me another shot and some pills. The following afternoon was an off day for players, so the finger had time to settle. Our trainer, Bud Jurgensen, fixed a brace for me so I was able to practice. Once I made it through practice I knew I could play in a game.

My thirty-seventh birthday came in October—not exactly a spring chicken in football years. But honestly, I still felt fine physically. My body had aged, no question. I wasn't as fast, and my legs weren't as strong, but I never lost my quickness. The aches and pains of football were the same as always. I don't care who you are, if you play football on Sunday, you're going to be hurting on Monday. Maybe Tuesday you're still feeling banged up, but by Wednesday you're ready to go.

Bumps and bruises could come in a variety of ways. In the early sixties we wore Riddell helmets, and the helmets didn't have padding on the inside. It was very protective, but that helmet was not designed to support a big face mask like the one we started wearing. When you hit someone head-on, as I did on virtually every play, the face mask pulled down, and in doing so pinched and tore the skin. The fact that I had a prominent brow made the effect worse, and once the skin was peeled (usually in preseason), I played with it the entire season.

Our equipment man showed the Riddell people what was happening with my helmet, and they built padding on the inside. It didn't eliminate the problem, but it helped.

I remember another incident with my helmet that also involved bumps and bruises. We were playing the Vikings, and I was up against Carl Eller, who was just coming into his own. On one play Carl head slapped me and knocked my helmet off, got by me, and sacked Bart. Everyone assumed the reason I got beat was because Carl knocked my helmet off, but I just got beat on the play.

Many years after the incident Carl and I were both being inducted into the East-West Shrine Game Hall of Fame. When I got to the podium to accept the award, I decided to tell them a little story about Carl.

"I'd like to tell you how I disappointed Carl Eller years ago," I said. Carl was sitting there on the dais, and he gave me a funny look.

"We were playing one year back when head-slaps were legal. Well Carl knocked my helmet off and sacked the quarterback. He then walked over and picked my helmet up and looked inside. A look of disappointment

145

covered Carl's face…he was hoping my head was still in the helmet."

Yes, it's a brutal game. But sometimes you can laugh about it.

————

In the spring of '70 Barbara and I attended the National Prayer Breakfast in Washington. We saw Vince Lombardi and Marie sitting at a table, and the two of us went over to visit. That was the only time I ever saw Vince emotional. He had tears in his eyes as he spoke. I could sense that something was wrong with him. He skin was gray and he just looked bad. At the time we didn't know anything about his health, but obviously something wasn't right.

A short while later he was admitted to the hospital. I phoned him, but he couldn't speak. Instead, I talked with Marie, and she told me the grim prognosis. He was a man we all thought was indestructible, but Vince was suffering from terminal colon cancer. Because of my duties as a coach, I didn't have an opportunity to visit him in the hospital.

Vince Lombardi died on September 3, 1970.

We were in training camp at the time, and the Green Bay Packers decided to fly the whole team to New York for the funeral. The coaches gathered to discuss our plans before we left Wisconsin.

"Coach," I said to Phil, "do you think we ought to let them know we're coming so they'll save us a place to sit?"

"I don't know if we need to do that," Bengston said. "St. Patrick's is a pretty big cathedral. Vince is popular, but I don't think he'll fill that place up."

After giving it a little thought, Phil decided he probably should call. It's a good thing he did, because St. Patrick's was overflowing that day. Bart Starr, Willie Davis, and Paul Horning served as pall bearers for Vince. He'd touched all of our lives in ways we could never repay. Three of his favorites represented all of us—the men who played for, fought for, and won (oh, how we won) for that man.

Vince Lombardi and I at The Thousand Yard Foundation, in Appleton, WI. I received an award as Offensive Blocker of the Year and Vince was the guest speaker.

Our 1970 season was bookended by losses to the Detroit Lions, a 40–0 home opener and a 20–0 defeat at Tiger Stadium. In between we struggled to reach mediocrity. Even before we lost that final game to the Lions, rumors flew that Phil Bengston would either resign or would be fired. I took the field that day not knowing my future with the Packers. Physically, I felt good. I was relatively healthy, but there's not much of a market for a nearly thirty-eight-year-old offensive lineman. If it wasn't my final game as a player, I was fairly certain it would be the last time I suited up for the Packers.

Standing with (left to right) Wellington Mara, then owner of the New York Giants, Marie Lombardi, and Willie Davis at the dedication ceremony for the Lombardi Athletic Center at Fordham University.

Little about the day stands out in my mind, though I do remember that Detroit's Lem Barney picked off one of Bart's passes. Barney returned the interception for a touchdown but not before I completely whiffed on a tackle.

At the end of the season, Phil resigned. Dan Devine replaced him. Some members of Phil's staff quickly took jobs elsewhere. Usually a new coach wants to bring in his own people, and Olejniczak told us that Devine would have the freedom to choose his own coaches. But, he added, we would be interviewed, and he wanted us to be working on the draft until Devine had made his final decisions.

In my interview Devine as much as told me that he had some other people in mind. I told him that I certainly understood. He then said that, as far as bringing me back as a player only, he was going to start from scratch with his own players. Barbara and I had already made the decision to move back to Texas. The movers had come to our house and began packing things when Devine phoned me.

"Forrest," he said, "I would like to offer you the job of offensive line coach of the Green Bay Packers."

I was shocked. After all, he had just explained to me that he had someone else lined up. (He told me sometime later that he had wanted Mike McCormack, who wasn't available.) I hadn't received an offer from any other team in the league, and I had made up my mind that I would do something else with my life. Still, I wanted to discuss it with Barbara before declining Dan's offer.

As she and I talked, I realized that it was time to move on. We continued with our plan to return home to Dallas.

———

It's funny how things happen. As the summer came and training camps around the NFL opened, I thought football for me was over. I had settled into my job at Steven's Sporting Goods; it wasn't coaching, but I enjoyed it. My role at Steven's was to sell a variety of sporting goods to high school and college programs. Jerseys, basketballs, footballs, shoes, whatever might be needed to field a team, I helped sell. Being a salesman isn't easy work, but I wasn't half bad at it.

Still, it wasn't football, and when the phone rang, my interest was piqued. On the other end of the line was Tom Landry, head coach of the Dallas Cowboys. Tom and I had recently seen each other at an SMU event. Perhaps that encounter prompted him to think of me when his offensive line ran into some problems during camp.

"We're having some injuries to our offensive line," Tom told me. "Would you be interested in playing one more year?"

I was a little taken aback, but the possibility certainly intrigued me.

"Yes," I replied, "I sure would."

"Well, come by my office tomorrow afternoon," Tom said.

The next day the coach and I had an open and honest talk. There were a couple of issues I wanted on the table right off.

"I don't want to go out with the Cowboys and then get cut," I said.

"Here's what we'll do," he replied. "We have two preseason games left. I'll play you a lot in those games. After that we'll sit down and make a decision on whether you should play or not."

That was reasonable, but there was one more thing I needed. "If I do make it, I want a nonrelease clause in my contract." Both Landry and the Cowboys' general manager, Tex Schramm, agreed, and I was back in the game.

The next day I walked into the Cowboys' locker room carrying my football shoes. Boy, did I feel the eyes on me. *"What the hell is he doing here?"*

I went into Tom's office, and he told me where to get my equipment. On my way out I ran into Bob Lilly. "What are you doing here?" he asked.

"I'm going to see if I can help you guys out," I told him.

Other than Bob, nobody else in the dressing room was particularly friendly. But then I understood—I probably wouldn't be either had I been in their shoes. Those two championship games weren't all that long ago, and a lot of the Cowboys who played in those games were sitting in that locker room.

I practiced with the team for a few days before we played the Kansas City Chiefs at the Cotton Bowl. Following the game I got a call from Hank Stram, the Chiefs' head coach.

"If you don't make it with Dallas, would you have any interest in coming with us?" Stram asked. "Oh, and Lamar [Hunt] said to tell you hello."

Just a few days earlier I was hustling sporting goods, and now I had two NFL teams interested in my services. I thanked Coach Stram for the phone call and told him I would consider the Chiefs if the Cowboys didn't work out. As it happened, however, Tom was pleased with what he saw of me in the last two exhibition games. And I was happy with how my body responded to the test. I felt good physically, but then again I wasn't thirty-five any longer. With the Cowboys, however, I wasn't going to play every down. Tom brought me in to back up his starters; I was there if needed. He was confident I would step up if called on, and I was comfortable with the situation.

———

It was to be an interesting and eventful season in Dallas. Fourteen years with one organization and you get used to the way things are done. Joining a new team was an eye opener on many levels, on and off the field. The Cowboys treated their players well. For tickets, the older you were the better tickets you received. The Cowboys gave their players tickets between the 35-yard lines. Barbara told me her seats were on the 50. The Packers gave their players seats on the 10s.

When I was at Green Bay, if you needed pictures for fan letters, you had to buy them. After I joined the Cowboys, I got a bunch of letters asking for an autographed picture. I went to the team office on our day off, walked up to the desk, and said, "Excuse me, I've been getting some fan mail. I wanted to know if it was possible to buy some pictures to answer the mail."

The receptionist looked at me funny. "Oh, yeah," she told me, "We've got pictures over there on that shelf. You just take as many as you want."

That year we had a quarterback controversy of sorts in Dallas. The Cowboys had two good ones, Craig Morton and Roger Staubach. Craig had lead Dallas to the Super Bowl the year before, and he began the 1971 season as our starter. But for a period Tom rotated his quarterbacks from one play to the next. Rather than use a messenger guard to carry in his

Still running hard—but for the Dallas Cowboys, in my last year as a player.

play call, Tom used Roger and Craig on alternate plays to implement his call. It was an unorthodox system, certainly, but Tom wanted to get Roger more playing time while keeping Craig in the mix.

As the season wore on, Tom knew he had to settle on one quarterback. At a team meeting he told us that he was going to continue to call plays, but Roger was going to be the starting quarterback. It was the right decision because we ended up winning seven in a row.

Lombardi and Landry worked together on Jim Lee Howell's staff in New York—Vince as the offensive coordinator, Tom as the defensive coordinator. I was very fortunate in my career to have the opportunity to play for Vince and Tom. The two men shared many traits, yet they were as different as night and day.

Vince was volatile, very expressive with the players. He wore his emotions on his sleeve during the ball game.

Tom, on the other hand, was quieter, easygoing.

Vince was Catholic, and Tom was Protestant. Both were very religious. Both were extremely dedicated coaches. That was their life. They were very studious about the game, and each man knew football inside out. Both believed in discipline, though Tom went about it in a different way. Vince attacked it straight on. At the Monday meeting, Vince would call you out in front of everybody.

Tom never yelled. Instead he would say, "You missed this block and it put us in a tough position." It wasn't that you feared hearing it from him. Tom used peer pressure to motivate; you didn't want to let your teammates down.

Every once in a while Tom would mention Vince. Sometimes he'd walk up to me and say, "I wonder what Vince would think about that."

There was a situation that Landry handled that year with running back Duane Thomas. Duane left the Cowboys during training camp and later rejoined the team mid-way through the season. When he came back, he wouldn't talk to hardly anyone. He completely shut out the media and there were very few players he would speak with. At the start of each meeting, Tom would have one of his assistants, Dan Reeves, call out roll. Duane wouldn't answer the roll call. After a couple of days I asked Herb Adderly, "Why doesn't Duane answer roll? It's just common courtesy."

Herb answered, "I asked him that same question and he said, 'I'm here, they can see that I'm here. They don't have to call my name.'"

The rest of us just sat back in awe. We'd never seen anyone buck the system before quite like Duane.

Before practice everybody went out early. Duane had his own way of warming up. He had a whole regiment of warmups before practice. While we were running laps to loosen up, Duane would run back and forth across the field. Once we started practicing, though, Duane did everything the rest of us did.

The coaches wanted us to jog a couple of laps around the field prior to practice. Everyday I would run those laps. Everyday I would see Duane down there. He never said a word to me. He'd look at me out of the corner of his eye just to see who was there. I grew accustomed to that; it was just his way. And then one day I was going around the field, and I saw Duane down there as I jogged past.

"How's it going, Forrest?" he said.

I thought I was dreaming. *Was that Duane?* "I'm doing good," I said. "How are you?"

"I'm doing good too."

He wasn't the malcontent the press made him out to be. So what if he didn't answer roll call? Duane's biggest crime was not talking to the media. He always put out on the field, and that's where it mattered.

————

So much was different for me that season. A new city, a new team. Old rivals were now my teammates, and perhaps the biggest difference was that I wasn't a starter any longer. Since early in my rookie year and then again in '58, I was always in the lineup. But I joined the Cowboys understanding the situation. I wanted to be there when they needed me and contribute when called upon. I didn't get on the field much with the Cowboys; my role was to be ready in case someone was injured. My whole career, except for the first two years, had been under the same system. It was enlightening playing under Tom Landry. Dallas was right on the cutting edge of pass blocking and run blocking. It helped me considerably, especially when I started coaching full time.

We won the NFC East with an 11-3 record. Beginning the year before, the first year of the NFL-AFL merger, there was now another tier to the playoffs—the three division winners and a "wild card." Our first playoff opponent was the winner of the Central Division, the Minnesota Vikings. Beating the Vikings in late December at Metropolitan Stadium was no easy task. We went up there thinking it would be another Ice Bowl, but Bob Lilly didn't believe it.

"I don't care how cold it gets in Minnesota, it will never be as cold as that day in Green Bay," he said before we left Texas, and he was right. The temperature in Minneapolis that day was about twenty degrees, and we didn't have any problems with the Vikings either, beating them 20–2.

One week later, on January 2, we played the 49ers at the Cowboys' new home, Texas Stadium, and beat them in a tight game, 14–3, giving us a date with the Miami Dolphins in Super Bowl VI.

There was a two-week break between the conference championships and the Super Bowl. We spent a full seven days in New Orleans preparing for the game, but the outside distractions had grown enormously since I'd last played in a Super Bowl. I was in the first two, though those games weren't even called the Super Bowl. I never thought I'd see as much press attention as those games received, but I was wrong. It was amazing how much the game had changed in just a few short years. Upon arrival in New Orleans we were overwhelmed by the media. I think every major paper in the country had representatives there, plus radio and television reporters. I wasn't even a guy who contributed much to the team, and they were interviewing *me*.

Bart Starr was there as a member of the media. I don't remember which news outlet he was with, but when Bart interviewed me…now that was a switch! Duane still wasn't talking, however. During media day he sat silently until his required time was up.

Looking at Miami, I thought we could beat them. We were a more experienced team. Roger Staubach had come into his own, Duane was playing great, and the Cowboys defense, "the Doomsday Defense," was one of the finest in the league. Still, we heard a lot of talk leading up to the game about how "the Cowboys can't win the big one." True, the Cowboys had a history of fielding fine teams only to fall short, including the championship games against the Packers and their last-minute loss to the Colts in Super Bowl V. They were a great team, close calls not withstanding. And though it didn't become our battle cry, everyone in the Cowboys locker room was aware of recent history. If anyone didn't remember, the media was there to remind them.

It didn't take long before the demons were being exorcised. Larry Csonka fumbled early, his first of the season, which was recovered by Cowboys linebacker Chuck Howley. The fumble led to a field goal. With a little more than a minute to play in the first half, Roger hit Lance Alworth with a 7-yard touchdown pass. The 10–0 lead was not insurmountable, but on our sideline there was no doubt about the game's outcome. Roger played great and was named the Super Bowl MVP, but he wasn't alone in his heroics. Bob Lilly, Jethro Pugh—all those guys who had played in those past championship games—all felt they had something to prove, and prove it they did. The Cowboys won going away, 24–3.

Though I had some playing time in both playoff games, I didn't get into the Super Bowl. In all honesty, I didn't mind. Those fellas on the field deserved the victory and the opportunity to savor the moment on the field as the final gun sounded. After the game, we had a team party in New Orleans. Barbara and I walked into the party at the same time as Duane. He had a big smile on his face as he said hello to us. It was the first time I'd seen him show any emotion off the field.

I had tremendous respect for the men on that Dallas team. Someone came up to me and said, "You showed those guys how to win a Super Bowl."

"No," I corrected them, "Lilly, Pugh, Staubach, Calvin Hill, Duane Thomas...they won the championship. I was just fortunate to be along for the ride."

———

The time was right. Even before the end of the season, I knew it would be my last year. After the conclusion of the regular season I began trying to ascertain all the coaching positions that were coming open. Coaching was my future, and I was ready to jump in with both feet. Shortly after the Super Bowl, I called Tom Landry to let him know I had been contacted by other organizations and offered a chance to coach.

"You do what you want to do," he told me, "But I was interested in having you go through a whole training camp with us."

I thanked him for the sentiment, but it was time for me to hang it up. My mind knew where I needed to be, but my legs wouldn't take me there. I knew when the year was over that I should get on with my life.

7

STARTING ANEW

IN THE MIDST OF OUR PLAYOFF RUN IN DALLAS I RECEIVED a couple of coaching overtures. John Ralston, the Broncos' head coach, and Harland Svare of the Chargers called me. Word of my desire to coach had gotten out around the league, and both John and Harland were interested in having me join their staffs for the 1972 season. It was gratifying to hear from them, but any further discussion had to wait until the season ended.

Neither man waited long after the final gun in New Orleans to get back in touch. I traveled to San Diego to interview for the position of offensive line coach. There was a comfort level with the Chargers. The offensive coordinator was Bob Schnelker, who used to be on the Packers staff. Behind Bob, the Chargers were going to run a system I knew. I also knew Harland Svare from our knockdown fights with the Giants, where he played linebacker.

I did receive another call from Ralston, who was referred to as, "Win Friends and Influence People," because he liked to attend motivational seminars. The Broncos still wanted me, but I had already decided on San Diego. There was a comfort level with the Chargers, and, man, did I fall in love with that town.

Barbara and I started searching for a house immediately, and it didn't take long to find one we liked. The house we chose was still under construction, and while it was being built we moved into an apartment in town. Our new house in Delmar was completed as training camp started. We could see the ocean from our living room and dining room. Each of the three bedrooms had an ocean view as did our front deck.

During training camp, Dallas called Svare and asked if we would like Duane Thomas. Since I'd spent time with Duane, the team asked for my opinion. I told Harland, "You may have to put up with some eccentricities, but he was a heckuva back." I had talked to the Chargers' staff about Duane a lot during the offseason, about his skills as a running back. There was no condition to the trade, two players for Duane—under normal circumstances that would have been a good deal. But Duane didn't report. The situation lingered on and on until finally he reported after the season started. He wasn't ready to play because he didn't know our offense. We planned on using him on kick-off returns to get him in the game. But then one week he just left and never came back. San Diego ended up trading him to Washington.

We had a pretty good team in 1972. John Hadl was our quarterback. At tailback we had Mike Garrett, a small back with a whole lot of moves. We had a good offensive line including Russ Washington, who made All-Pro, and Carl Mock, our center. While I was familiar with the offensive system Schnelker brought out to San Diego, it was all new to Hadl, and a new system takes time to sink in.

The following year we traded Hadl to Los Angeles, and then we acquired John Unitas in a separate transaction. Being on a staff watching John play was a memorable experience. Through the years I had the chance of being at a number of Pro Bowls with John. Boy, he had a terrific arm. When he threw a ball, it made a special sound as it passed over your head, one I'd never heard before or since. John still had his arm in 1972, but time had caught up with him. He had never been a great scrambler, and now he struggled to escape the pass rush. He also was learning a new offense.

Through eight games we were 1-6-1, and had been shut out in the last three. Under mounting pressure from the fans as well as Charger owner Gene Klein, Harland resigned as the head coach on November 4. Though he stepped away from the field, he remained the team's general manager and was replaced on an interim basis with Ron Waller.

It had been a tumultuous season for us. Harland attempted to build the team through experienced veterans. The acquisition of Johnny U was just one of his moves. He also traded for Deacon Jones and Coy Bacon. Unfortunately, none of these moves worked out well for the Chargers. A third of the way through the year, he fired the offensive coordinator, and that was followed by his own resignation. His tribulations were a good indication of pro football's volatility.

The year, however, wasn't all bad. In the third round of the college draft, we had selected a quarterback from Oregon. Dan Fouts was the Chargers' future, and when we fell out of the running, Dan began receiving more and more playing time. By the end of the season he had shown great development behind center. Still, we ended the 1973 campaign with the dismal record of 2-11-1.

———

We knew Waller was only an interim coach, but at the end of the season there was no hint of who the next man would be. Anytime there is a change at the top, assistant coaches are left in limbo. More often than not, the incoming coach wants to bring in his own people. I was waiting to see who the Chargers named as their head coach when a couple of organizations reached out to me.

New Orleans called, but the Saints were still a young team. And though I didn't dismiss them out of hand, they took a backseat when Art Modell, owner of the Cleveland Browns, called. He wanted to know if I would be interested in coaching the Browns offensive line. I jumped on a plane for Cleveland. Modell conducted the interview, accompanied by Nick Skorich, the Browns' head coach. They offered me the job, and I quickly accepted.

I chose the Browns over the Saints, in part, because I thought they had a better chance of winning, but there were other factors involved in my decision. Cleveland—and the state of Ohio—is the heart of football. The people of the region live for the game. I looked forward to joining one of the NFL's great franchises, and I was hoping to become part of the Browns' championship legacy.

———

I loved San Diego. It was a great place to live for many reasons, but it was particularly tough to leave because of the kids. Forrest Jr. and Karen were just blocks from their school, and they both had made a number of friends during our short stay in Delmar. But Barbara and I had decided sometime before that if we needed to relocate to advance my career, we would do so.

After I accepted the position in Cleveland, Tommy Prothro was named the Chargers' head coach. Tommy called and offered me a place on his staff as the line coach. But I had already made up my mind. I'd given my word to Art Modell, and there wasn't any way in the world I would go back on that. Integrity means a lot, and one broken promise will stay with you in professional football.

———

Nick Skorich and I went back to 1958, when he was the offensive line coach with the Packers. Every coach has his own style, and Nick, though he was a good coach, had a few idiosyncrasies. One was his penchant for scheduling meetings. Meetings are sometimes necessary, but meetings can also be redundant. Still, Nick liked to gather the entire team together. Each week we would have a meeting the night before the game, and we'd discuss who was going to start the next day. We'd been practicing all week long with our starters getting the majority of reps, but Nick still had to go through the ritual.

"Who's going to kick off?" Skorich would ask.

Well, that would be Cockroft, he's our only kicker.

The lineup changed very little from week to week unless we had injuries, and yet we still went through the lineup every Saturday night. One man's meeting is another man's waste of time.

As the 1974 season unfolded, and we showed little improvement on the field, the pressure mounted on Nick from fans and from the media. To their credit, the writers showed some mercy in Nick's last days as the coach—maybe sensing a change would be made at the end of the year, and feeling it was unnecessary to pile on. It wasn't as if Nick was a complete failure as a head coach. The Browns made the playoffs in '71 and '72 under his guidance, but we finished the 1974 season with the worst record in team history at 4-10. Modell didn't waste any time in dismissing Nick. The day after our season-ending 28–24 loss to the Oilers in Houston,

Modell held a news conference where he said, "with deep regret I have asked my friend to step aside."

My immediate reaction was to wonder what would happen to me. Though I had comparatively little coaching experience—and no experience as a head coach—I threw my hat into the ring. There were some eighty applicants for the position, but the number was quickly whittled down. At the beginning of January, Modell was only giving serious consideration to me and to Monte Clark, the Dolphins' offensive line coach. Art brought me in for an interview to get a feel for my philosophy.

"You haven't been coaching very long in the NFL," he said. "Do you have coaches in mind that you'd like to bring with you?"

"I know a lot of coaches. Some I'm interested in, some I'm not."

"Do you think we need to totally rebuild, or do you think we have the men on the roster now, with a few additions, to be competitive?"

That was a difficult question to answer because I recognized at some positions we didn't have the quality of athlete we needed. My answer was honest, but diplomatic.

"We can improve this team with just a few players. I don't think we need to completely disassemble and reassemble in order to be competitive."

He then wanted to know how I valued the personnel. We went over the players individually, discussing their abilities. I knew who we could win with and who we needed to replace.

"I know one thing for certain," I said. "That little running back, Greg Pruitt, will no longer be a part-time player in our offense."

Modell listened to my ideas.

"The one thing you need to know about my coaching," I continued, "is I'm going to make sure my players are in great physical condition. I'm going to be very demanding of those players, and I'm going to expect them to give us everything they've got. Some players aren't going to like me, but I don't care about that because they'll like winning, and that's what I intend to do."

Before I left the meeting, Modell told me that regardless of whether I got the head coaching position, the Browns wanted me back as the offensive line coach. When it was over, I felt good about the interview. I believed I explained what could be expected of me and had shown I was ready to be a head coach. I'm sure that it helped that I was already on the staff. Looking back on Modell's history, after he fired Paul Brown, he hired Blanton Collier, a member of Brown's staff. When Collier retired, Modell hired Nick Skorich from Blanton's staff. He liked to hire from within, liked the sense of familiarity.

He also liked to work the media—to test the waters, and I think he did that with me. He threw my name out there as the leading candidate and waited for the response. He heard a positive reaction, both from the writers and from the Cleveland fans, which helped me. I also received a good recommendation from my offensive line. At first they didn't like me much because I was tough on them, but by the end of the season they had an idea of what I was talking about. Marie Lombardi also spoke to Modell for me, which I appreciated.

I later learned that Art approached Willie Davis and asked if I would be my own man should he name me as the Browns coach. Willie told him the story from the 1965 season when Vince stood before the team and told us, "Nobody here wants to win," and my reaction to that statement. I don't know how much Willie's story aided my cause, or if Marie putting in a word for me helped. Heck, on the morning of January 22, I knew nothing. I went to work that day just like it was any other. Modell was taking his time making a decision, and I was beginning to get a little antsy. The coaching staff was gathered to prepare for the draft when I got the message that Modell wanted to see me in his office.

Here it is one way or the other: I'll either come out of this meeting the head coach, or I'll still be the offensive line coach—for now.

I walked into Modell's office and found a seat. In the room with

Art was Bob Nussbaumer, the Browns' vice president in charge of player personnel.

Modell spoke first. "Forrest, we're going to hire you to be the head coach of the Cleveland Browns."

That got my attention.

"We're going to have a press conference at noon; did you bring a coat and tie to work?" he asked.

Assistant coaches never dressed up to go to the office. "No, I didn't, but I'll take care of that."

I called Barbara to tell her the news and then headed downtown to buy a nice, stylish checked coat, white shirt, and a tie.

A press conference was called and before the gathered media, I laid out what I would expect from my players.

"Motivation is the key to this thing," I told the press. Practices will be harder next summer, more physical…. There will be curfews, the players will be neat, and there will be no place on this team for any player who gets involved with drugs."

Following the press conference I was accompanied by the Browns' public relations man, Nate Wallach, for the rest of the day. Nate spent the afternoon shuttling me from one interview to the next. Radio, television, and newspapers—I think I talked to everyone in the Cleveland media that day. A new job with new responsibilities: but the next day it was back to the business at hand—building a winning football team.

My first full day on the job started with an organizational meeting during which I spoke up.

"Art, one thing I'd like to do is move the team offices to Baldwin-Wallace [College] year round."

We already used Baldwin-Wallace during the season, but in the winter and spring, the team set up at Municipal Stadium downtown, where there were too many distractions. It seemed as if something was continually happening at the stadium. Baseball season was coming soon, and rock concerts were scheduled as well.

After I spoke, a moment of silence enveloped the room. Modell looked at the other men in the office.

"We were going to make the same suggestion to you," he said.

Those first few months it seemed as if he and I were on the same page on most everything. He was pleased when I decided to retain a few of Nick Skorich's men for my own staff. I wanted Richie McCabe as the defensive coordinator. Richie had a great reputation and a fine defensive mind. I also asked Dick Modzelewski to stay on as the defensive line coach. I'd known Dick for years, having played against him when he was a member of the Giants and Browns. Mo and I were to become great friends. There was also Al Tabor, the special teams coach. I liked Al and what he brought to the staff and wanted him to continue with me.

But there were other positions that needed to be filled. I had to hire a receivers coach and a quarterback coach, among others. I was in the midst of researching possible candidates when, during a meeting one day, Art asked me how I was coming along with my coaching interviews. After I gave him a brief update he said, "I just thought about something, and I'd like to know what you think about it. What if you hired Blanton Collier as your quarterback coach?"

Blanton had been a member of the Browns organization since its inception, except for a brief time in the mid-fifties when he left Cleveland to become the head coach at the University of Kentucky. He had been Paul Brown's right-hand man and good friend when Brown was in Cleveland. And then, when Modell fired the legendary Brown, Blanton was picked to be the successor. The decision to replace his friend was difficult, but Blanton accepted the position and within two years led the Browns to the 1964 World Championship. Following the 1970 season he retired as head coach, but he remained with the team, working with personnel. In fact, on a number of occasions during the 1974 season I stopped by Blanton's office and spent time talking football with him. His knowledge of the game was deep, and I enjoyed tapping that reservoir.

I paused for a moment, letting the suggestion sink in. "I think that would be a good idea," I said. "Do you think he'd be interested?"

Modell said, "All you can do is ask him."

After we broke up the meeting, I walked down the hall to Blanton's office. We talked for a while, and then I asked him.

"Anything you need," Collier told me, "I'll help out."

And Blanton proved to be a big asset to me, especially from an organizational standpoint. He mostly helped clean up the language in our playbook. When Nick Skorich took over, he adopted Blanton's playbook, but over the course of a few years there had been so many changes that the playbook barely resembled Blanton's original. We went through all of that, and put the train back on the track, so to speak.

———

Shortly after I was named head coach, Art approached me one afternoon at the team's offices in Berea.

"How do you like training at Hiram [College]?" Modell asked.

Though I only spent one camp at Hiram, I found there was much to like about the campus. It was isolated—boy, was it isolated—and the people at Hiram treated us very well. I felt bad about the move, but we had only one field at Hiram, which would get torn up quickly. They had kept the same dorms through the years with no updates, and the dressing rooms were not fit for a professional team. Heck, the dorm rooms weren't even air conditioned, which is a real necessity in the dog days of training camp.

Modell informed me that Kent State University was willing to host the Browns' training camp. We took a ride to the campus and inspected the university's facilities. They had a number of fields, a good dressing room, a nice dorm, a big meeting room. Everything needed for a successful training camp was already in place. The Browns had called Hiram home for twenty-three years, but I agreed on the spot that we should make the move to Kent.

At our new summer home we had four practice fields. I had laid out the fields so the playing surfaces wouldn't get chopped up and the turf would last the whole training camp. On one I held the "skill" positions workout—the running back, quarterbacks, and the receivers. On another we put the defensive backs and linebackers. And on the third field the offensive and defensive linemen practiced, so that's where we placed the sleds and tackling dummies.

On the second day of camp, Modell came to the field before practice.

"There is something I'd like to go over with you," he said to me as we stood near the first field. "On this field here, you need to do calisthenics; throw the ball here on this field."

Well, I had part of that covered; they were throwing the ball there.

"Now these sleds," he said, moving on to another field, "I'd like to move them here. When the people come out…" He stopped speaking as he placed his hands in front of his face, like a film director setting a scene. "…there will be guys here, and here, and here. And then there would be this big sled right here in the middle. I'd like to spread the sleds around."

Here I was trying to prepare a football team for the coming season, and Art was just concerned with the cosmetic look of practice for the fans. I'm not discounting the importance of making the spectator's experience as enjoyable as possible, but my priority was the team's preparation. I did compromise, though. I moved the sleds to the edge of the first field, which assisted Art's cinematic vision.

He had purchased the Browns in 1961 for what was then an astounding four million dollars. He arrived in Cleveland, a thirty-six-year-old bachelor, with a new toy on his hands. He bought the team and vowed to work in partnership with Paul Brown. Brown, however, had successfully operated for years without interference from management, and he wasn't about to change his timeworn ways for some young upstart. The relationship was destined to disintegrate.

I wasn't Paul Brown, and Art Modell had matured over the years. Our relationship was never presumptuous. He would come to training camp, watch the players work out, and listen to my instructions to the team. Not that he understood what I was saying because he didn't know much about football. But at this point, he did not meddle in my coaching.

My style, to say the least, was a great deal different from Nick Skorich's style. I was very demanding of the players, and I was vocal. Whether at practice or in a ball game, I wanted every man to give the best that he had to give. I was also more critical of the players' performances in meetings than Nick had been. It takes time to adjust to that type of tough critique. The players were grown men, and they didn't like to be criticized. Myself, I didn't see it as criticism. I was simply demanding the best they had to offer. Some members of the Browns didn't care for my motivational techniques, but that wasn't my concern. A coach can't worry about being liked by his players. If he does, he'll never be able to function.

By the end of the season I could tell who was buying into the program. Most of my players were on board, but I can think of maybe three guys who definitely were not. There might have been more, but only three of any significance. Yes, there were a couple of malcontents on the '75 Browns, but we also had a number of quality individuals.

Greg Pruitt was a little guy, about five feet, nine inches, 185 pounds, but he liked the challenge. And if you challenged him he usually answered. In fact, I probably asked too much of Greg that first year. In '75 my plan was occasionally to utilize Larry Poole, a rookie from Kent State, to give Greg a break. But Larry sprained an ankle and missed a few weeks, and

Coaching a preseason game with the Cleveland Browns in August 1975. Behind me are assistant coach Rod Humenuik and wide receiver Reggie Rucker.

then broke his arm in the next-to-last game, against the Oilers. In the end, Larry only appeared in three games, which forced me to use Greg more than I wanted, though I started to give him some rest late in the season.

Greg was a terrific ball player. He was our best running back, our best kick returner, and our best punt returner.

Earlier in the year I put in the short trap. Greg took a look at the play.

"Coach, you want me to run *that?*" he asked.

"Let me tell you about that play," I explained, "The key here is to crack the line of scrimmage; once you do, you'll be in the secondary very quickly. Most of the time you'll have just the safety to get by, and then it's one on one."

I was always getting on Greg in practice about something. It seemed

170

he was always trying to get my goat, and I'd yell some more. It didn't seem to faze him one bit. In fact, I later learned he liked to laugh about it behind my back. One day after chewing Greg out, I looked at our backfield coach, George Sefcik, and said, "He's driving me crazy."

George smiled, "That's exactly what he's trying to do."

I really believe if Greg's timing had been a little different, had he been on a championship team, that he'd be in the Hall of Fame.

We came out of the gate slowly, with losses to Cincinnati, Minnesota, and Pittsburgh. After the loss to the Steelers in early October, a devastating 42–6 defeat, I got my first real taste of Art Modell. Following the game he spoke with a reporter from the *Plain Dealer*, saying, "We've lost before, but I don't like to be embarrassed. These have been three terrible, terrible weeks.... I made certain recommendations to Forrest when he became head coach. Some may not have been sound."

I wasn't used to this—the owner of the team throwing coaches under the bus. We were struggling offensively and defensively, trying to get on our feet. The worst thing an organization can have is more than one person speaking on behalf of the team.

Despite Modell's outburst, the losing continued for another six weeks. We'd get close, and we never played anybody that said we didn't compete with them, but we just couldn't get beyond it. In the ninth week we were playing at Oakland, a game we lost 38–17. But afterward, the Raider assistants told a few of my coaches that "you guys don't play like an 0-9 team."

When those words reached me it made me feel good. We just kept plugging away and the next week we beat the Bengals. That victory gave us the bounce that kept us going for the next two years. In fact we won three of our last five. I think we were a little better than the '74 team, but our record was a little worse at 3-11. Still, I could see the light at the end of the tunnel. All my energies went towards improving the team, and we were getting better, not by yards but by inches.

That '75 Browns squad never quit on me, and I admired the hell out of them for that. The last game of the year we were playing the Chiefs at home, and Greg Pruitt finished up his quest to get 1,000 yards. During the game I wasn't thinking about the 1,000 yards, I was focused on winning the game. We got a lead, and began making some substitutions. One change involved a young lineman, Barry Darrow, who we put in for Doug Dieken. We wanted to give a few men some playing time and give ourselves a chance to evaluate them.

Dieken, our starting left tackle, always played hard, and he was always there for us. He came up to me on the sideline and asked to go back into the game. The position coach did the substitutions, and I rarely stepped in. This was one thing I wish I could do over—put Doug back in the game so he could be on the field when Pruitt reached the milestone. When you're 3-11 you don't have much to hang your hat on, and Doug wanted to be there with Greg as he attained that 1,000th yard. He'd earned that much.

———

In the summer of '75 we were taking a summer family vacation in Dallas before the start of training camp. Along with us were some friends, Bill and Ann Forester, as well as Jerry and Jean Norton. I had been in the hotel pool with the kids and Barbara, and when I got out of the water Jean saw a mole on my left thigh and told me to get it checked.

"Oh that, it's been there all my life," I said.

Looking back, I'm sure I was in denial. I certainly didn't want to acknowledge a possible illness. But Jean's words were in my mind when after that season, as we were preparing for the college draft, I noticed a change in the mole. The Browns' team doctor, Vic Apolito, was on vacation so I contacted another doctor on the team's staff, Mal Brahms. Dr. Brahms scheduled an appointment for me to visit with a dermatologist on St. Patrick's Day. I wasn't in the office of Stuart Fischer a moment before the doctor took one look at my mole and remarked, "How long have you been hiding that?"

"Well, I've had it all my life, but six months ago the mole developed a bump on it and started to change color."

The doctor got straight to the point. "You have melanoma," he told me. "You've got cancer; the mole has to be removed. I have no idea how far along it is."

That's all I needed to hear.

"When can we do it? Can we do it today?"

"I'm not a surgeon," Dr. Fischer explained, "but I have a surgeon in mind to perform the procedure." The specialist Dr. Fischer had in mind was Dr. James Sampliner, a well-respected surgeon in his field.

Two days later I was in Mt. Sinai Hospital.

Obviously, I came through the ordeal, but it was touch and go for a while. Barbara was advised to prepare for the worst, that it might be best to get our affairs in order. During surgery Dr. Sampliner had removed a four-inch square piece of skin from my left thigh, on which he grafted skin from my hip. I was given an update: They looked at the lesion; it was melanoma in its third stage.

"What do we do from here?" I asked.

"We have to do a lymph node dissection, but first you have to recover from this surgery."

I returned home following the surgery, and as I was getting out of the car a little neighbor boy named, Carl, came up to me.

"Mr. Gregg, are you going to die?" he asked.

"I hope not. Why do you ask?"

"This lady we know who works at the hospital as a nurse," Carl explained. "She said you were going to die."

"I feel pretty good right now."

Carl wasn't the only one wondering about my mortality. Barbara and I went shopping after I was released from the hospital.

"You need some new slacks," Barbara informed me.

"Maybe we should wait on that," I said.

"*No*, you need some slacks," she insisted.

I know better than to argue with Barbara. I picked out three pairs of dress pants, and she took them up to the register. "We'll take all three," she said.

The cashier looked at her. He seemed to be on the same wave length as me. "Why don't you take one pair, and come back and get the others later?"

Barbara was adamant. "*No*, we'll take all three."

Neither Forrest Jr. nor Karen was sure what to think. Despite our own concerns, Barbara and I both tried to reassure them, but we couldn't protect them from the rumors or the talk. A neighbor of ours told Forrest Jr., "You're going to have to be the man of the house now." At his young age, Forrest Jr. wasn't ready to accept his father's mortality or the responsibility this neighbor placed on him.

I had been concerned how the kids would react when we left San Diego for Cleveland. That first summer in Ohio, Forrest Jr. went to training camp with me and served as a ball boy. I didn't learn until later that he and his friends endured practical jokes and good-natured harassment from a few Browns players, most notably Doug Dieken. Among other things, the boys were tied up with athletic tape and stuffed into trash cans. I was proud that Forrest Jr. never ratted out any of the players to me, and I was happy to see how well he had adjusted to the move. He'd quickly made some friends and played Little League baseball. It didn't take Karen long to acclimate either. As it turned out, you ask either of the kids where they were happiest and both will say, "San Diego and Cleveland." But it was difficult for them during the time I was fighting melanoma. Not only was their father ill, but my medical problems were public knowledge and fodder for gossip that they heard.

————

I was happy with Dr. Sampliner, but Modell thought I would be better off with a doctor he knew of in New York at Sloan-Kettering hospital. I talked to Dr. Sampliner about it.

"You can do anything you want; it's your life," he told me.

"But what do you think?" I asked.

"I think I know what I'm doing, and I know exactly what needs to be done. In New York you're just going to be another number. Here, you'll get better care."

I trusted Dr. Sampliner and told Modell as much. I appreciated his efforts and believed his heart was in the right place. Though he never said anything directly, I got the impression that Modell wasn't happy with my decision. I always felt that it might have been one of the things that put distance between us.

While I was in the hospital, the wife of a high-ranking Browns official demonstrated the lack of tact sometimes present within the organization. The very first words this woman spoke to Barbara were, "How has the cancer affected your sex life?" This insensitivity wasn't limited to one rude individual. A member of the Browns medical staff advised me to never tell anyone I had cancer. He was afraid of the stigma attached to the disease. *Cancer*—that was a dirty word back then.

A couple of weeks after the surgery I was back in Dr. Sampliner's office. Up to that point I hadn't felt sorry for myself or wondered, "Why me?" Nor had I gone through the "anger" stage that happens to many who suffer from serious illness. But as I was waiting in the doctor's office, I looked around the room and the many pictures of Dr. Sampliner and his family having a good time at the beach, in the mountains…I looked at those photos and something snapped.

"Why should he have all that fun with his kids while I'm not going to be with mine?"

A few moments later the doctor came in and examined me. "What we'll do is remove the lymph nodes in your left groin," he said. "If the cancer has spread, the next step is chemotherapy."

He didn't pull any punches in his diagnosis. "We've got to get in there and get out all the bad cells, and just hope the cancer didn't travel."

I left the room not feeling real good about my chances, and I also was feeling a bit ashamed of myself. The doctor had done nothing but help me. I had no reason to resent him.

I returned to Mt. Sinai, and to be honest, the doctors believed my chances of ever leaving the hospital were slim. Dr. Sampliner as much as told Barbara that the odds of my survival were not good. He added, "But when you walk into that room you can't cry. Seeing you upset might send Forrest into shock and kill him."

Barbara was under a great deal of stress in those arduous days. On several occasions, as she rode the hospital elevator to my floor, she had to listen as doctors and nurses imprudently discussed my health.

"Have you heard that Forrest Gregg is dying?"

These careless conversations occurred daily until somebody realized that Mrs. Forrest Gregg was one of the occupants in the elevator.

Throughout the whole ordeal, Barbara was my strength, as were Karen and Forrest Jr. Barbara was by my bedside practically around the clock for the month that I stayed in the hospital. Doug Dieken came by nearly every day I was at Mt. Sinai. I cherish Doug's visits and thoughtfulness for they not only helped my spirits but gave Barbara a much-needed break. The kids relieved her on weekends, and during the weekdays Doug allowed her to go home for a change of clothes or a nap, or to just get away for a few moments to collect her thoughts. A number of my players checked in on me as did my coaching staff. In fact, we had a couple of coaches' meetings in my hospital room, though we couldn't get a lot of work done. The NFL wasn't going to wait for my recovery, and we had to prepare for the draft.

My second surgery took about seven hours. When I awoke—standing before me was the nurse who predicted my doom.

"Why did you tell Carl I was going to die?" I asked her. "I'm not going to die."

Without saying a word she hit the road out of there.

A few moments later Dr. Sampliner came in and explained the procedure. "I removed all the lymph nodes in your groin and scraped some muscle and skin off the ephemeral artery. Everything that could possibly be cancerous has been taken out, but we won't know for sure until we do the biopsy."

When the results came in, I was called into Dr. Sampliner's office. The doctor was the only person in the room. Uh-oh, I thought, we've got some bad news coming.

"I've got some good news."

"Tell me about it!"

"It looks like your cancer has not traveled," the doctor said. "Your lymph nodes are as clear as they could be. It looks like we got all the cancer."

There are no words to convey my emotions at that moment. Winning a football game doesn't compare to the feeling I had when Dr. Sampliner gave me that news. People who were around me the most say the cancer mellowed me. You know, I can't argue with that. The thing I thought about the most was my family...I'm going to be here to be with my kids while they're in high school; they won't have to make it on their

Receiving the American Cancer Society's Courage Award in 1982 at the White House. (From left to right): Actor Kirk Douglas, First Lady Nancy Reagan, me, my daughter Karen.

own. I was happy as hell to have my family and my health back.

Yes, I had mellowed; until the first preseason loss, that is.

The Browns were a fairly young team, and our philosophy was to build through the draft. With our first pick in the '76 draft, we selected Mike Pruitt, a running back from Purdue. We had picked up Cleo Miller on waivers from Kansas City late in the '75 season, and I put him in the starting backfield with Greg Pruitt. They worked well together, but my decision to keep the pair in the lineup was a bone of contention with Modell, who wanted Mike Pruitt in the lineup immediately. I was trying to work Mike into the system, but I wasn't doing it fast enough for Modell.

"I believe that if you draft a player number one, he should start for you that year," Modell told me.

I didn't buy into that thinking. My philosophy was to give younger players time to develop. Besides, we were winning, and I believe that changing for the sake of change is always the wrong move. There was never any doubt in my mind that Mike Pruitt was going to be a good football player, but I wasn't going to rush him.

The season started very slowly for us. We won our first game against the Jets, but in the course of the contest we lost quarterback Mike Phipps to a separated shoulder. Our back-up quarterback, Brian Sipe, was a thirteenth-round pick in the 1972 draft and therefore not someone we assumed would be more than a competent fill-in. We dropped three in a row while the offense got accustomed to Brian.

But everything started coming together in the season's fifth week, when Pittsburgh came to Municipal Stadium. The Steelers had already handily beaten us, 31–14, three weeks earlier. They were a physical team. When you took your team into Three Rivers Stadium, your players had better be ready or they'd get the hell knocked out of them. When I arrived in Cleveland, the Browns were not a very physical team. There were some physical players on the roster, but the team did not play hard-nosed football. From my first day as head coach, I preached to them that the road to the division title and a trip to the playoffs went through Pittsburgh. To beat the Steelers they needed to out-physical them.

How do you make a team play more physical? As a coach, you talk about it, preach it, and demand it. If you don't get what you want, you have to demand it again. I coached my team to play hard, aggressive football.

"This is how you compete against the best teams," I told them. "If we're going to beat them, we have to out-tough them."

When we met Pittsburgh on October 10, the Browns hadn't beaten them since 1973. We ended the ignoble streak by beating the Steelers,

18–16, but the game is most remembered for an over-exuberant Turkey Jones play. Jones spiked Terry Bradshaw head first into the unforgiving Municipal turf, injuring the Steeler quarterback. Jones was penalized on the play, as well he should have been, but it had been a long time since the Browns turned the tables on the physical Steelers. There wasn't a malicious bone in Turkey. In fact the incident was probably the only real foul of his career. But in the heat of battle, players sometimes cross the line.

Counting the Pittsburgh game, Brian Sipe led us to three wins in the next four weeks. Mike Phipps returned in the ninth week against Houston. I started Mike against the Oilers, a decision that was questioned by many in the media, given our success with Brian. The second-guessers were proven right because Mike just wasn't on his game, and I recognized the situation early. Before the end of the first half I called for Brian. With him behind center, we beat the Oilers and won the next four games as well. We were 9-4 heading into the season finale against Kansas City. Despite the great turn around, we had been eliminated from the playoffs, effectively making the final game meaningless. Well, believe me, the game meant something to the Cleveland Browns' head coach.

I learned a great lesson that day. The players were ready to go home before they even took the field. As far as they were concerned, the season was over, and that's how they performed. Players from the western part of the country had their cars, with U-Hauls attached, driven to Kansas City and made a quick escape after the game. I decided that day to institute a new rule the following season. If the final game was away, the club would come home together on the team plane and we'd have a meeting the next morning. We lost 39–14 to a bad team, the only blemish on an otherwise rewarding year. At mini-camp six months later, I played the game film of the Kansas City debacle and painstakingly went over each frame of celluloid. The message was being sent; they wouldn't be mailing in a game again.

———

As our success increased, so did the enthusiasm of our fans. Years before the Municipal Stadium end zone was dubbed "The Dog Pound," defensive end Mike Sinclair claimed those fans for his own.

"Those are my fans in the end zone," Mike declared. "I brought them in to come and see me."

Whether he was right or not, I can't say, but we did notice that the fans cheered us with a new level of enthusiasm.

———

Years earlier I served in the Army with a couple of guys from Cleveland. Boy, did I get sick of hearing about that town. Little did I know that I'd be coaching there one day. And it didn't take long for me to appreciate the loyalty and the depth of football knowledge the Cleveland fans had. Despite our terrible start in '75 our fans never deserted us. They continued to come out to the games, cheered for the good stuff, and when the good stuff was hard to come by, they didn't get on us too bad. When Greg Pruitt reached the 1,000-yard milestone on the final day of that season, the fans at Municipal Stadium went crazy. Unfortunately we didn't give them a lot to get excited about that year. But they knew the game, and they were patient.

———

In January of 1977, I was busy preparing for the draft when I got a phone call from Peter Hadhazy.

"You've been named Coach of the Year," he told me.

"Really?" I said. "That's nice."

"You know this is not just the AFC Coach of the Year," Hadhazy said. "This is the big one. This is the AP, the NFL Coach of the Year."

I was pleased with the honor, but I had more pressing issues. I had signed a three-year contract with the Browns, and I really didn't want to head into the '77 season with just one year remaining on my deal. Art Modell always preached continuity, and a lame-duck coach doesn't speak to continuity, especially in the aftermath of what everybody believed to be a good year. No, we didn't make the playoffs, but after 3-11, everyone in Cleveland was tickled to death with 9-5.

I went to Peter Hadhazy with my concern.

"I have one more year on my contract," I said. "Everybody on the team knows that. I think that extending my contract now would show we were all interested in stability."

My request didn't come because I was trying to cash in on winning the Coach of the Year. But I believed our record showed we were on the right track. And given that fact, I did receive a one-year extension. Every indication was that we were in lockstep together—Hadhazy, Modell, and me. Before the year was out, however, I discovered that we couldn't be further apart.

———

On January 7, 1977, my staff and I were in Mobile coaching the North squad in the Senior Bowl. Following the game, I returned to my hotel room where I received a phone call. It was Earl Schreiber, the director of the Hall of Fame, on the line. "I'm pleased to tell you," he said, "that you have been elected to the Pro Football Hall of Fame."

The news surprised me, quite frankly. I thought that someday I might make it, but this was my first year of eligibility!

Barbara was with me in Mobile, and we both sat for a few minutes just soaking in the moment. I then asked if she had Marie Lombardi's phone number. We had remained close to Marie in the years after Vince died. She often stayed with us, sometimes for days at a time. And when I considered who would present me for induction, Marie was my first choice—the only person I considered.

I dialed the number and, after telling her the news, I asked if she would stand with me in Canton and present me to the crowd. She said, "I would be more than happy to, Forrest."

More than seven months later we were in Canton. I was going into the Hall with a great group of players—Gale Sayers, Bill Willis, Frank Gifford, and my quarterback, Bart Starr. Boy, I was happy to be going in with Bart. I had taken a couple of days off from my coaching duties, and we arrived in town on Thursday evening for the festivities. The whole weekend was an incredible experience, from the mayor's breakfast on Friday morning, to the banquet that evening, to all the speeches, dinners, cocktail parties, and the parade.

The parade may have been the most emotional part of the weekend. Marie and I were sitting in the back of a convertible riding through downtown Canton. Crowds lined both sides of the street, some shouting to me as we rode by. I waved until I thought my arm would fall off. A couple of longtime friends were in the crowd, but I didn't think there would be any chance I'd see them. And then I heard a familiar voice holler out. I looked and saw Bill Forester, my old teammate with the Packers. Next to Bill was Jack Pogue from my hometown of Sulphur Springs. Seeing those old friends…the memories washed over me. It didn't get much easier for me when the actual induction ceremonies began.

Before we went out on the dais, a Hall of Fame official put all the new inductees in a room together, saying, "We'll give you a few moments to collect your thoughts."

Gifford and I looked at each other.

"What are you going to say?" I asked.

He said, "I'm not sure."

One of my proudest days—being inducted into the National Football League Hall of Fame in Canton, Ohio. Marie Lombardi kindly agreed to introduce me.

PHOTOGRAPH
JAMES H. McC
COLUMBUS, OH

If Frank Gifford, a national TV broadcaster, didn't know what he was going to say, why should I be worried? I had a little bit prepared, but basically I decided to just say what was on my mind. In the audience, of course, were Barbara, Forrest Jr., and Karen, and they were foremost in my mind. This is what I ended up saying:

What happened this morning was the most emotional thing that has happened to me in my lifetime. When I was going down the street in that parade, I saw friends that I knew, and I saw my family sitting on the side. It made me think back to how it all started, and I don't want to get too deep into this right now, about how it all got started because I'm already pretty emotional about it. But as I look out and see my family, I think how empty it would be, how little it would mean, if I did not have them to share it with.

Sometimes in the game of football, not just professional football, but in all football, the families are left a little bit to the side. But I can tell you this much right now. If it had not been for my wife, Barbara, her love and encouragement, I would not be standing here right now. My two children, Karen, my daughter, and Forrest Jr., my son: they have known nothing in their lives but professional football."

The entire weekend was a humbling and emotional experience. I never thought I would have the opportunity to stand on that stage, the ultimate individual recognition in my profession.

———

Unbeknownst to me, during the '76 season, Modell made a promise to Mike Phipps. He told Phipps we wouldn't ask him to come back and compete with Brian Sipe for the starting quarterback position. Early in the offseason Peter Hadhazy had called me into his office shortly before the January 28 draft.

"We're trading Mike Phipps to the Bears," he told me. "Art made a promise to him."

Modell and I had an agreement; either he or I could have veto power over any trade, and this was one trade I wanted to nix.

"Let me ask you one question before we do this," I said to Hadhazy. "How many games do you think we'll win if Phipps is gone and Sipe gets hurt?"

"None," Peter replied, "but don't worry about that. If that happens it won't affect you and your status as Browns coach."

I didn't like the deal. In exchange for Phipps, the Browns received Chicago's first- and fourth-round picks in the 1978 draft. My disagreement wasn't over the compensation we received from the Bears. (The number one pick, in fact, was Ozzie Newsome.) Rather, I knew by dealing Phipps that we then had no quality backup at quarterback. Draft picks are how teams are built, but I believed we were on the verge of winning in 1977, and the loss of Phipps severely hampered that opportunity.

Despite my reservations, I played the good soldier. I never spoke out in the press or publicly expressed my misgivings. In fact, later in the fall, Howard Cosell asked me on camera why we traded Mike Phipps.

"We had decided Brian Sipe was our starting quarterback, and we felt Phipps was expendable," I said, but I didn't believe it. And, unfortunately, I was later proven to be a prophet of sorts when Brian got hurt. Hadhazy was wrong, though. We won *one* game after Brian went down.

————

In 1975 our ambition as a team was to play well enough to make Howard Cosell's *Monday Night Football* highlights. In the years before ESPN and round-the-clock sports news, Cosell's halftime narration of that weekend's best games was nearly as popular as the *Monday Night* game itself. When we beat Cincinnati in the tenth week of the '75 season, we finally made Howard's highlights. Two years later we got our own shot at the primetime

On the sidelines at practice with Browns' owner Art Modell.

in the second week of 1977 against the New England Patriots.

We had a fine football team in '77. A 13–3 victory over the Bengals got the season started on the right foot before we made our *Monday Night* debut on September 26. Before the game my players were like kids— they couldn't wait to get on the field. Following our warmups we returned to the dressing room. I always liked to address the team before taking the field for introductions. However, when I walked into the locker room there weren't five players in the room. I looked around and decided to look up the tunnel, which led to the dugout. We had to watch our heads as we walked down that old tunnel toward Municipal's playing field. When I reached the dugout, half my team was there waiting for me, waiting for the ABC cameras to come on.

"Come on, Coach, let's get this thing going!"

Mike Sinclair had the whole group singing, *"To the Supe, to the Supe, to the Super Bowl!"*

I like to think it was my fine motivational tools that got them up for the game, but I'm pretty sure it was the bright lights of *Monday Night Football*. The Patriots, coming off a 10-4 record, were one of the league's better teams, and few experts believed we could beat them. A thrilling game was still tied at the end of regulation play, 27–27. We won the coin toss and took the ball down field all the way to the Patriot 15, mostly on the back of Greg Pruitt. On second down I told my staff, "Let's get this over with," and we sent in Don Cockroft, who was money in the bank from that short range. Don made the kick and we won the game, but, boy, I got criticized like hell for kicking on second down. I heard later that Don Meredith said on the broadcast, "Forrest had to get his babysitter home."

Midway through the season, we were sitting at a comfortable 5-2. The only thing we didn't have is what they traded away, a backup quarterback. I knew when Hadhazy traded away Phipps that the move would come back to haunt us, and when Sipe suffered a broken shoulder blade in Pittsburgh on November 13, we had no experienced quarterback to step in.

We came back the following week and beat the Giants, 21–7, but things fell apart seven days later when the Rams shut us out, 9–0. In the aftermath of that loss, Modell went to the press and said he had asked Hadhazy to "reevaluate the team from top to bottom."

Reevaluate? What did that mean? Everything was out in the open;

it shouldn't have been too hard. Our record at the time, 6-5, was in all the papers.

Reevaluate?

The result of the assistant coaches' work was visible on the field.

The players, anyone with some football sense, could tell who was playing well and who wasn't, providing they were paying attention. So Modell's call for a reevaluation was a signal to me to get ready for a change.

This was Modell's modus operandi. Test the waters in the press first, stimulate the media, and wait for the reaction. Up until that point I wasn't feeling any pressure. Even without Brian behind center, we had played well. But after reading Modell's words in the *Plain Dealer*, I knew the writing was on the wall.

One week later we got waxed in San Diego. I don't know if I was pushing them too hard, or if they were reading the papers, but it looked to me like they were just going through the motions. Perhaps they were thinking, "Why should we put out for this guy when he's not going to be here much longer?" Modell's words not only put me in a tough position, but the players were also in limbo.

Against the Chargers, the defense wasn't doing a good job tackling, covering, or applying pressure on the passer. It was really an embarrassment, and I think I took it personally. After the game I vented my anger in the press. I made the statement that the team had "laid down," and they looked "dead and buried." Both statements were unfortunate and born in the heat of the moment, as was my decision not to join in the team prayer following the game. In that moment I wanted to pray alone.

The next day I spoke to the players and apologized. "I got too emotional about the game," I told them. "You guys have played hard for me and I appreciate it." I also said, "I was wrong yesterday."

———

My days in Cleveland were numbered, that was certain. I just didn't know if the end would come before the close of the season or after. Chuck Heaton of the *Plain Dealer* called me to find out where things stood. Chuck had been very fair to me during my stay in Cleveland. He had been covering the city's sports scene for a couple of decades and had been doing it better than anyone.

"You're a lot like Paul Brown," he told me.

"I didn't know that," I said. I had met Brown a couple of times over the years, but our acquaintance never went beyond cordial greetings. "I would like to talk to him."

"I'll get in touch and tell him you're going to call," Chuck said.

A few days later I phoned Paul at the Bengals office. Fifteen years earlier Paul was living through a very similar drama with Modell. Paul was the only coach in Cleveland Browns history—heck, the team was named for him—but Modell fired him nonetheless when the two men couldn't see eye to eye. I told Paul that I was thinking of resigning my position.

"No," he said emphatically, "that's exactly what he wants you to do."

"That's what I thought," I said, but working under those conditions was stressful, to say the least.

"Just stick it through," he advised. And I'm glad I took his advice.

As the Browns' coach, I wasn't told what to do, but things were happening that made me suspicious. I sensed that a couple of players had turned on me. I'm not comfortable giving their names on these pages, but a defensive back and a wide receiver, in particular, had begun working against me. Modell had a history of using players to do his bidding against the coaches he hired. Most famously, after purchasing the franchise in the early sixties, Modell ingratiated himself with several players and fed their disenchantment with Paul Brown. He also used the media against Brown, and he tried to do that with me, but the press wasn't biting this time.

————

A couple of days after our loss to the Chargers, I asked Blanton Collier to come to my office. He had seen all this happen before to his friend Paul Brown, and I was hoping he might have some advice on how I should handle the press, the players, and Modell. Blanton, though, was uncomfortable offering me advice under the circumstances. I went to him for counsel, and he offered nothing. I think he'd already heard the word from above that there was going to be a change.

On Sunday, December 11, we played the Houston Oilers at home. We must have fumbled six times that day. It seemed like everyone who carried the ball for us fumbled.

We lost for the third straight week, and, perhaps worse from Modell's point of view, only thirty thousand people were in stands.

Following the game Hadhazy and Modell came to me and said, "We're going to make a change at the end of the year, and we would like you to resign." I listened without saying a word for a moment. I wasn't surprised. I knew a change was coming since Modell publicly demanded a "reevaluation." But I took their statement to mean I would be able to coach the last game at Seattle. We still had a chance to break even. That's what I was shooting for. Under the circumstances, 7-7 wasn't bad. It might even help me get another job down the road. I agreed to their "offer," and said I would resign after the season was over.

The next day, however, Modell floated a story to the press.

I came home late that Monday night, and at eleven o'clock Chuck Heaton phoned me for a reaction to a story the *Plain Dealer* was going to run the next day.

"You're being fired before the season is over," he told me.

"He's not firing me," I snapped. "I'm resigning!"

I hung up the phone and immediately changed my mind. I wasn't going to resign. I was going to make Modell fire me. Some months earlier we negotiated another year onto my contract. If I resigned Modell wouldn't be obligated to pay me, and I was determined to make him live up to that commitment.

I awoke the next day to a headline on the front page of the *Plain Dealer*: "Forrest Gregg to Resign as Browns Coach." I arrived at the team's offices and told Modell in no uncertain terms that I was not resigning, but even those words didn't stop him from calling a press conference. In front of the local media he and Hadhazy announced that I had, indeed, resigned.

Resigned or fired—to many it made little difference. The bottom line was that Forrest Gregg was no longer the head coach of the Cleveland Browns. Semantics or not, I wanted to set the record straight. On Tuesday I held a press conference of my own at the Hospitality Inn. I spoke for ten minutes and took no questions from the press

"I did not want to quit before the season was over," I told the media gathered before me. "I had a commitment to my coaches and players. I did consider resignation, but to resign before the season is finished because of pressure is to be a quitter. I leave here unashamed. If I could go back, I can't think of anything I would change if I could."

The Browns gave me my first experience as a head coach, and I walked away from Cleveland grateful for the opportunity. Had I been given a fair shot? That's debatable, and I certainly have an opinion on that subject. But feeling acrimony over how matters turned out would serve no purpose. There was one thing I learned from my stay in Cleveland. With the Browns there was no room for two strong personalities at the top.

———

Dick Modzelewski was named the interim coach for the final game at Seattle. We had basically formed our game plan for the Seahawks, both offensively and defensively, before I was fired. Mo just needed to put everything together for Sunday.

Let's face it—when you get fired, you don't want your old team to ever win again. Anyone who says anything different is a liar; there's just too much emotion invested. Still, as I sat at home watching the game, I viewed it with mixed emotions. The Browns still felt like they were my team. At one point they took the lead over the Seahawks and I began thinking, "I'm going to be 7-7." And then I stopped and thought, "No, *you're* 6-7."

There was one particular play that we had practiced before a game against the Rams, but we never used it. It was a trick 'em play. The quarterback bent over like he was tying his shoe and the center snapped the ball directly to Greg Pruitt, who then acted like he was going to run while the quarterback eased out into the flat. Greg then turned and passed the ball to the quarterback.

Raymond Berry, who I brought in as an offensive coach, put the play back into the game plan against the Seahawks...and it worked. They scored, and when they did I cheered. We had worked hard on that play and seeing it implemented felt good.

I wouldn't have missed watching that game for anything.

———

As a kid I set some goals for myself: to be a good enough football player to get a scholarship, and then to get a degree so I could have a career as a coach. I worked really hard, and I did what I was supposed to do and success came to me.

And then I went to Cleveland. I basically repeated the formula. I worked hard and took the Browns from a 3-11 team to 9-5. And then I was named the NFL Coach of the Year, battled cancer, was elected to the Hall of Fame, and then was fired...all in a year's time.

And what did I take from these lessons? I got knocked down, I got up, and I went right at it again.

8

REDEMPTION

IN THE DAYS AND WEEKS TO FOLLOW I DID A LOT OF soul searching.

When exactly did things fall apart in Cleveland? What could I have done differently? My mind kept returning to the biggest chasm between Modell and me, what I saw as the beginning of our falling out was my reluctance to play Mike Pruitt as a rookie. I really liked Mike personally, and after I left the Browns he had a very productive career. But to play Mike when he wasn't really ready was not something I believed in. That's not to say I had all the answers or that I made no mistakes. At times my emotions got the best of me. But my core beliefs—discipline, prepared-ness, and fielding the best players available—these remained with me and guided me. And I would not alter those principles in order to satisfy an owner's whimsy.

In February I received a proposal from Tommy Prothro, the Chargers' head coach. Tommy wanted to know if I was interested in joining his staff as the offensive line coach. I appreciated the offer, but I first wanted to explore a couple of head coaching vacancies before accepting an assistant's job. Those available head positions, however, were quickly filled without me. I called Tommy and accepted his offer.

For the next few months I worked with the Chargers staff as they prepared for the draft and examined personnel needs, but I had a hard time getting into the job. It's difficult to go from a head coach's position to the subordinate role of assistant, especially when you're itching to get back into the role of head coach. And in retrospect I should have declined the position. In mid-June I told Tommy that my heart wasn't in it, and that it was best I resign.

I spent the summer and fall checking on all available jobs and keeping myself as close to the game as possible. I visited the training camps of a few teams, including Cincinnati, Detroit, and Cleveland. And once the season began, I went to a game practically every weekend. I attended contests in Washington, Buffalo, Pittsburgh, Cincinnati, a couple in Detroit, and even the Browns, thanks to a couple of tickets courtesy of Dick Modzelewski. I was keeping my name out there as well as maintaining my knowledge of league personnel.

Though I was still being paid for the final year of my contract with the Browns, I wanted to do some kind of work. A friend of mine put me in contact with Sam Luccarelli, who owned a company that provided temporary help to a variety of businesses. Sam and I met over lunch, and he asked me if I would like to join his organization. I worked with Sam for the better part of a year. My role was rather simple: I would go out with Sam's representatives, who were trying to sell the idea of temporary help to clients. My function, however, was simply to talk football. It was something I could do fairly well, and the pay was fine, but I never stopped looking for the opportunity to quit talking and get back into the game.

In February of '79, I saw that the Toronto Argonauts were in search of a head coach. Though it was the Canadian Football League, the Argos job seemed to be a good opportunity. I reached out to the team's president and general manager, Lew Hayman, and expressed my interest in the job. Lew invited me to Toronto to visit the city for an interview.

When we sat down, it became apparent that Lew had done his research on me.

"I can't find anybody who will say anything negative about you," he told me. "But I noticed you had cancer in '76. How are you with that?"

Dr. Sampliner had written a letter for such an inquiry. Teams, both north and south of the border, were shying away from hiring me because of my medical history. I produced the document for Lew, which stated the opinion that my chance of getting cancer again was no greater than someone who never had cancer. The letter satisfied Lew, who cast aside any concerns he might have had, and the two of us began talking contract.

I had seen some Canadian games, and I realized there were a lot of rule variations when compared to the American game. Still, I thought I could adjust and began studying the rule book as much as possible, but in the heat of battle things don't always come to you as quickly as you'd like. I needed to alter my way of thinking—and I didn't always do a good job.

For instance, the most obvious rule difference is that the CFL only allows the offense three downs rather than four to make a first down. Pro football in Canada is based on the quality of a team's passing game, but I spent too much time with the running game. Initially, when faced with second and one, I would substitute like it was third and one in the NFL, getting my big people on the field for the short-yardage situation.

Thankfully, I had Lew Hayman to go to for advice. There was no greater name in the Canadian Football League. He had a distinguished career as a player and as a coach, winning five Grey Cups before becoming a respected executive. After a couple of games, Lew pulled me aside.

"In this league a lot of people just run the quarterback sneak on second and one or third and one," he explained. "In the CFL the defensive line has to line up a yard off the line of scrimmage. The sneak isn't a given, but it's kind of hard not to make that yard."

When I looked at the league statistics, I realized that, by God, everyone always made it in short-yardage situations.

On one occasion we had the lead at the end of the ball game, and I was trying to run out the clock. Unfortunately, the rules in Canada differ—the clock stops after every play. On third down our kicker/punter, Ian Sunter, came up to me on the sideline and said, "I know what you're wrestling with here. Send me in and I'll end the game for you."

I listened to his advice. Ian took the snap and ran around, killing off the final seconds.

Another difference: There was also no such thing as a fair catch in the CFL. On punts, the receiver has to catch and return the ball, but the coverage team has to allow him a 5-yard "halo." While followers of American football look at the Canadian game as a bastardized version, the fans up there are very proud of their football. And it's a good game, too. Every now and then an American coach will go up there and suggest, "Why don't we change it from three downs to four?" Well, let me tell you, that's not the thing to say in Canada. They wouldn't change it for anything.

Canadian fans also take winning very seriously. The rivalry between Hamilton and Toronto reminded me of the Bears and Packers. Toronto was the big city and Hamilton the small industrial town. Hamilton fans are very avid, perhaps a bit too avid at times. As we were leaving the field after falling to the Tigers 42–3, Hamilton fans pelted us with everything they could lay their hands on. One guy threw a Coke can at me; I caught

My wife Barbara sitting in my office during my tenure as coach of the Toronto Argonauts. Forrest Jr. snapped the picture.

it and threw it back. They were throwing hot dogs, too. I even got mustard on my shirt. The last time I was in Hamilton I noticed a canopy had been built above the entrance to the visiting team's dressing room to stifle such fan expression.

———

We were a competitive team at the beginning of the year, rolling up a record of 6-4 after ten games. But we fell apart in the second half of the season, losing nine of our final ten contests. I don't want this statement to be mistaken for criticism, but there is a different attitude in the CFL, especially among the Canadian players. One of my players, whose name escapes me, told the press, "The trouble with Gregg is he prepared for every game like it was the Super Bowl." What this player intended as criticism, I took as quite a compliment.

When Lew Hayman hired me, I told the Canadian press, "I have no intention of using the Argos as a stepping stone to the NFL. I have no thought ahead of me other than what it's going to take to build a winner in Toronto." My ambition was simple—to win a Grey Cup. And that is where all my energies were focused throughout 1979. Still, I never shut out the idea of someday returning to the NFL.

Just prior to the holidays, Lew put together a letter that was sent to season ticket holders in which I wrote, *"Next year we will have the type of football team on the field that will warrant your support. I can assure you that we will do everything in our power to justify your loyalty."*

I gladly placed my signature on the letter. The timing of the note, however, could not have been more suspect. The mail carrier had probably just placed the envelope in season-subscribers' mailboxes when I received a phone call from Paul Brown.

"You've probably heard that Homer Rice has resigned as our head coach," he said. "Are you interested in the job?"

Indeed, I had read about Rice's resignation, and the thought of returning to the NFL was appealing.

"If you're interested in me, I'm interested in the job," I told Paul.

He arranged for me to come to Cincinnati for an interview. I flew from Toronto to Columbus, rented a car, and drove to Paul's home. The subterfuge was for a good reason. The press had the Cincinnati airport staked out, and Paul wanted to keep my visit out of the papers and off the sportscasts. Paul had been known for his paranoia as a coach, but I appreciated him allowing Toronto to prepare for the media blitz that was sure to follow if I were to leave the Argonauts. I had immense respect for Lew Hayman as a man, and I owed that much to him. I arrived at Paul's house around noon, in time for lunch with Brown and his son Mike. The three of us talked at length about football. They asked for my thoughts and philosophies.

It wasn't as if I were a complete stranger to Paul. Throughout my whole football life I had heard about Paul Brown. He was the legendary coach of the Cleveland Browns and had won countless championships. But I met him for the first time in the summer of '69. At the time I was a player/coach with the Packers, and we were preparing to play the Bengals in a preseason game in Milwaukee. The Packers' director of player personnel, Pat Peppler, and I were on the field during warmups when I saw Paul across the way.

I asked Peppler to introduce me to Paul.

Pat agreed and we walked over.

"I've got a guy here, one of our players who is also new on our staff, and he would like to meet you," Peppler said.

Paul looked at me and said, "You're a big one, aren't you?"

While coaching the Browns, I had the occasion to speak with Paul a few times, but the conversations were just cordial small talk. In fact, other than the call I made to him as my days in Cleveland were winding to a close, I had never done much more than exchange hellos with him.

Still, I think Paul saw us as sort of kindred spirits. He had phoned Barbara at our home not long after he heard the news that I'd been fired by the Browns.

"I see my whole life passing before me," he told her. "Don't worry. Forrest will be coaching again. We won't let Modell destroy him." I'm pretty sure Paul wasn't thinking of me coaching for him at that time, but two years later, here we were meeting to discuss such a proposition.

We wrote up a contract and signed it right there in Paul's house, but before I officially became the Bengals' head coach, I had to get my release from the Argonauts. Paul and Mike Brown gave me two days to get the release. If I failed to do so, the contract we signed would be void. I returned to Toronto and sat down with Lew Hayman.

The Argos wanted me to stay and even offered me more money. The temptation was there because the organization had been really good to me, especially Lew. But I couldn't get it out of my mind that with Cincinnati, I would be playing Cleveland two times a year. That fact, in itself, was motivation, but I also wanted to prove myself in the NFL.

We sat for several hours until Lew finally said, "I see how important it is to you. We won't stand in your way."

I called Paul Brown to inform him that the Argos would put it in writing that I was free of my contract. By this time, however, the two days had run out on my contract with the Bengals, and I wasn't sure if the offer was still on the table. Brown listened and then said, "Here's what we'll do. I'll make the same arrangements. You'll fly into Columbus, drive to my house, bring your release, and then we'll sign another contract. We'll call a press conference for the next day."

Everything played out once again as Paul planned. I spent the night at his home, and the following day I was introduced to a surprised Cincinnati press corps as the fourth head coach in Cincinnati Bengal history. All of the subterfuge had worked. Until I walked into the room, no one in the media had any idea who would be coming through the door as the next Bengal coach.

Stepping to the microphone, I looked out at the gathering of writers and broadcasters wearing more than a few looks of surprise. I couldn't help but think of how different the decision-making process was in Cincinnati compared to Cleveland. Paul kept the press at bay during the interview process, while that owner up north used the newspapers to test the waters before making a decision—any decision.

The particular questions thrown at me that day have receded from my memory, but I do remember the recurring theme: Was I going to be my own man? Paul Brown was such an imposing figure, the press believed it to be a natural question. And while I assured those assembled that, yes, I would be my own man, only time would assuage their doubts.

———

Earlier, as we sat in Paul's home in the suburb of Indian Hill, Paul, his son Mike, and I discussed a number of issues. Who would be selected for the coaching staff was one topic on the table. Paul recommended a few men, but the final decision was left to me. Two men who were with me in Cleveland were on Homer Rice's staff in '79—George Sefcik and Dick Modzelewski. I wanted to keep them, and I took Paul's advice on Frank Gansz, the tight-ends coach.

Foremost, though, I knew I wanted Hank Bullough as the defensive coordinator. I wanted to run the 3-4 defense, and nobody knew that formation better than Hank, who had done a great job in Baltimore and New England. I also wanted Dick Lebeau, who I knew from his playing days in Detroit. If Dick could get our secondary to play as physical as he was with the Lions, we would be all right.

On the offensive side of the ball, Paul suggested, Doug Scovil who was a respected coach at BYU. While on the coast scouting the East-West Shrine Bowl, Scovil and I sat down for an interview, and I offered him the job as our quarterback/receiver coach. A short while later we gathered in Mobile for the Senior Bowl. In fact, all of our efforts were geared toward scouting. Each coach was responsible for his own area of the country.

One day Doug asked, "When are you going to start working on the offense?"

"We'll get to that," I said, "but first we need to prepare for the draft, to see if we can find players better than what we've got."

Scovil didn't say anything at the time, but a couple of days later he came up to me wearing what Hank Bullough called the "trout" look—that look in the eye implying you don't know which way to swim, upstream or downstream.

"Coach," he said to me, "I called BYU this morning. They haven't replaced me yet. I miss Provo. I have a house there where I come out the front door and look out at the mountains. I would just prefer to coach in college."

So we were back in the market for a quarterback/receiver coach. I called Gil Brant in Dallas and told him what had happened. "Yeah, some guys just like coaching in college better, there's nothing wrong with that." I agreed. I understood Doug's desire to return to BYU, but I needed a coach.

"The best coach I can recommend to you is a guy down in Tulane, Lindy Infante," Brant told me. "When I've been down there to scout his players, I've had the chance to spend some time with Lindy, and he has a great knowledge of the game."

I called Infante and was impressed by his football knowledge. I needed someone well-versed in the passing game, and Lindy knew how to coach quarterbacks as well as receivers. We weren't long into our conversation when I knew he was the man we wanted. The Bengals made arrangements for Lindy to fly to Cincinnati, and when he arrived the two of us spent about a day and a half together. I was convinced he was our man, and after they interviewed him, Paul and Mike were convinced as well.

I also had Mike McCormack on the staff, another holdover from Homer Rice's staff. Mike and I went back to our playing days when he was on the Browns' offensive line, but he was offered the head coaching job in Baltimore, and so I needed a new offensive line coach. Through the recommendation of Mike Faulkner, a member of my staff in Toronto, I learned about a coach at Wake Forrest.

"Would you be interested in interviewing for the offensive line coach of the Cincinnati Bengals?" I asked Jim McNally over the phone.

"You're kidding, right?" was Jim's response.

"No, I'm quite serious," I told him, and then explained about Mike McCormack moving on.

Jim listened intently and then said, "There's one thing I need to tell you. I'm not very tall."

"You're not?" I said.

"No, I'm not very tall."

"Well," I told him, "I worked for a guy once who wasn't very tall, but he was the damnedest coach I ever saw. His name was Vince Lombardi. All I need to know is—do your feet touch the ground?"

When Jim came to the stadium for his interview, I took him up to Paul's office for an introduction. Paul got up from behind his desk and eyed Jim up and down. When the small talk was over, Jim and I went to the interview room. We started talking at 10:30 in the morning and stayed there until 4:00 in the afternoon. Paul came by every once in a while and poked his head in, saying, "You guys still talking?"

We talked and talked, and eventually Jim and I began to demonstrate different blocking techniques. I got down in a three-point stance, and Jim got down in a three-point stance, and we went through every aspect of blocking. We blocked tables, chairs, doorways....

With my staff set, everyone focused on preparing for the draft. During one meeting we specifically discussed the offensive line. The Bengals already had the pieces of a solid line in place with Dave Lapham, Max Montoya, Blair Bush, and Glen Bujnoch. In fact, we were good everywhere except at left tackle. With the number three pick overall, we could basically select whomever we pleased, and there was one player who fit the bill to fill our needs: Anthony Munoz of Southern California.

Munoz was a physical specimen at six feet, six inches, 280 pounds, but there were questions about his health. Knee injuries had limited him to just eight games in his junior and senior seasons. In fact, the only contest he played in his senior year was the Rose Bowl.

Paul suggested I go out to USC, watch as much film as necessary, and give Munoz a workout.

I flew to Los Angeles and talked to the Southern Cal coaches. To a man, they told me I would be pleased with Anthony, both as a person and a player. Then I studied film. And though he was impressive in that junior season, his timing was off in the Rose Bowl, and he didn't dominate his opponent the way he had done in his junior year.

I then went to Munoz's apartment, which was near campus, and had a nice lunch with him and his wife, Dede. After our meal he and I went to the practice field and ran through some drills. First, I put him through some agility drills, and he was awesome. There wasn't anything that slowed him down or affected his dexterity.

Since I already knew what he bench pressed, I wasn't concerned with his strength, but there was one more aspect of his game that needed to be explored—his blocking technique against a real defender. Unfortunately, we didn't have anyone to put on a pass rush, so I said, "I'm not going to be much of a challenge, but I want to see your technique and movement."

So, I ran one inside and one outside rush. Certainly I wasn't a great defensive lineman, but I could see he had excellent movement. Next, I took off outside but cut quickly inside and then back outside. I was getting close to the corner when he jammed me in the chest, knocking me head over heels.

He looked at me with great concern, saying, "Coach, Coach, are you all right?"

I said, "I don't need to see anything more."

———

I returned to Cincinnati and told PB and the rest of the staff that Anthony's knee was healed and rehabilitated. "I think this guy has a chance to be one helluva player."

On April 29, after the Lions selected Billy Sims and the Jets chose Johnny Lam Jones, the Bengals stepped forward with their pick: Anthony Munoz.

The pieces were coming together, and now it was time to start coaching my new players. It was written later that I had come to Cincinnati and "cleaned house." That wasn't the case. In the previous four years the Bengals had struggled to find success. In fact, since Paul Brown stepped aside as the team's head coach at the conclusion of the 1975 season, the Bengals had gotten progressively worse: 10-6 in '76, followed by 8-6, and then consecutive years at 4-12. But I knew the talent was there.

During our December meeting at Paul's home, Mike and Paul explained how the Bengals prepared for the college draft. Paul's youngest son, Pete, was the head of the team's scouting department, and he took information gathered by the club's scouts and coaching staff and prioritized, ranked, and organized the reports. I had been a firm believer that the coaches should have a say in selecting the players they would be working with, and I was pleased to learn that Paul thought along the same line. Everyone had an input in the draft.

It was a democratic process, though Paul's vote carried the most sway. When our turn to pick came on draft day, we would have a discussion, bounce some names back and forth, and more often than not we would have a consensus. In my time with the Bengals, we usually got every player I really wanted.

If one of the assistants was especially high on a player, their opinion carried weight in the draft room. Prior to the 1981 draft we had heard reports on a receiver from the University of Florida, Cris Collinsworth. We had a picture of him, and he was the skinniest thing I'd ever seen in my life. Because of his slight build, we had reason to wonder if he could handle the physical aspect of pro ball. Lindy Infante went down to Florida and had a look at him on the practice field.

"Can this guy beat the 'bump and run'?" I asked Lindy when he returned to Cincinnati.

"Yep," Lindy said, "he's get the speed to do it."

The next year we took Cris with our second round pick, and he turned out to be a great selection. He performed as Lindy promised, but he brought so much more to the team than natural talent. He was a mature young man who caught on to our scheme right off the bat—a big reason for our success in his rookie year.

A couple of years later Dick Modzelewski was high on a defensive lineman from Wisconsin, Tim Krumrie. Krumrie wasn't a highly rated prospect, but Mo went to Madison, worked him out, and studied film. He came back to Cincinnati with a much different grade on Krumrie than other scouts. Mo really wanted this kid and went to bat for him. Paul and I agreed to take a chance on Krumrie, and we eventually grabbed him in the tenth round.

I was also able to use my experience in the CFL to benefit the Bengals. After I left the Argonauts, I continued to stay in touch with my replacement, Willie Wood, my old Packer teammate. I liked to call Willie to see how he was doing, and at one point I mentioned a player we had in Toronto, M. L. Harris, who I liked a lot.

"If you ever get to the point where M.L. doesn't fit in your plans, we would be interested in him down here," I told Willie.

Sometime later Willie phoned me to say the Argos were looking for a smaller and faster end and were releasing Harris.

As soon as he cleared waivers in Canada we grabbed him.

My kicker in Toronto, Ian Sunter, also followed me to Cincinnati. He kicked 2 game-winning field goals against the Steelers, but he didn't make it through the whole season. One day at practice he told me he had a problem.

"What's wrong?" I asked.

He pointed across the field at Frank Gansz, our special teams coach. "That guy right there," Ian responded.

Ian told some people he was homesick and wanted to return to Canada so I don't know for certain if it was Gansz or not that caused Sunter to give up on the NFL. He made it about halfway through the season before leaving Cincinnati and Frank Gansz behind.

———

Before I arrived in Cincinnati I saw a story in one of the local papers in which a reporter asked Reggie Williams, a linebacker on the team, "Do you think the Bengals need a coach like Forrest Gregg?"

"I don't think we need *that*," Williams answered.

As it turned out Reggie was one of my biggest supporters on the ball club.

Two games a year builds some familiarity, and I was knowledgeable of the Bengals personnel from my days in Cleveland. They had some good talent, but they also had some underachievers who weren't playing up to their ability. It's the coach's job, the head coach as well as the assistants, to get their players to perform to the maximum of their abilities. Sometimes you can get that done, and sometimes you can't. Sometimes they aren't buying what you're selling. My job was to get them to buy into my philosophy. It wasn't easy, though. After Tiger Johnson and Homer Rice, who were both mild-mannered coaches, I was a drastic change. Admittedly, Bengal players took some time adjusting to me because I wasn't always nice.

On the first day of training camp, I walked into the meeting room and noticed a piece of tape with a player's name affixed to each chair. I called for Tom Gray, the team's equipment man, and told him to remove the tape. The next morning, the same thing—each chair had tape with a player's name written on it. Again, I asked Tom to remove the tape. When I saw that the tape had returned on the third day, I asked what was going on.

"Paul likes everyone's name on their desks," Tom explained.

"Take 'em off," I said.

Later in the day I asked Paul about the tape.

"This is how we take roll call," he said. "All you have to do is look, and if there's someone not in his chair, you'll see who's missing."

"That may have worked for you, but I really like to call roll," I told him.

PB couldn't wrap his head around that one. "Why?" he asked.

"Because they have to respond," I explained. "You can read a lot into the inflection in their voice."

Paul listened and said, "Okay, if that's the way you want to do it."

The tape didn't appear again. Well, not in the summer of 1980, but in '81 there it was again, the names on each chair. "Tom," I said, "we don't need names on the chairs."

That was the end of the tape.

———

Long before I came to Cincinnati, I had heard stories about Paul from Willie Davis, who told me Paul was stern, taciturn, and in charge. One incident that Willie passed on stands out in my mind. Following one poor series of downs, Willie returned to the Browns sideline where he was met by a severe-looking PB.

"Davis, just so you'll know, we'll be looking at your position in the draft," Paul said.

If that doesn't motivate a player, I don't know what would.

Critics of the Bengals during the Homer Rice and Tiger Johnson years were certain Paul was pulling the strings from upstairs. I'm not certain what happened during those years, but I can speak to my tenure, and PB never tried to influence or pressure my coaching decisions.

———

Our philosophies weren't all that different, but we disagreed on game preparation—more specifically, the hours involved in game preparation. My staff worked long hours, putting in all the time I thought necessary to properly prepare for the next game. None of my coaches ever said they were working too much, or "I'm tired." As a group they were dedicated to their craft. Our longest day was Tuesday, when I arrived at the stadium at 7:30 in the morning and went home at eleven or twelve that night. For the most part, though, we were home by 8:30 or 9:00. PB, however, liked to have his coaches home in time for dinner. We disagreed on that point, but it was never an issue between us.

My favorite times with Paul were when we traveled. We always went to the visiting team's stadium and worked out. If we didn't have time to work out, we would at least walk around the field and get a feel for the stadium, so come Sunday things wouldn't be strange to the players. Paul and I both agreed on this routine.

He and I always sat together on the bus and on the plane when we traveled. After we practiced, we'd get back on the bus together. I was always intrigued by the All American Football Conference and all the players he brought with him to the NFL. I loved to talk with him about those days—guys like Gatski, Groza, Lenny Ford, Motley, Jim Brown, Bill Willis.

After the conclusion of the baseball season we worked out frequently at Riverfront Stadium in all kinds of weather, especially when we were going to play on Astroturf in the coming week. Following significant precipitation, there were certain places on the field that would stay wet for two or three

Watching practice with Bengals' owner Paul Brown.

days. During that 1980 season I remember sitting with Paul watching film, and one of our players slipped and fell down on a wet spot. "You have to be aware of the wet spots," Paul said. "This is your home field."

We laughed about it at the time, my coaching staff and I, but we started paying attention to it, and we made the players pay attention, telling them, "You have to be aware of the wet spots." That was PB—always be prepared, always know all the angles.

There were also some unforgettable moments away from football with Paul. On several occasions Barbara and I spent some time with him and his wife, Mary, at their home in LaJolla. Paul loved to play gin, and he was as competitive at cards as he was at football. Though I knew little about the game, the two of us partnered against our wives. The ladies were beating us pretty soundly, but PB was quick with the pen. When the women fell behind in points, Mary got suspicious and she asked to see the score sheet.

"You've pencil whipped us!" she shouted.

As I said, PB was competitive.

———

Early one morning I arrived at the team offices and found someone standing outside my door waiting for me.

He said, "Coach, I just got out of the hospital. I noticed you need players, and I'm here to help you."

From the wild look in this guy's eyes I knew the "hospital" he'd been let out of was a booby hatch.

"Well," I told him, "First we need some information from you—your history, where you've played—and then you need to try out."

That wasn't acceptable to him. "No, I'm not trying out," he said. "I want a contract."

I started looking around, hoping one of the players would show up and help me get rid of this guy. No one was in sight.

"How about I go to my secretary, get a contract, and we'll sign you up," I said. I went to open my office door but he put his hand up and pushed it shut.

Uh-oh.

It was time for fight or flight, but I thought I would give diplomacy another chance.

"Look, I don't carry contracts around in my pocket. Let me get my secretary to call downtown and get a blank contract and we'll sign you up."

He thought for a moment, and then said, "Okay, go ahead."

Quickly, I went inside my office, latched the lock, and called the police. It didn't take long for them to come and carry off my visitor.

About a week later I arrived at work early. Jim McNally was there studying film, but I decided to leave him alone and continued on to my office. The hallway was very dark, making it difficult to see clearly. I noticed a figure walking toward me—a guy wearing a cowboy hat so low over his eyes it nearly covered his face. Between the darkness of the hallway and the hat, it was nearly impossible to make out any of this guy's facial features. As he got close to me, the figure stopped and spoke.

"Coach, I'd like to play for your team."

Oh, Jesus, not again.

"What's your name, son?" I asked

"Bench," he told me, "Johnny Bench."

Sonofabitch

———

In their most recent drafts, the Bengals had spent a lot of high selections on the defensive line, but the unit continued to struggle. Wilson Whitley,

Eddie Edwards, Ross Browner—we expected more from guys with that level of talent. I went to Dick Modzelewski.

"Let's have a meeting with these guys, Mo. I want to talk to them."

We went into Mo's meeting room. I didn't want it to be a "coach/player" thing; I wanted it to be an open discussion on what we needed to do to get better results.

"Look," I told them, "let's be out front about this. I'm not satisfied with how you're performing. We've got a lot invested in this defensive line. Either you're not as good as advertised and we made a mistake drafting you, or you're just not getting it done."

They sat and listened. I like to think the talk did some good because we started seeing an improvement within a couple of weeks. There was an attitude change on the line. They began pulling together and helped one another do a better job.

———

The Bengals scattered some wins throughout the 1980 season. We beat the defending champs, the Pittsburgh Steelers, twice. And late in the season we won three in a row against Kansas City, Baltimore, and Chicago. Of our ten losses, five were by 5 points or less. The last game of the year was against Cleveland. Paul was motivated. I was motivated. All I needed to do was get my players motivated. "Let's send them home for Christmas" was our battle cry for the game. The Browns were fighting for a spot in the playoffs. Everything was on the line for them, and we knew they would play hard. On our side of the street, we were playing for nothing but pride. When you've got players putting out for you when there's nothing at stake, you're building a winning ball club.

Late in the game we were behind when Pat McInally scored a touchdown, but that wasn't the story. The story was that McInally was

**Discussing a call with a referee during a Bengals game.
(We apparently had different opinions about the call.)**

knocked out of the game in the third quarter by a vicious forearm blow
from safety Thom Darden. After McInally was taken from the field on a
stretcher, it looked for certain that his day was over. A short while later,
Pat came up to me and asked to be put back in the game. I asked Marv

215

Pollins if Pat was physically able, and Marv cleared him by saying, "He can't hurt himself further."

By trade Pat was a punter, but if you asked him, he would say he was a receiver. Pat ran a fly pattern and Kenny Anderson threw a beautiful pass just over Pat's out-stretched hands, out of reach of the Browns defender. Pat dove for the ball and pulled it in. As he was falling, he used the Cleveland defensive back's body and rolled over him into the end zone. His valiant touchdown demonstrated that the team was buying into the program. Cleveland came back in the last series to score and beat us by 3 points, 27–24. We lost the game, but we had turned an important corner. I could feel it. The players felt it. The fans felt it too. Even the local media felt it.

We all couldn't wait to get on the field again.

———

After the season-ending game against the Browns, I told one of the local writers that I'd like to take two weeks off and start over again with this same bunch. Well, seven months passed before we got together again, and the roster was basically the same as the year before with the exception of the addition of Cris Collinsworth. Our first-round pick was spent on David Verser, a big, strong receiver, but it was Collinsworth, our second-round pick, who broke into the starting lineup. I had only seen Cris on film before that summer, but once he came to camp it was pretty much a done deal that he was going to be the guy. In 1980 opposing defenses doubled Isaac Curtis. But with Isaac on one side and Cris on the other, we were now a dangerous club. And though Cris likes to take credit for the whole season, being the new guy and everything, men up and down the roster were fulfilling their potential. And more importantly, like any great team, they came together as one.

The entire team worked hard that summer at Wilmington; their concentration and sense of purpose was evident. As the regular season approached I began to notice that the team had a swagger in their step. They knew they were good. They knew they could beat anyone they lined up against.

———

Our opening game was at Riverfront Stadium against the Seahawks. Seattle jumped out to a 21–0 lead before we could blink our eyes. The Seahawks were just putting it on us, and offensively we were out of synch. Kenny Anderson had thrown 2 interceptions and just wasn't getting the job done so I sent in Turk Schonert. Ordinarily Turk was our number-three man, behind Kenny and Jack Thompson, but Thompson was out with an injury. Behind Turk we rallied and cut the Seahawk lead to 21–10 at halftime. Turk continued to move the club in the second half, and our defense picked up, shutting Seattle out for the remainder of the game. We came all the way back to win, 27–21.

During the press conference after the game a reporter asked who would be our starting quarterback the following Sunday. "Turk Schonert," I said without hesitation, and immediately I knew I should have kept my mouth shut. The words came out before I had given the issue due diligence. Next we faced the Jets and their two dominating defensive linemen, Mark Gastineau and Joe Klecko. I have always been a firm believer that if a player steps in and wins a game for you, you give him a chance to win again. Turk had earned the opportunity to start in New York, yet as the week began and we prepared our game plan for the Jets, I struggled with the decision.

During the week I stopped by Paul's office and asked him to put on his coach's hat. There are times when you like to talk with someone who had been there. And I don't know of any coach who had seen more than

Paul Brown. Besides, I have never known a coach who wouldn't give an opinion if asked.

I explained the situation and said, "My first inclination is to start Turk."

"Think about this," Paul said, and then we discussed Kenny's experience. He was bigger physically, and Kenny was a better scrambler, which would help him avoid the vaunted Jets rush. Everything Paul said made sense, but before I made a final decision I needed to see if Kenny *wanted* to play. I needed him to *tell* me that he wanted the ball. Over the years I have seen men who didn't want the responsibility that came with running a team's offense. Some players were content to stand on the sideline out of the fire and hold a clipboard.

I called Kenny into my office and presented my dilemma to him. After looking into his eyes I got the answer I needed and expected. He was our starting quarterback, and behind him we won a tightly contested game, 31–30. Over the next few weeks we played well but were not consistent. A loss to Cleveland was followed by an overtime win over Buffalo and then a loss at Houston. At the mid-point of the season our record was a so-so 5-3. But from there we hit our stride.

———

One belief I carried over from my days under Lombardi was players should dress like professionals. I insisted that Bengal players wear a coat and tie when we traveled. For the most part, the players did what was expected of them and dressed appropriately. That is with one exception: Pat McInally. With his worn-out coat with its leather elbow patches, Pat looked like "Professor McInally" when he stepped on the airplane.

Early in my first Cincinnati season, I called him into my office following a road trip.

I didn't know for certain, but I assumed he was being well compensated by the team. I said, "Do you make good money with the Bengals?" "Yeah," he said, "but I'd like to make more, and I've been meaning to talk to you about that."

"Well, you are a professional football player, but you don't always dress professionally on road trips. I want you to buy a proper sport coat."

On the next trip Pat was dressed better, but I guess he didn't get enough attention from me. We came home and were preparing for our next opponent at the stadium. Pat was being held out of practice because of a pulled muscle. At one point I heard a bit of a commotion and some of the players laughing. I looked up, and across the field I could see somebody dressed in a top hat, tails, and sporting a cane.

What in the hell... That's Pat McInally!

McInally walked over to me and said, "Is this dressy enough for you?"

"Yes, Pat," I said. "I think that will do."

————

In my playing days we had Fuzzy on the Packers to keep the guys loose. And with the Bengals we had Pat. But he wasn't the only cut-up on the squad. I didn't know it at the time, but I've been told that defensive lineman Gary Burley used to do a pretty good impression of me. One thing Gary liked to do is imitate me calling roll, which always had the guys in stitches. I'm sorry I never got to see that side of Gary.

And then there was fullback Pete Johnson, who was one of my favorites in Cincinnati. A big, powerful runner, Pete claimed that he could run a 4.4 in the forty-yard dash. We never knew his speed for certain because we never timed him; I didn't see the necessity to put him on the clock because Pete was a veteran. But he was a strong runner, who could not only go through people, but also around them.

Whenever Pete would be late for practice, or tardy for a team flight, the excuse was inevitable: "My grandmother died."

"Pete," I'd say, "your grandmother just died."

"Yeah," he'd respond, "she did. This is another."

Guys like Pat, Gary, and Pete were good for a team. Pat, in particular, kept the club loose throughout my stay in Cincinnati. He was quite a character, never malicious with his jokes. I'm certain Pat always let Isaac, Kenny, and Turk in on his pranks because they were never surprised when he would pull one of his stunts.

I don't recall which year it was, but we were in training camp and had just lost an exhibition game. We had really stunk up the joint, and I intended to let the guys know what I thought of their effort. I was primed and ready to go when I started calling roll. I got to Pat's name and called it.

"McInally!"

And there was nothing.

Again, "McInally!"

Nothing.

Then I heard a commotion down the hall, someone shouting, "I'm coming, I'm not late, I'm not late!"

It was McInally. A moment later he walked into the meeting room wearing a belt and a pair of slip-on sandals and nothing else.

I was so flabbergasted that I was struck dumb.

I can't top this.

I dismissed the meeting without a word.

———

When I came to Cincinnati, the Bengals were far below the Reds in the pecking order of the city's sports fans. Several years of dismal performance on the field will do that to a fan base. In fact, not long after my family moved to the city, we arrived at our home to find that vandals had spray-painted "F**k the Bengals" on our front lawn. Yes, the team was held in low regard in 1980, but as we found out in the fall of '81, winning cures all.

Since the team's inception, the Bengals wore drab uniforms that closely resembled the Cleveland Browns. The similarities surely weren't coincidental, given Paul's history with his former team. But I thought we desperately needed a new identity. Mike, Paul, and I got together and discussed a new design for our uniforms. The result: Bengal tiger stripes on our pants, jerseys, and across the helmet. With the new brassy duds, we had a new identity.

As the '81 edition of the Bengals began to turn around the franchise's recent poor fortunes, practically the whole town jumped on the bandwagon. The fans really got behind us and a new chant was born: "*Who dey! Who dey! Who dey think gonna beat dem Bengals?*"

And the response came in a roar: "*Nooooooooobody!*"

I could feel the charge in the air when we played at home. And it wasn't just Sundays at Riverfront. When we would go out to eat, people in town now recognized me.

"*How are you going to do this week, Coach?*"

"*We're pulling for you!*"

There was also a noticeable difference in the media coverage we received. Typically I met with the press on Mondays, usually in front of not more than twenty journalists. Any coach worth his salt, if he hadn't yet seen the pictures of the previous game, would respond to questions with, "I haven't seen the film." But I preferred to watch the movies before my Monday press conference. Under ordinary circumstances, the beat writers from the *Enquirer*, the *Post*, and the *Dayton Daily News* would be present along with representatives from local TV and radio stations. As the season wore on there was an increased media presence from Columbus,

Lexington, and Louisville. Even the locals who would normally only appear for the Monday press conference, began showing up for the brief Q&As I gave during the week. We had turned a corner, and people were beginning to take notice.

———

One of the players who I most admired on that team was cornerback Ken Riley. From the day I arrived in Cincinnati I felt like I knew Ken already. He was one of our adversaries while I was with the Browns. "The Rattler" was one of those players who did his job and never asked for anything. I never worried if Ken Riley would be ready on Sunday because he was always prepared. Week in and week out he gave his best on every play.

And the best Ken had to offer ranked among the best to ever play the game. From time to time I get phone calls from sports writers asking me why Ken Riley isn't in the Hall of Fame, and I don't have an answer. If anybody deserves to be in the Hall of Fame, it's Ken Riley. He played fifteen years as a cornerback in the National Football League, all of them as a starter, facing the best receivers every weekend. I don't think the average football fan understands how remarkable an achievement it is to play cornerback for that length of time in the NFL. It's not just unique, it's miraculous. At the time of his retirement, Ken ranked fourth all-time with 65 interceptions.

Still, no Hall of Fame for Ken, not even a sniff. I don't know exactly how the pro football writers select members for the Hall; what I do know is I wouldn't leave that room until they put Ken Riley in Canton.

———

On November 29, we went to Cleveland. If we won this game, we were going to the playoffs. Late in the game we were driving for a score. Lindy Infante came to me and asked, "Pass, or give it to Pete?"

"Give it to Pete three times in a row," I said.

On the second play Pete just bowled over everyone and reached the end zone. One of the men Johnson barreled through, Thom Darden, was one of my biggest detractors in Cleveland.

I let a lot go when Pete crossed the goal line. I couldn't get the smile off my face. Usually, I never smiled on the field, feeling that the game isn't over until the final gun, and I don't believe in celebrating a moment too soon. On the sideline I never let up on my players, my coaches, or myself. But reaching the playoffs, and doing so by beating the Cleveland Browns in Memorial Stadium, was extremely gratifying.

Earlier in the game I had told Pat McInally, "If you score a touchdown, I'll spike the ball in the end zone."

As we were running off the field, Pat came up to me with the ball. I laughed, "No, I lied to you, Pat."

We had a lot of fans make the trip up to Cleveland for the game. Most of them were seated in the corner of the end zone near the entrance to our dressing room. Just before we headed into the tunnel I heard a few of the fans yell out. With a big grin still plastered on my face, I threw up my hand with the index finger raised. "*We're number one.*"

In the locker room there was a lot of back slapping and a whole lot of shouting. I quieted the guys down for a moment and spoke to them briefly. It was the biggest and most fulfilling win in my coaching career, and I thanked them all for their effort. But I also reminded them that this win was just one step toward our ultimate goal.

Following each game, the team's captains would step forward after I addressed the room. The captains highlighted the most important performance of the day with a game ball. Jim LeClair, our defensive captain, held up the game ball and said, "We know how much this game meant to Coach Gregg. Winning this game was extremely important to him personally and to us as a team. And he got us ready to play today."

Jim then told everyone that they were giving the game ball to me.

For a moment I struggled to find the words. "You don't know how much I appreciate this honor," I told them.

PB shook my hand. We didn't need to say a word. He knew what I was thinking, and I knew what he was thinking...*Redemption*.

Still, we had a long way to go. The division title hadn't yet been determined, nor had home-field advantage or the bye. The following week, though, we lost to the 49ers at Riverfront. But a 17–10 win at Pittsburgh on December 13 captured the Central Division for us. Glenn Cameron and Jim LeClair carried me off the Three Rivers turf. I appreciated the sentiment, but the division crown was just the first piece of the puzzle.

I met Steelers' coach Chuck Noll at mid-field. In my previous encounters with the Steelers, both in Cleveland and Cincinnati, the post-game exchange with Chuck consisted of nothing more than a nod and a handshake. There was much to admire about Chuck. He was a quality player for Paul Brown in Cleveland and a great head coach with four Super Bowl titles in Pittsburgh, but through the years I never got to know him well. As a coach and player, Chuck was composed, an introvert. This late-season game in '81, however, eliminated the Steelers from the play-offs, and when Chuck reached me, he put his arm around my shoulder.

"I just want you to know, you've done a good job with this team and I congratulate you," he said.

"Coming from you, that means a lot," I replied.

———

We couldn't rest on our laurels, however; a division title was just the first leg of our journey. Before our final game in Atlanta, I preached to my players about the importance of home-field advantage throughout the playoffs. A win over the Falcons would give us the best record in the AFC and allow us to play all of our postseason games at Riverfront Stadium. But they weren't paying heed to my admonition. We didn't prepare the way we should have for the Falcons, and at Fulton County Stadium, my players struggled to maintain their focus all day. Against an inferior opponent, we won, but barely, 30–28.

At 12-4 we had the best record in the AFC, which allowed us to take a week off as we awaited the outcome of "wild card" weekend. The Jets and the Bills met at the Meadowlands for the opportunity to play the Cincinnati Bengals. The game was decided when Buffalo defensive back Bill Simpson intercepted a Richard Todd pass at the 1-yard line, sealing a thrilling 31–27 Bills victory.

Buffalo came to Riverfront Stadium on January 3, a relatively mild winter day—rainy and overcast but temperatures in the forties. The two teams had already played in the third week of the season, a game that we won with a field goal in overtime. This time we jumped out to a 14–0 lead, and it briefly looked as though the game was destined to be a blowout. Buffalo came back, though, and tied the score at 14, only to see us jump ahead again 21–14. The see-saw battle continued when Joe Ferguson took the Bills down the field to a game-tying score, but in the midst of their comeback they lost two running backs, Joe Cribbs and Roosevelt Leaks, to injury

Charles Alexander unexpectedly had a great day for us. We hadn't planned on calling his number so much, giving him only a few carries to see how the Buffalo defense reacted. When they struggled to adjust, we kept handing the ball to Charles. At the end of the day, he had gained 63 yards on 17 carries with 2 touchdowns. You never know who the heroes are going to be.

Early in the fourth quarter Ken Anderson hit Cris Collinsworth with a 16-yard touchdown pass. After that score our defense stiffened and held the Bills scoreless for the remainder of the game. The Bills threatened and were driving for a potential game-tying touchdown late in the fourth quarter. Ferguson completed a first-down pass to the our 14-yard line only to have to play nullified by a delay-of-game penalty. That infraction turned out to be a backbreaker for the Bills. We wrapped up the game when our defense forced the Bills to turn the ball over on downs on their final possession. The first January game at Riverfront, my first playoff game as a coach, ended as a 28–21 Bengal victory.

There was another AFC playoff game that weekend, and it was one for the ages. The San Diego Chargers and Miami Dolphins played one of the most memorable contests in league history. The Chargers and their high-powered offense led by Dan Fouts came out on top, 41–38.

A couple of months earlier, on November 8 we beat the Chargers easily in San Diego, 40–17. But I had no misapprehension that the second time around would be so easy. The Chargers were too explosive to dismiss. The weather wasn't a factor as we worked out all week in preparation for San Diego. It was cold, but when Sunday arrived, the severe weather snuck up on us. The night before the game we stayed at a Marriott hotel in Sharonville, a few miles north of the city. On January 10, 1982, I woke up, and the sun was shining. I knew it was cold, but I had no idea just how cold until Marv Pollins told me it was ten or twelve below zero. The thermostat would reach fourteen below, and the wind chill factor was an unbelievable fifty-nine degrees below zero.

Following our pre-game meal, I gathered our team for a meeting. Foremost in my thoughts: How do I explain to these guys what it's going to be like playing in this weather? I had been in those circumstances as a player, and I understood what it was going to be like, but it was hard for me to express in words. I wanted them to accept the fact that it was cold and to understand that they had to deal with it.

One thing I used to tell my players was, "If this game was easy everybody would be doing it, because it's a lot of fun." On a day like that, though, I really felt the need to emphasize how difficult the conditions would be.

"You are going to be uncomfortable. That you must realize, but this game is scheduled. This game is going to be played. And we're going to have to be out there in the weather, and there is nothing we can do about it. It's kind of like going to the dentist," I told them. "You know it's going to hurt, but you're going to have to put up with it."

I also hearkened back to the story of George Allen from our playoff game against the Rams in '67. I told them how George came out for the pre-game warmups wearing just a dress shirt. "'Ol George was trying to pull a Woody Hayes on us; he was trying to show us that the cold didn't affect him. But we all had been around long enough to know it was cold, and by the time George came back out for the kick-off he was wearing so many coats we could barely recognize him. Know that it's going to be cold," I said. "Don't be proud. Wear what you need to keep warm."

Even with those words of advice lingering in the air, as we went on the field for warmups, I saw that our offensive linemen had their sleeves rolled up. They wanted to show me and everybody else that this weather wasn't going to be an issue for them.

As a coach, there are certain things you look for in those conditions. Ball handling would be affected by the adverse conditions. Can our quarterback throw? Can our receivers catch? We watched closely in warmups.

Being able to maintain your footing is probably the most important thing for a football player. If you can stand up, cut, and run without falling down, that is extremely important. The Ice Bowl was played on the frozen natural turf of Lambeau Field. We couldn't get any footing at all that day. The artificial turf on Riverfront Stadium, though hard as concrete, supplied good footing.

The wind, too, would affect my decisions. It was obvious that the wind was prevailing from the river end of the stadium. We had a choice to make: if we win the coin toss, do we kick or receive? Do we take the wind and kick off to San Diego? Or, do we elect to receive? There was some risk involved in giving the high-octane Charger offense the ball to begin the game. But after some deliberation, I thought it might be a good way to welcome those Chargers to southwestern Ohio during the depths of winter.

When we returned to the locker room, I told Hank Bullough, "We're going to put pressure on the defense."

Hank replied, "We'll be ready."

———

My old friend Jack Pogue had flown into town for the game. When Barbara picked him up at the airport, she realized that Jack was unprepared for the harsh weather. He had brought only an unlined topcoat and a pair of leather gloves with him to combat the cold. At one point I looked up in the stands where Barbara was sitting with Nancy Brown, Mike's wife, and I saw some guy standing with them. This fella looked like he was wearing everything in his closet. It took a moment before I realized that it was Jack, and it was my closet that had been emptied.

When the offensive line came back out on the field for the game, they had rubbed Vaseline all over their arms to better protect their skin from the elements. Vaseline or not, they still looked intimidating as hell. I'm certain that the Chargers were discouraged by the sight. Here they were freezing their tails off, and they looked across the line and saw those crazy Bengal linemen wearing short sleeves.

On the bench we put on every article of clothing we could find. The players on that day had better cold weather gear than we did in 1967. Gloves had been developed that helped keep the chill off their hands and still allowed dexterity to play the game. The quarterbacks had a pocket sewn into their jerseys to protect their hands between plays.

We won the toss and determined to defend the goal from the river side of the field, the stadium's west end, leaving San Diego with the ball going into the wind. After the game, Charger coach Don Coryell claimed that we purposely left a door open on the end of the field allowing gusts of wind to blow into the stadium. This door was supposedly closed while we had the ball and were driving toward that goal in the second quarter. In the third, Coryell said the door was again open to the Chargers disadvantage.

"I'm not accusing anybody of anything," Coryell said after the game, "but we had to request that the door be shut."

Home teams often do what they can to gain a competitive advantage. If we were playing a team that was faster than us, Vince would let the grass at Lambeau grow to slow down the quicker team. As far as the Freezer Bowl, I knew nothing about any of this door stuff until after the game. To this day I don't know if the story is true or if there was anything to Coryell's complaints. What I do know is this: if it was an advantage to us, I appreciate it.

We struck first on a 31-yard Jim Breech field goal, and on the ensuing kickoff we recovered a San Diego fumble. A day before the championship I noticed that M.L. Harris, our backup tight end, wasn't wearing "receiver" gloves while we were working out. Instead, Harris had on a pair of sheepskin-lined leather gloves.

"M. L." I said, "Wouldn't you rather wear those receiver gloves?"

"No," he answered, "my hands get too cold in those."

"Well, I'll watch you in practice and see how you do with those," I told him. I kept my eye on M.L. during the workout, and he didn't drop a single pass.

On our way off the field I caught up with him and said, "If you catch the ball tomorrow as well as you did today, I don't care what you wear on your hands."

He didn't catch many in the championship. In fact, he only got his hands on one pass, but it was a big one, an 8-yard touchdown in the first quarter that put us up 10–0. We were determined not to relinquish the lead, but the Chargers and their "Air Coryell" offense were dangerous. Coryell was a good offensive coach, and Dan Fouts was a very good quarterback. It came down to which quarterback handled the weather better, and I have to give it to Kenny Anderson. He played very well. I believe it was one of the finest games of his career. He threw for 161 yards and 2 touchdowns with no interceptions. His second touchdown pass came in the fourth quarter—a connection to tight end Dan Ross that gave us an insurmountable 27–7 lead.

I was very proud of my guys that day. They handled the weather well. In fact, they played better than anyone could have expected under such conditions. Our defense forced four Charger turnovers while we didn't give the ball up until late in the fourth, after the outcome was decided.

It's hard to put into words my feeling when the final gun sounded. I had been in this position a number of times as a player, but coaching that group of men who played so exceptionally under such trying conditions was enormously gratifying. As I was hoisted up again on the shoulders of my players, one thought ran through my mind: "We're going to the Super Bowl!"

———

It was just our luck—if ever a team needed a respite from winter, a nice visit to a balmy climate, it was the Cincinnati Bengals. However, Super Bowl XVI was the first ever played at a cold-weather site, the Silverdome in Pontiac, Michigan. Our opponent, the San Francisco 49ers, provided

Being carried off the field after the "Freezer Bowl" victory over the San Diego Chargers, January 10, 1982, in which we won the AFC Championship.

a good story line for sports writers to follow and expand upon in the days leading up to the game. The 49ers, too, were making their first appearance in the Super Bowl, and they were led by a fair-haired quarterback, Joe Montana. And like the Bengals, San Francisco had made a dramatic turnaround from 2-14 in 1979 to become NFC champions just two years later. Joe Montana certainly played a big role in this transformation, but it was a Paul Brown protégé who brought the 49ers to the brink of a world championship.

Bill Walsh was on PB's staff from the Bengals' first year in 1968 until Paul retired from coaching following the '75 season. When Paul tapped Tiger Johnson to replace him on the sideline, Bill opted to leave Cincinnati for San Diego, where he worked on Tommy Prothro's staff. The media jumped on this connection and played up Bill's hard feelings about being passed over by PB. Whatever happened between them was none of my concern. Even legitimate stories can be blown out of proportion during Super Bowl week. I was grateful that no one asked me to comment on the Walsh/Brown "feud."

———

The entire week following the championship game was so damn cold in Cincinnati we didn't want to be out there on the field, to tell the truth. Not the players or the coaches. The frigid weather hadn't let up, and the conditions made it impossible for us to practice effectively. Following our workout on the Monday of Super Bowl week, Mike, Paul, and I discussed our options. We agreed we should take the team to Detroit early so we could get in some work at the Silverdome.

During that week the league had mandatory media gatherings for players and coaches. Because we were coming into town a few days early, I assumed that we wouldn't have any media obligations until Tuesday. I wanted to get the players settled and have a schedule laid out for them so they would know exactly what we were doing all week. I didn't want them wondering about anything; I wanted them focusing on the San Francisco 49ers.

While we were en route to Detroit, our public relations director, Al Heim, told me, "They want all the players and coaches as soon as we get to the hotel."

I was not pleased to hear this news, to say the least.

"We don't need this right now," I said. "I'll go. Let the players settle into their rooms. The media pressure will be enough later in the week."

When the Packers played that first Super Bowl, before it was even known as the Super Bowl, we were amazed by the media coverage for the game, but it seemed quaint compared to what we faced now. None of us in Los Angeles in 1967 could have imagined the event that the Super Bowl would become. The distractions were many, and keeping my team focused through the week was a priority. There were a number of media gatherings throughout the week—sometimes it was the coaches, sometimes it was the players, and sometimes it was just me. Everybody was looking for an angle

Whatever work a coaching staff is going to get done to prepare for a game needs be done before the team travels to the site. We had played the 49ers in the last part of the season, and they beat us pretty bad, at Riverfront, 21–3. But we thought we had a good handle on them and what they did. Still, I never thought we got the type of practices we needed for the Super Bowl, even though we had an opportunity to use the Silverdome. It wasn't anybody's fault; it was just the way things fell. We had time to prepare our game plan, but little time to work with the players on executing the plan. Had we known we were going to Detroit early, perhaps we would have been in a better frame of mind to handle it.

Super Bowl week turned into one long social event with numerous parties held during the days leading up to the game. I went to just one of them, along with Mike. Paul, however, kept a low profile while we were in Detroit. He was at our practices, but even though he was a focus of many media profiles, he wasn't seen socially at any of the many league-organized events. His old nemesis, though, was busy making the rounds. Barbara ran into Modell at one party. He gave her a hug and a kiss and said, "I'm so happy about Forrest. I always knew he could do it, that's why I hired him."

––––––––

With all the hoopla, sometimes it was hard to remember there was a game to be played. Once we took the field on Sunday, things did not begin well for us. The 49ers jumped out to a 20–0 lead, while we couldn't hold onto the ball. There was something about that field—the cold weather outside combined with the warm temperatures inside the Silverdome to make the turf particularly dry, which caused the ball to bounce funny. This little fact was something that San Francisco discovered during their week of practice. The 49ers took advantage of the anomaly by having Ray Wersching squib the kick-offs. David Verser had a hard time handling a couple of kicks and averaged only 10 yards a return, half of his season average. Archie Griffin fumbled one return, which the 49ers recovered at the 4-yard line.

After falling into that 20–0 hole our defense tightened up. We came out in the second half and scored quickly. And then, later in the third quarter, we drove the ball inside the 49er 5-yard line.

On first and goal at the three, we ran Pete Johnson, who picked up two, taking us down to the 1-yard line. There was a play that we had worked on for just such an occasion. We sent in an extra tight end with Johnson and Alexander lined up in the back field. David Verser was also in the game at flanker. He was our strongest wide receiver. Kenny made a special call at the line of scrimmage to signal the play, and I think David missed the audible because of the crowd noise. At the snap, David and the tight end both blocked the wrong man, and Pete was met by an army of 49ers before he could reach the end zone.

On third down Kenny threw a pass in the flat to Charles Alexander, who caught the ball and tried to turn up field. If he had just fallen forward he would have landed in the end zone, but it just wasn't to be. Dave Bunz took Charles to the ground inside the 1-yard line.

On fourth down we ran the same short yardage play that failed on second down. This time we ran it to the right rather than the left side. The play was designed to go right over Mike Wilson, but 49'er linebacker Hacksaw Reynolds took a calculated risk and he was right. Reynolds filled the hole and caught Pete at an angle, keeping him from driving up field.

After the game I told reporters, "That was an important play." Well, that was an understatement. The game wasn't over, but we were running out of time.

We got the ball back quickly, preventing the 49ers from making a first down on their next possession. Following the punt, Kenny marched the offense down the field, capping the fifty-three-yard drive with a touchdown pass to Dan Ross. There was 10:06 left on the clock, and we were behind, 20–14. But that was as close as we would get. San Francisco was able to put two more field goals on the board. The last of the field goals came with under two minutes to play. With time running down Kenny completed six consecutive passes on a drive that culminated with a second touchdown to Ross. It was now 26–21 but only twenty seconds remained on the clock after we scored.

Our attempt at an on-side kick was recovered by Dwight Clark, effectively bringing our championship dream to a close.

———

I know it sounds cliché, but I was very proud of my team in defeat. They fell behind by a large margin but they never quit. Players who lack character would just roll over after falling behind 20–0 in a championship game. But they came out of the locker room in the second half and played great football and took the game down to the wire.

In the dressing room I let my team know how I felt. Yes, I was disappointed, just as they were. But the fight never went out of them. In the face of adversity they never quit, and I will always remember them for that.

Following the game there was a party held at the Troy Hilton, the team's home for the previous ten days. No one felt much like celebrating, but the party had been planned—win or lose. Barbara and I went, and though it was difficult to disguise the disappointment, I did my best to put on a good front.

The next morning we flew home to Cincinnati. On the plane Barbara and I sat near Mike and Nancy Brown. Not a whole lot was said on the short flight. When we arrived at the airport we were told there was a gathering to welcome us at Fountain Square. Three busses carried the players and their families up Interstate 75/71 toward the city. All the way through northern Kentucky people lined up wearing their Bengal jerseys and jackets, cheering for us.

We felt bad about losing the game, but the homecoming helped fill the void and made us proud to represent the city of Cincinnati. I had the chance to say a few words to the crowd—thanking them for their support and assuring them there would be another opportunity.

It was a great year, one worth saluting. We went beyond expectations, but we didn't close the deal. And that's something you never forget.

———

Discussing football with San Francisco 49ers coach Bill Walsh in Kansas City at a 101 Club banquet, where he was named NFL Coach of the Year and I was named AFC Coach of the Year.

After falling just short at the end of a long, hard-fought season it would be easy to have an emotional letdown. But just as I did in 1960 after the Eagles beat us in the championship game, I wanted to get right back at it. There was no time to dwell on the loss. Playing so late into the season allowed little time to prepare for the college draft, and we had a lot of catching up to do. We had already missed the East-West Shrine Game as well as all the other postseason all-star games.

There was no "Super Bowl hangover" for us. The team reported to Wilmington in the summer of '82 with a chance to redeem itself. If there was a distraction during camp, it was the threat of a player's strike, which hovered over the entire league. I could sense that the team was preoccupied with all the labor talk, and I felt it necessary to address the situation with the players.

"Look, I know what's on your minds," I told them. "A strike is looming, but right now it's only talk. We need to focus and prepare for the season as if there won't be any work stoppage."

The season began as scheduled, and we started off with a victory over Houston, which was followed by a tough overtime loss to Pittsburgh. And then the strike became a reality. All the teams closed up shop. We were not permitted to contact the players in any way. During the season the coaches set up at Spinney Field, a practice facility not far from Riverfront Stadium. We were still making our scouting trips to college campuses on the weekends, and on weekdays we tried to operate business as usual. But it was anything but business as usual.

Before the strike was days old, Paul had Spinney Field totally locked up. "We can't have the coaches down there or any of the players," he said.

I tried to explain that the coaches liked to work out during their lunch break and all the equipment was at Spinney. "I understand that we are in a total lockout," I said, "but what does it hurt for the coaches to work out?"

But Paul was emphatic: "No." His fear was that some players might get in the facilities and "get some information." So we had Tom Gray move the exercise equipment to Riverfront. If nothing else, our coaching staff was in pretty good shape.

One week and then another went by, and the two sides were no closer to an agreement. As game after game was lost because of the strike, the owners announced that the entire season would be canceled if the work stoppage eliminated more than half the season. But that turned out to be nothing more than a threat. Seven of the sixteen games

Standing with the captains of the AFC Champion Bengals: (Standing, left to right): Jim LeClair, Tom Dinkel, Isaac Curtis. (Kneeling, left to right): Ken Riley, Archie Griffin.

scheduled were canceled before an agreement was reached. The strike, which began on September 20, lasted fifty-seven days. Following the settlement, we had only four days to prepare for our November 21 game at Philadelphia.

Once the players returned to Spinney, I gathered them and welcomed them back. "It is important that you put all the labor strife behind," I said. "It's time to get back to business."

And the players responded. We won six of the seven remaining games and qualified for the "Super Bowl Tournament." Because of the strike, the normal playoff set-up was cast aside for a truncated tournament. The new plan allowed the top eight teams from each conference to be seeded one through eight and placed in brackets. We were the number three seed in the AFC and drew the sixth seed New York Jets.

The game was played January 9 at Riverfront. We jumped out in front of New York, but the Jets then jumped all over us. Their defense overpowered our offense, and once New York's offense generated a lead, they never relinquished it. I was not pleased with our performance, and the final score, 44–17, was evidence enough that my discontent was warranted.

———

Drugs, holdouts, defections...the summer of 1983 was nothing but one long headache for me.

Just before the start of training camp Lindy Infante told me he was offered the position of head coach with the Jacksonville Bulls of the newly formed United States Football League. The USFL had begun play in the spring of '83, and they had decided to expand from twelve to eighteen teams for the '84 campaign. The Bulls would be one of the expansion teams joining the league that spring, which was when Lindy was expected to join the franchise.

"You'd better tell Paul," I said to Lindy.

He made an appointment to meet in Paul's office. Lindy divulged his opportunity and offered an explanation, saying, "I want to coach this season and fulfill my contract with the Bengals."

Paul didn't need to hear anything else. He fired Lindy on the spot.

A short while later PB called me. I'd be lying if I said I was happy with his decision. Though I'm sure he already knew the circumstances, I let Paul know what a jam this put us in. We didn't have an offensive coordinator and we couldn't bring anybody in with such short notice.

"Well, I can't have him here," Paul said curtly. "He's under contract to another organization in a competing league. We just can't have it. All he'll do is gather information about players who would become available."

At the time I was upset with the decision; it was one of the few disagreements we had. In retrospect, if I had been in Paul's shoes, I probably would have done the same thing. But I was the coach, not the owner, and Lindy was an important part of my staff. The first person that crossed my mind to fill his spot was Raymond Berry. But there wasn't time enough for him to learn our system. I then looked to Bruce Coslett, our tight end/special teams coach. We made Bruce our offensive coordinator, but that still left us one coach short. Bruce continued to handle some of the special teams' duties, but a few other coaches chipped in also, including me.

If the USFL hadn't intruded on our team enough, two of our better players signed "futures" contracts with the renegade league. Cris Collinsworth agreed to play for Tampa Bay when his Bengals' contract concluded following the 1984 season. Dan Ross, too, would be leaving once his obligation to the Bengals was fulfilled, after the '83 season. Ross was to join the Boston outfit in the USFL. But at least we had Ross and Collinsworth in camp. Anthony Munoz was a hold out and wasn't present when players reported to Wilmington. Contractual disputes had been around football long before I joined the league, and I had to accept the situation with Anthony.

But in that summer I was confronted with a new problem: drugs.

Ross Browner and Pete Johnson both appeared as prosecution witnesses in a federal drug trial. Under immunity, both testified to purchasing cocaine from defendant John F. Schultz. The revelation came as a complete surprise to me, and I was especially shocked that it was those two men involved. For their indiscretion, Johnson and Browner were suspended the first four games of the regular season by Commissioner Rozelle.

I was disappointed, and I expressed that frustration to the team. But the commissioner had issued the penalty, and we as a team had to do what we could until they returned.

The most tumultuous training camp I'd ever experienced was capped with an embarrassing 34–7 loss to the Lions, giving us a 0-4 preseason record. Following the game I commented that it was, "the worst exhibition of football I have ever witnessed."

The next week we opened the season against the Raiders with a lineup that barely resembled the team we fielded in Detroit for Super Bowl XVI. In addition to the absent Johnson and Browner, ten starters on the Super Bowl team were no longer members of the Bengals. We added a young back, Stanley Wilson, to step in for Johnson during the suspension. When Pete returned and everyone was healthy, we had a pretty good backfield with Johnson and Wilson.

Our season ended with a 20–4 loss to Minnesota, leaving us with a 7-9 record. I couldn't contain myself following the Viking contest. "I can't tell you how happy I am this season is finally over. I've never been this happy that a season had ended this early before."

Football teams live together six months. As a coach you see your players every day, you talk to them, you learn about them and what's going on in their lives. And I knew my team was distracted in 1983. The focus wasn't on football. This isn't necessarily something you *know*, it's something you *feel*. I don't know how many times I told them, "Only worry about things you have control over."

They didn't have their mind on business. During the season it seemed as if half the team was in conversation with, or flirting with, USFL teams. Before the players went home for the winter I sent them all a message: "I am not going to live with this complaining, bitching, and moaning for another year. I can prevent it and I will prevent it. I can't keep people from complaining to each other, but there is no reason to continually air this thing publicly. It got completely out of hand this year."

9

A PACKER AGAIN

BART STARR HAD BEEN COACHING THE GREEN BAY Packers since he replaced Dan Devine in 1975. In those nine seasons the Packers had two winning seasons and one playoff appearance. When it was announced that Bart had been fired less than twenty-four hours after the Packers' season-ending December 18 loss to the Bears, my thoughts went out to my friend and teammate. I wished things had worked out better for him, but I must confess the possibility of returning to Green Bay crossed my mind briefly, and I do mean briefly. I didn't give the idea much consideration because I still had a year on my contract with the Bengals. Paul Brown did not allow his coaches to move on to other teams. Besides, I was happy in Cincinnati.

A couple of days after I learned of Bart's dismissal, Mike Brown called me.

"Green Bay has contacted us," he told me. "They would like to talk to you about the head coaching position."

I think a whole minute passed before I said anything. Finally I managed to ask, "Well, where do we go from here?"

"We're going to give them permission," Mike said. "All we ask is that you call us before you make your final decision. You do know they'll probably name a street for you up there."

"I don't know how I feel about this, Mike."

Admittedly I was surprised that Paul and Mike granted the Packers permission to speak with me, and I was curious to hear what Green Bay had to say and what they had in mind. The Packers' team president, Judge Robert Parins, and I made arrangements to meet in Chicago at O'Hare Airport. Along with Parins, Tony Canadeo, a member of the team's executive board, was present at the meeting. We talked a great deal, and I was pleased with what I heard. The money the Packers offered was better than my salary with the Bengals but not significantly. The big difference was length of contract. Green Bay put five years on the table, while Paul wouldn't consider offering a coach a deal of that duration. I was also being given what I believed to be complete control of player personnel.

I gave my word to Paul that I would be in touch before making a final decision, so I called Mike, and he in turn got in touch with PB. When I explained the Packer offer, it was understood that I would be leaving, but first I had something to say to Paul.

"I owe you a tremendous debt of gratitude," I told him. "You gave me a chance to get back into the National Football League as a head coach, and I will be eternally grateful for that opportunity."

Some in the press tried to play up the angle that I was leaving Cincinnati because the town "isn't big enough for Paul Brown and Forrest Gregg." There was speculation that my dissatisfaction with Paul's handling of the Lindy Infante situation influenced my decision to sign with the Packers. Indeed, I was unhappy with that decision, but I understood his reasoning. There was never anything hidden in our relationship. I

Our time in Cincinnati was full of great friendships. (Top) Barbara and I with Jack and Lynn Schiff in Puerto Rico. (Middle) Barbara and I with Mike and Nancy Brown at the World's Fair in Knoxville, Tennessee. (Below) Forrest Jr. and I on a fishing trip with ex-Packer teammate Bill Forester (far left) and Shannon Little, for many years a coach at Tennessee State.

always felt that I could go to Mike or Paul anytime I needed.

In fact, Mike and I developed a close friendship. Starting in 1980, we occasionally went out for dinner along with our wives and the Schiffs, Jack and Lynn, from Cincinnati. The following year it became a regular Friday night thing for the six of us. We went out to dinner or to a movie, even made trips to Indiana for whitewater canoeing. You wouldn't know it to look at him, but Mike knows how to loosen up—in the canoe he wore a sport coat and Florshiem Imperial shoes. The good times we had together were many. Every Fourth of July the Schiffs had a big party at their home. Jack had a big pasture where we'd line off a softball field. Anyone big enough to hold a bat could get up and take a swing. The summer after our Super Bowl appearance, the Browns, Schiffs, and Greggs all vacationed together in Knoxville. Mike's kids—Paul and Katy—were with us as well as Forrest Jr. and Karen, who were home from college. We fished, swam, played golf, and visited the World's Fair, which was held in Knoxville that summer.

Sometimes for our Friday night gatherings we would go to an upscale restaurant, while on other occasions we'd just go to a hamburger joint. One of my favorite places was a small tavern on the east side of town, the Millcroft Inn in Milford. They had a house band, a little three-piece combo that played music we could all understand. Occasionally we went out to the movies. One evening we took in a decidedly lowbrow comedy called *Porky's*. When the movie was over Mike and I emerged with our faces covered so we wouldn't be seen coming out of the theater. I have to say, though, *Porky's* did make me laugh.

Those friendships continue to this day. Every time Barbara and I return to Cincinnati, we always make a date with Jack, Lynn, Mike, and Nancy.

———

On Christmas Eve, 1983 I was introduced to the Wisconsin media via a telephone conference. Speaking from team headquarters in Wisconsin, Judge Parins explained, "Forrest will have full responsibility of the football operation."

From the outside I thought I was inheriting a good situation with the Packers. A couple of months earlier I had turned fifty years old, entering what I hoped would be my prime years as an NFL coach. Before we took the field for the first time in 1984, I told a local writer, "Regardless of what any coach says, deep down he believes he will take his team to the Super Bowl." Some ridiculed me for this statement, but the ultimate goal is the Super Bowl, and if you don't believe, then your team doesn't have a chance to win. If you don't believe, then you're not coaching.

Part of it is dreaming. Part of it is belief in yourself and belief in your players. This I know: If a player has the physical and mental attributes to be in the NFL, there is no limit to what he can do. If a coach puts limitations on his team, then he is telling them, "You're just not good enough." And if he does that, what kind of message does that send? There is no need to advertise, "We're going to the Super Bowl."

But you have to believe.

You never know. Your team gets a few wins in a row, and then the players start believing things are possible that maybe at one time they thought were impossible. And then the coaches start believing, then the fans start believing…and there you go.

The bottom line is: Don't sell yourself short.

————

Having been in the AFC for the better part of the decade, I wasn't overly familiar with the Packers personnel. I needed to know more about them, individually and as a team. What were their physical limitations?

Because I was a new coach, we were permitted to have two mini-camps, which allowed us to get acquainted. In those mini-camps we put them through a lot of tests. I wanted to know what kind of athletes we had up and down the roster. Players came expecting to bluff their way through the camp, but there was no faking it through one of my camps. League rules wouldn't allow us to have the players put on the pads; I would have if I could have, though.

At quarterback, the Packers had veteran Lynn Dickey. He was one of the best long ball throwers I'd ever seen, but he couldn't move at all. He was susceptible to the rush, but as long as we kept him healthy, we had a chance.

He had a few good receivers to throw to—Phillip Epps, James Lofton, and John Jefferson. Jefferson was the quietest guy on the team during the week. When I first observed John I thought, "Does he really want to play football?" But when Sunday came and the games counted, his whole personality changed. John had a sparkle in his eye and he talked. Man, how he could talk on Sundays! He had some great years with the Chargers earlier in his career. By the time I got to Green Bay, though, John had lost some speed but still had quickness and great hands. With James Lofton we had a good guy and a great receiver. James was tall and could go up for the ball. The trio provided us with fine targets for Lynn Dickey, but we lacked a "Pete Johnson." Our offense had no ability to move the ball on the ground. We didn't want Lynn Dickey throwing the ball on every play.

During preseason we had two kickers, Jan Stenerud and Eddie Garcia. Jan was nearing the end of a great career and his leg didn't have quite the strength it once did. Therefore we used Eddie to kick off and Jan to kick field goals. Before the end of camp, Jan came to me and asked to be traded.

"If I could play in Minnesota or a dome stadium I could last a few more years," he told me.

It was a reasonable request. I knew we were only going to keep one kicker, and I wasn't sure if Jan would be able to kick off adequately for us on the natural turf of Lambeau. We traded him to the Vikings—a move that probably cost us at least one ball game. In a 17–14 loss to the Broncos in Denver, Eddie Garcia missed 3 short field goals on October 15. He just couldn't handle the footing at Mile High Stadium. Trading Jan was a move I lamented, one that might have been the difference between us making the playoffs and staying home for the holidays.

We began the season 1-7, but came on strong to finish 8-8. Winning seven of our last eight games was a mixed blessing. We came very close to the playoffs, but the '84 Packers were an old team. Changes were necessary. We needed to revamp the roster and make the club younger. But I was lulled by the chance to reach the postseason. And I also knew there would have been serious fan repercussions had we torn the team apart after that great finish. So we sat pat and made no major roster changes leading into the 1985 season, a year that was more of the same—eight wins and eight losses, a struggle in mediocrity.

Before we played the Dolphins on December 8, Lynn Dickey made a statement that got a lot of play in the press, something along the lines of, "I wish I had Don Shula as my coach."

Lynn had been in the league a long time, and he had the reputation of being injury prone. Some of his teammates accused him of picking out the games he wanted to play, of coming down with ailments before we went up against an opponent he didn't want to face. He approached me after the Shula quote was made public. He didn't mean it "in that respect." Dickey told me. His explanation was fine with me, but the players knew what he said, and they knew that I knew. The team was waiting to see how I handled the situation.

A day later the team was in the locker room. "We got a game to play Sunday against the Dolphins," I told them. "They are coached by one of

Coaching the Green Bay Packers in 1984.

the greatest coaches of all time. Lynn and I talked about this. I apologized for not being Don Shula, and he apologized for not being Dan Marino. We both agreed to see what kind of coach I'll be Sunday and what kind of quarterback he is."

The Dolphins beat us 34–24. Dickey didn't play, though. He came down with a crick in his neck on Friday and missed the game on Sunday.

———

After two years of mediocrity with an old team, I was tired of sitting still. In 1986, after final cuts on September 1, only eleven players remained from the fifty-seven I inherited in 1984. Our 7-1 finish in the '84 season had raised expectations for the following year, and had we dismantled the team at the point, I might have been run out of town, but waiting a year to do it was a mistake. Nevertheless, for all the roster changes, we showed no improvement on the field. In fact, we took a dramatic step backward. We lost our first six games, the worst start ever for a Packer team, on the way to a 4-12 season.

Overshadowing our dismal performance, however, was a seemingly endless flood of arrests, accusations, and bad press that would mar the remainder of my stay in Green Bay.

———

The Packers and Bears rivalry goes back a long way—back even further than my arrival in Green Bay. It was something I was aware of while playing, certainly. Vince would talk about it, but not a lot. He didn't have to. In Green Bay everyone in town reminded us. Wherever we went fans reminded us, "It's Bears week! It's Bears week!"

The Packers had Curly Lambeau and later Vince Lombardi. The Chicago Bears *were* George Halas. Most of our games against the Bears were held at Wrigley Field. The fans were right on top of us there, but Wrigley wasn't the best facility in the world. Going toward the outfield, from left to right, the field seemed to be slanted down toward the outfield. Many times we had to take cold showers, which we all attributed to Halas. "Papa Bear" was one of the great legends of the game. He was practically the father of the NFL, and I had heard his name throughout my life. I'd see him twice a year on the field when we played Chicago, sometimes three times in those years when we played the Bears in the exhibition season. It wasn't until 1964, at the Pro Bowl, that I had personal contact with him. Jim Taylor, Jim Ringo, Paul Hornung, and I were named to represent the Western Conference in the Pro Bowl, but we had to play the Browns in the "Runner-Up Bowl" in the Orange Bowl. We were all late reporting to the Pro Bowl because of the game, and Halas needled us about it when we arrived.

"Just to make sure all you Green Bay players are comfortable, we'll use the Packer offense this week," he told us, "since we know your offense well."

One of the more violent incidents in my playing career occurred in a game against Chicago. I believe it was during the 1960 season, and I was blocking a linebacker with the Bears when my helmet came off. The play had concluded, and I was on all fours when I started looking for my helmet. The Bears linebacker stood in front of me, and I saw him pick up my helmet by the facemask. We locked eyes for a split second, and I thought, "He's not going..." but before I finished the thought he swung and hit me flush in the jaw with my helmet. The blow cracked all my front teeth...but I didn't lose any of them.

In 1965 the Bears selected two future Hall of Famers in the first round of the college draft—Dick Butkus and Gale Sayers. Each, in his own way, added much to the Bears-Packers rivalry. With the third pick overall Chicago selected Butkus, a linebacker out of Illinois. He was a great player, there's no doubt about that. He played with a vicious ferocity. He had what coaches call a "good motor," meaning he ran full throttle on every play. He delighted in hitting people. And at the Pro Bowl, when the rest of us were getting to know one another a little bit, he kept to himself. He didn't like you on the field or off. He was the same all the time. I never did get to know him even after it was all over.

While Dick Butkus brought unmatched intensity, Gale Sayers was polish and grace. After selecting Butkus, the Bears used the next pick in the draft on Gale, a running back from Kansas. With a football in his hands, he was exquisite, the smoothest runner I've ever seen. God, he was beautiful.

In those years it was a tough, physical rivalry, though not bitter. During my tenure as coach, though, the rivalry heated up, to put it kindly.

During the summer of '84 we were playing the Bears in a preseason contest at County Stadium. I was still learning about my team and our personnel, and in this game I wanted to see Lynn Dickey handle the two-minute drill in game conditions. One thing I like to do in training camp is to cover every phrase of the game. Whether it's throwing late in the game, trying to come from behind, or trying to run out the clock to preserve a lead. I wanted to test every aspect of our team under game conditions if the opportunity allowed. As time was running down in the first half, I called a timeout. At County Stadium, because of the field configuration, both teams used the same sideline. After we signaled for a timeout, the Bears' head coach, Mike Ditka, came charging down the sideline yelling.

"What in the hell are you doing?" Ditka screamed. "It's an exhibition game."

I was not about to be intimidated by Mike Ditka.

"You coach your bleeping team, and I'll coach mine," I said. Coach Lombardi would have frowned on my lack of vocabulary, but my temper got the best of me at the moment.

In the locker room at halftime I told the team, "You guys handle the Bears and I'll handle Mike Ditka."

In the sixties we played against one another, and later we played together on the '71 Cowboys. But from that August night in 1984 on, Ditka and I would be forever linked as bitter adversaries. This "clash" was played up in the Chicago papers and exacerbated by two on-field episodes in particular. But what stoked the rivalry from my point of view was simply the desire to defeat Chicago. They were the team to beat in the NFC Central, and the 1985 edition of the Bears were the measuring stick for the entire league.

As a player Mike was a good, tough tight end, very physical. His style as a player was typical of his 1985 squad. Those Bears fielded what might have been the best defense I've seen. Linebacker Mike Singletary set the tone for that defense, playing all out on every single play. Walter

Payton was one of the finest backs in football history. Behind center, Jim McMahon was molded in the image of his coach. I firmly believed that if you're playing a team that is physical, and the Bears were physical, then you have to be physical. As Chicago marched to their first championship in more than two decades, the storied rivalry between the Bears and the Packers was taken to another level.

Kenny Stills, a defensive safety, had been with us in training camp that summer but was cut before the start of the season. Later in the year, however, after we suffered some injuries in the secondary, we brought Kenny back. We were playing at Lambeau in November when Stills hit Bears fullback Matt Suhey after the whistle had blown, drawing a 15-yard penalty. Just a week earlier, Stills was on the street without a job, and now he was the starting strong safety for the Green Bay Packers. In a game where there were six unsportsmanlike penalties called, Kenny wanted to prove he belonged.

The following season, in the second quarter of our November 24 game at Lambeau Field, a play unfolded that has gone into Bears/Packers lore.

Charles Martin was an undrafted free agent who we brought into camp. He was an aggressive defensive tackle who didn't save his aggression for Sundays. He went full bore in practice also—to the point where some of our offensive linemen talked to him about slowing down in practice. Charles had a good motor, and he went full tilt all the time.

On the play in question, Charles rushed McMahon, who had dropped back to pass. Charles broke through and was chasing McMahon, who then threw an interception. When a pass is intercepted, a defensive player looks to block the quarterback; somebody has to get him because the quarterback is the first guy to see the interception. Later, when Charlie and I discussed the play, he said he had a moment of confusion—sack the quarterback or block the quarterback? In a flash, he body-slammed McMahon to the turf seriously injuring the quarterback's shoulder. The hit was obviously flagrant and illegal, but I've never believed it was malicious.

Over the next couple of days, Ditka appeared on his radio and TV shows blasting Charles, the Packers in general, and me obliquely.

"Ever since Bart Starr left Green Bay, the Packers have been playing like a bunch of thugs," Ditka said. "The character of the ball club is tremendously lacking. Over all, for that kind of attitude to permeate throughout, something is lacking. They had high character when Bart was there. I don't see that anymore."

He was very outspoken, and had I been in Ditka's shoes I'm sure I would have been also. With that said, I didn't appreciate my players being called thugs. Nor did I like the implication coming from Ditka and a few of his players that we encouraged dirty play. We played hard, clean, aggressive football. I didn't teach dirty football. I don't think it was a coincidence that the only time we were accused of playing dirty was when we played Chicago. I apologize for nothing...we were out there trying to win, and what we did was play the Bears the way the Bears played us. My only regret is we only beat them once in eight tries while I was coaching the Packers.

———

When I was playing with the Packers, I remember Willie Wood and Willie Davis telling me there was no place for the black players on the team to get a haircut or to eat in Green Bay. They would have to drive into Milwaukee on their day off to get their hair cut. After I became coach of the Packers, I was determined to make Green Bay as hospitable as I could for our black players. There were a few little things I could do, like when we played in Milwaukee I changed our day off to Monday. That allowed players to stay in the city for any personal business, if necessary. Housing was an issue in Green Bay, but the problems weren't limited to black players. We were a family of four living in a one-story house with one bathroom. Before my second season as Packer coach, I had the idea of bringing somebody in to serve as a liaison for the players to the community.

I wanted to hire someone I knew, someone who knew what I wanted, and I had a specific person in mind for the job. Al Dennis had played for me in San Diego and Cleveland. Al fit the bill in every way, in addition to being a good guy. He would be someone the players could go to if they had a complaint with me, or if they had trouble in the community or with a teammate. Al would be there to head off any difficulties. I brought Al and his wife up to Wisconsin to discuss the position, but unfortunately Green Bay was like a foreign country to them. Al Dennis was the man I envisioned for the job, and when he turned down my offer, I didn't pursue the idea any further. That was a mistake.

For Packer players, life in Green Bay was like living in a fishbowl. If you went to the grocery store, the whole town knew what you were having for dinner. A spilled drink in a bar becomes "disorderly conduct." If a player has an argument with his wife, that becomes an item. And for a period of time it seemed as if everything that could happen did happen. A number of my players ran into trouble with the law for a variety of transgressions. There was a D.U.I. and a bar fight. Some accusations, however, were more serious than others. As a coach, I don't know how you prepare for those occurrences.

In December of '86 the third Packer in three years was charged with sexual assault. So much time has passed that I don't want to rehash the accusations and indiscretions. Two of the players accused of assault were Mossy Cade and James Lofton, and their trials were conducted simultaneously. And in each instance when one of my players was accused of a crime, I stood by his side because he was innocent until proven guilty. When the Lofton and Cade cases went to trial, I was in the courtroom every day to show my support. Lofton was acquitted while Cade served two years in prison. James had a sharp lawyer who didn't allow a jury that was stacked against his client. Mossy may have been guilty as hell, only he knows for certain, but things that came up in the course of his trial didn't add up.

Upon release from prison, Cade signed with the Vikings, but the outcry from women's rights groups forced the team to reconsider. I understood their outrage, but in America, when you've paid your debt to society, you've paid. And Mossy paid a very, very steep price. Football was his job. He shouldn't have been blacklisted.

Don't get me wrong—we didn't have a team of choirboys. But there are two sides to every story. Charlie Martin, for instance, ran into trouble on a Friday night in a Green Bay bar. He came to me after the episode, and we had a long talk. The bar incident happened not long after he was suspended by Commissioner Rozelle for his hit on McMahon. I received a "fan" letter at the time. I had never read such prejudiced vitriol in all my life. People who didn't know Charlie thought he was an animal, but he wasn't. He was really a good guy. He couldn't understand why he was suspended. "Coach," he told me, "I don't know what happened to me on that play. I saw McMahon and I thought, 'do I block him? Tackle him?' I didn't intend to hurt him."

He gave me his side of the story concerning the "altercation" at the bar. I contacted the other parties involved, and we had a lengthy conversation. "What do you want Charlie to do?" I asked. "Do you want him to apologize? Pay for the damaged clothing?" In the end Charlie did what was asked of him. He apologized to the woman (he had spilled a drink on her dress). As far as all parties were concerned, the issue had been resolved.

And then it appeared in the papers.

It is the job of the press to find stories and report what they discover, but I have to ask how many bar fights are there on Friday nights in Green Bay? How many of them become news? Bob McGinn, who covered the Packers for the *Press-Gazette*, discovered the story, and it was splashed across that paper's front page.

I had a history with McGinn. When I first got to Green Bay in the summer of '84, he pulled me aside as I was coming off the practice field. "Look," he said, "I'm young. I'm new at this. I know you have a press conference immediately after practice. But I'd like to have some private time with you. There are some things that I'd like to ask you that I don't want other writers to know about because it's my story."

"When I have time I will," I told him.

And so I did. "It can't hurt to work with this young man," I thought. Stirring up the Martin story was cheap journalism as far as I was concerned, and I let McGinn know it. This guy thought he was investigating the next Watergate. At times things were confrontational. I called him "a muckraker," though I understood he had a right to print the article. Still, I believed it was totally unnecessary.

On the whole I enjoyed good relationships with writers through the years, as a player and as a coach. I understood and appreciated their role in the promotion of the game. On the last day of training camp in the summer of '84, I informed the press corps that the writers would be required to participate in grass drills or "up-downs" as some call them, "so you guys have an understanding of what the players endure."

Earlier I told the team my plan. "I want you fellas to do five or six grass drills and then stop. After that, make some noise like you're still working out."

I put the writers in the front row and began the drill. After a handful of "up-downs," the players stopped but kept grunting and stomping their feet pretending that they were still doing the exercise while the writers continued the workout. I've got to hand it to the writers, they gutted it out. And when it was over, the players gave them a big cheer. It was one of the few nonadversarial moments between the press and myself during my Packers tenure.

Green Bay had changed a great deal since my playing days. There were a lot of new faces, new attitudes about the Packers. But the love for the team was still there. The media, however, was different. Young guys of a new ilk were covering the team and seemed to criticize first and offer very little praise.

Looking back to the buildup prior to the first Super Bowl, I recall that Henry Jordan was the happiest person in the locker room. "Just think of all the publicity we're going to get," Henry said to me. It is a double-edged sword, that's for certain.

In my playing days, writers were fair. We were not the enemy. That's how I felt about Art Daley, Lee Remmel, and Bud Lea, the men who covered the Packers in our glory days. They reported it like it was. If you played badly, that's how it was written. If you played well, that's what they reported. These guys weren't homers, but I thought they were aware of not being too negative. Then again, it's hard to argue with success. When a team is winning the way we were, it's difficult for the press to find much negative to accentuate. All the Packer players received their share of press. Mostly it was Bart Starr, Hornung, Taylor, and McGee…but they gave us linemen our share, too.

Today, with so many competing media outlets, I believe the press emphasizes the negative. That's what sells newspapers, brings the ratings, and produces Web site and blog hits. Unfortunately, too often today's athlete gives the press ammunition.

During my first season in Cincinnati, the Bengals' public relations director, Al Heim, asked me to speak at a function in Dayton attended by local sports writers and broadcasters. In the course of my talk I told those in attendance, "We're starting a new era in Cincinnati. You're not always going to like what I do. I am not always going to like what you're going to write and broadcast, but I will fight to the death for your right to say it."

I know that sounds like a cliché, but I was saying what I believed. I enjoyed relatively good relationships with the writers in Cincinnati and Cleveland. That's not to say I didn't come under criticism, especially in

Green Bay. On more than one occasion I told reporters, "You're writing about something you don't know about. I'm talking about something I know about."

There was one writer in Cincinnati, Joe Minster, who wrote for the suburban *Hamilton Journal*. I often called on him first at my press conferences. When he was writing an article, Joe would always phrase his questions as a statement, trying to get me to agree with him. "Coach, now wouldn't you say…"

One time Hank Bullough said to me, "I don't think this guy is really a sports writer."

"What do you think he is?" I asked.

"An eccentric millionaire who likes coming down here and talking football with us," Bullough answered.

———

In February of 1987 Robert Parins hired Tom Braatz to join the team as executive vice president of football operations. Up to that point I had complete charge of personnel; my job was to hire all coaches, players, and scouts. However, Judge Parins came to me shortly after the season ended and informed me that he was bringing in a general manager. "The job is too much for one person," he told me.

I didn't agree with him, and I told him as much. But there was nothing I could do about the situation. Legally, if Judge Parins wanted to hire someone he could, but my contract read that I was to have such control, under the direction of the team president.

I knew Tom. He had played for the Redskins and later at Dallas. After he retired as a player, he was a scout in the league for sometime before working in Atlanta as the Falcon's general manager. If Judge Parins was going to bring in somebody, I preferred it to be somebody I could talk to. Tom and I met before he decided to take the position. We both came away agreeing that we could work together.

And we did work well together. We communicated daily and discussed the team and the club's needs. The only thing I held against Tom was Brent Fullwood. In '87 we had the fourth pick overall in the college draft. Tom had gone to Auburn and spent the day with Fullwood, and came away impressed with Brent's abilities as a running back. I was skeptical. Fullwood only had one good season in college that might have been attributed to the fact that he was playing behind Bo Jackson, and I was wary of "one year wonders."

While we were sitting in the draft room, Tom said, "I think we should take this back from Auburn, Brent Fullwood."

"Tom," I asked, "what's he going to do when we're in Chicago, it's late in the season, and we need 1 yard for a first down to keep the clock running?"

"He's got gravel in his gut," Tom assured me.

"Okay," I said, and we selected Fullwood.

I was given credit (or blame) for the pick of Fullwood because he was taken during my regime, but he was never my player. In my mind a great football player is dedicated. Someone who will spend the time off the field or on to make himself as good as he possibly can be. Someone who works hard in practice, in games, and during the offseason—in short, someone who is dedicated to their craft. But, I could never keep Brent Fullwood on the field. There was a pulled muscle here, a strained neck there. He came in making a million dollars, and that was rare at the time, yet he wouldn't learn our offense. At one point during training camp, he approached me.

"I need to go home," he said.

"Why?" I asked

"My auntie is sick."

He was already behind, and I let him know it. Later in the year he made one run of significance. It came against the Bears on third and short. We picked up the first down, and I thought to myself, "Tom must have told him about my earlier skepticism." But you know what? He got hurt on that play.

———

As I entered my fourth year as the Packers' head coach in 1987, I thought we had improved the team by getting some good young players. It felt like we were turning a corner. Today we see teams go from one win in a season to the playoffs the following one. In the 80's, though, it was very difficult to turn a roster over in a short period of time. The options to improve your personnel were few since free agency did not yet exist. The most obvious avenue was through the draft, but you could also pick up undrafted free agents and players that other teams had released. We could also trade, but in the NFL those are few and far between.

To win in pro football you must have a quarterback. Without a good one nothing else is possible, and that is what we were lacking. We had Randy Wright, a great person and a hard-working dedicated player, but he just didn't have the physical tools that make up a franchise quarterback. In the tenth round of the '87 draft we found a quarterback who could one day lead us to the playoffs, Don Majkowski. Don started five games in his rookie season, and in one contest threw for more than 300 yards, a first for a Packer rookie. We were building the offensive line, which was anchored by Ken Ruettgers, and Kenneth Davis had turned into a solid running back. Though we lost defensive back Tim Lewis to a severe neck injury during the '86 season I still thought our defense was showing improvement behind the leadership of Tim Harris. Our record didn't represent the strides we were making, but we had assembled the beginnings of a good football team.

———

Talk of another players' strike was in the air throughout the summer of 1987. A walkout seemed inevitable, and following the second game of the year, the Players' Association called a strike. It was intimated to us earlier in the summer that we would continue the season with "replacement" players when and if a strike was called. Some preparations were made in advance. Tom Braatz and our scouts laid some groundwork by putting together a list of names. When the strike came, it took us about a week to put together our roster. We looked first at guys we had in training camp who didn't make the final cuts. But we needed more than them to fill out an NFL roster.

It was a group effort; everyone had a hand in building our "replacement" team. Our scouts, Red Cochran and Dave Hanner, worked in conjunction with Braatz, the entire coaching staff, and myself. Everybody had recommendations. We weren't slapping together a team for exhibition purposes. Whether it was one game or the rest of the season, the contests we played with replacement players were going to count, and our goal was to acquire the best players possible.

The players started reporting. Some were in shape, most were not. As a whole we were not a well-conditioned team, but throughout the league everyone was in the same boat. I was pleased that none of our regular players crossed the line. They all hung together and nobody broke the code. But we were left with a group of guys who were in no way ready to play a full sixty-minute game.

Once we gathered a roster of players, we only had a week to prepare them for play. By necessity we were limited when putting together our game plans. We couldn't put in our whole offense, and on defense we used three coverages and a couple of different fronts. We also had to deal with the kicking game, the coverage teams, short yardage situations…the list was lengthy and time was short.

NFL locker rooms are inhabited by young men at the pinnacle of their athletic careers, and many of these players happily enjoy the accoutrements of fame and fortune. As the replacement players began reporting, I was immediately taken by their lack of pretension. Some guys got out of their taxi cab from the airport carrying nothing but a paper bag. They walked into the dressing room and stuffed their paper bags into their assigned lockers. I watched as they began pulling out the contents of the bags—clothes, shaving equipment, toothpaste...everything they brought from home was crammed in those sacks. And the first thing they asked was, "When do we get paid?"

They left wives and kids at home, where they'd send their paychecks, leaving just enough to eat for the week. I admired them for their tenacity and passion. In the first few days of practice they were incredibly enthusiastic. They were just happy to be there, but I think they expected that the experience would only last a few days and then they'd be sent packing. Play in an actual game? Not a chance.

I gathered the entire team together.

"Get ready," I told them. "Word has come down from the league that we are playing, and *the games will count.*"

It was as if an electric current went through the room. The news that they would be playing made a marked difference in practice. During the next workout I leaned over to one of my assistants and said, "Whatever else we'll have, we'll have hungry ballplayers."

The striking players were none too pleased to see that the NFL was carrying on without them. They gathered outside our practice facilities and picketed each day. I didn't realize the depth of their enmity, though, until I took the replacement players outdoors to practice. The striking players began yelling and screaming at the replacements. "Scabs" was among the nicest things they yelled. It was difficult to work in those conditions, so I took everyone inside. That's where we stayed for the next few days, and while we where indoors the pickets disappeared. With the strikers gone, I thought it was safe to go back outside. The strikers must have had a man on the inside, though.

We were about a quarter of the way through our drills when the striking players began pulling up outside the gates. From the other side of the fence they began hurling eggs. They must have bought out every grocery store in the city because once the eggs started coming, there seemed to be no end to the barrage. The sky seemed to be raining eggs.

I blew the whistle and yelled, "Everyone inside!" and we all took off running. A lot of players were hit in the salvo. Eggs fell all around me, but other than a little yolk splash on my shoes, I escaped unscathed.

I'll tell you this, though: it wasn't because they weren't trying.

The third week of the season was canceled altogether, and we next took the field on October 4 at the Metrodome in Minneapolis. The players were ready to play, but they were nervous as they could be. They were "wide eyed" as the old saying goes. And when they took the field those guys played their hearts out and left everything out there. The Packers won two of the three "replacement" games before the strike was settled. Those three contests were memorable, if not for the artistry then for the fervor.

One play in particular stands out in my mind that epitomized the "replacement" games. We had put a couple of misdirection plays in the game plan; one was a reverse to a wide receiver. Prior to the strike Lee Morris, a wide-out for us, had been working a regular job and wasn't in football shape, which was evident in practice because he was getting winded during workouts. Ol' Lee had played the entire game against the Vikings including special teams. Still, we called his number in the fourth quarter. Lee got the ball on the reverse as cleanly as he could, and there wasn't a defensive man in sight when he reached the sideline and headed up field. But his legs just folded on him. He got back up but he was spent, and only gained a few more yards. There was no doubt in my mind that he would have scored if he had been in condition, but the poor kid just ran out of gas.

After Lee was tackled, George Sefcik and I just looked at each other and burst out laughing.

The primary goal of the strike was unfettered free agency. To that point, what the players had was the so-called "Rozelle Rule." Players had the right to sign with other teams when their contract was up, but the system in place required the player's old club be awarded compensation from his new team. The union's preparation for the strike was short-sighted and not well thought out, however.

The NFLPA hadn't set up a strike fund to assist players with their lost salaries, and there were cracks in union solidarity. While no Packer players crossed the picket line, eighty-nine players around the league did cross it. Fans across the country had directed their anger about the strike toward the players. And while the replacement games didn't draw great numbers in ratings or attendance, the fact that the games went on without them was effective in bringing a relatively quick end to the strike. On October 15, the union capitulated and voted to return to work having achieved none of its goals. When the regular players returned, I sensed there was some animosity directed towards management and the coaching staff. The air needed to be cleared, so I gathered the team together.

"Look, I know you didn't like it, and I understand that," I told them. "But our job is to coach. Our job isn't to say who we coach. We coach the players management tells us to coach. There are no hard feelings on our part. Now I want you guys to concentrate on Detroit and put the strike behind us."

When we got our regular guys back out on the field I was pleased to see that they had all stayed in shape. I knew going in that their arms remained strong from throwing all those eggs, but it was nice to learn that they were diligent in maintaining their playing condition while on strike. While we were standing on the sideline watching the team practice, I asked my coaches a question: "What's the difference between the men we were coaching for the last month and the guys in front of us now?"

I believe it was my linebackers coach, Dale Lindsey, who spoke up first.

"Speed," Dale said simply.

I nodded my head. "Yep, speed."

We beat Detroit, and as we walked off the field I heard a couple of our guys talking. One said, "Boy, we socked it to those scabs today!"

They had forgotten that their opponent wasn't the replacement players and I corrected them. "No, you beat the Detroit Lions today."

The following week we met Tampa Bay in Milwaukee. The 23–17 loss to the Buccaneers was one of the most frustrating and embarrassing losses of my career. Though it's never pleasant losing because your team is outplayed, its part of the game. However, losing because of lack of effort, is never acceptable. The pressure and stress, which had begun to weigh on me, was revealed when I spoke to a reporter.

"It's the toughest job I've ever had. Extremely challenging and at times it hasn't always been enjoyable," I said.

———

It was never my belief that I expected too much from my players. As a coach, if you ask less than their best, that's exactly what you get in return— less than their best. I expected everything they had to give in every practice and in every game. Still, I was bothered that there were some players who wouldn't give their all. I had many, many men play for me who gave every ounce they had to give in an effort to win. But I could never get over those few who wouldn't live up to their capabilities. I took it personally when that happened, feeling that there was some reason I wasn't getting through to the guy. I wanted it for him as much as I did for myself and the team.

After four frustrating years, I felt like we had the Packers moving in the right direction. But they were an exhausting four years. All the things that had happened had a collective effect on my mind, my attitude. It was constant. Suspensions, arrests, trials, strikes…we made the headlines an awful lot but not for the right reasons. Off-the-field incidents that were out of my hands, things that were out of my control…that's what bothered me. And then there was the fact that the front office had pushed Tom Braatz on me. Though I wasn't the general manager in name, I previously had the responsibilities that came with the job. My problem wasn't with Tom; we got on well. My issue was with the front office because they had backed out of our deal. When I went to Cincinnati, Mike and Paul told me exactly what the situation was and what my responsibilities would be.

"This is the way we do it here," PB told me, and I appreciated that. I knew what to expect. But in Green Bay I didn't know, and I have to take some responsibility for that. Perhaps if I had a lawyer study my contract beforehand there would have been no misunderstandings. But hindsight is always 20/20, isn't it?

10

MIRACLE ON MOCKINGBIRD

THEY SAY YOU CAN'T EVER GO BACK HOME. AND TO BE honest, the prospect of returning to SMU had never crossed my mind before the phone rang. Professional football had been my life since I left school in 1956, and my objective when I got the call had been to turn around the fortunes of the Green Bay Packers. Still, when the call came I listened.

My alma mater's football program had fallen on self-inflicted hard times. The university had been caught paying players in the mid-eighties, and they were disciplined by being stripped of some scholarships. And what did they do following these sanctions? They got caught doing the same thing again.

The list of infractions was lengthy, and the penalties incurred devastating. A published report uncovered numerous violations by the Mustang football program, including the assertion that thirteen football players were paid approximately forty-seven thousand dollars during the '85-'86 academic year and that eight students athletes continued to receive payments from September to December '86 of about fourteen thousand dollars. The most recent allegations against SMU football surfaced in November of '87 when former player Davis Stanley told WFAA-TV that he had received payments of $750 per month from recruiting coordinator Henry Lee Parker. Two days later, the *Dallas Morning News* reported that senior tight end Albert Reese had been living rent-free in an apartment provided by George W. Owen, a booster who had been banned from any contact with the SMU athletic department when the sanctions were handed down in August of '85 by the NCAA.

Later I learned that the football program had made commitments to some of these kids that they would receive a certain amount of money while they were in school. Lo and behold, the second time around the NCAA threw the book at SMU. On February 25, 1987, the NCAA handed down "the death penalty" against SMU's football program. The 1987 football schedule was canceled and the school was stripped of scholarships. Those players already under scholarship to SMU were freed by the university, setting off a feeding frenzy as coaches from around the country moved in to sign these kids to scholarships. Southern Methodist was made an example, and the NCAA wanted to make sure no one committed such egregious acts again. But only a naïf would believe SMU was the only guilty program in collegiate football.

It was said that SMU paid their recruits so much because they were in competition with other schools in the Southwest Conference. There was (and still is) a lot of money made in college football, and teams wanted the best athletes to represent their universities. That's not to say paying kids was the right thing to do, far from it. But the intense pressure to win, coupled with unscrupulous boosters, resulted in SMU football being a national story for all the wrong reasons.

Like everyone else, I read the headlines. "Why did the NCAA come down so hard at SMU?" I wondered. They were far from the only guilty program. Still, I just sat back from a distance and watched as events unfolded. Some time passed after the death penalty was handed down and then I heard about the dismissal of Mustang coach Bobby Collins and the university's athletic director. I had several friends involved in the program, including Ross Love who had been the president of the Letterman Association for a long time. From that position Ross was well aware of what was going on within the program, and he phoned me shortly after Collins was let go.

"Do you know about it?" Ross asked, referring to the death penalty.

"I don't know the specifics, but yes, I've heard about the sanctions."

We talked for a while before Ross broached the subject of coaching the Mustangs. Admittedly, I had always thought I would enjoy coaching at the college level, but this was totally out of the blue. Ross and I talked several more times on the phone, and the more we talked, the more interested I became. The differences between the college game and the pro version began swimming through my mind. Recruiting, obviously, was the biggest difference. All things being equal, the chance of returning to the Hilltop wouldn't be so bad. But SMU football was in bad shape. The common thought around the country was, "Could they run a program without paying players?"

The president of the University, Kenneth Pye, and SMU's athletic director, Doug Single, flew to Appleton to meet with me. We sat down together at the airport and had a lengthy discussion. Single and Pye laid everything out for me—the sanctions, the recruiting restrictions, and the de-emphasis of athletics. The challenge was daunting, certainly, but the lure of returning to SMU and starting a program from scratch fascinated me. Coaching kids after what we'd been through in the previous few years in Green Bay seemed like a breath of fresh air. I told Pye and Single that I was interested, but I wasn't ready to give them a definitive answer. The news was kept out of the papers while I debated the pros and cons. In fact,

Pye asked me to keep our discussion in complete confidence.

Several weeks passed before I approached Judge Parins, the Packers' president.

"I'm thinking of taking the head coaching position at SMU," I told him. Not for a moment did he try to talk me out of making the move.

"Well, if that's what you want to do."

We didn't talk long, and I didn't go over the reasons for my decision. I didn't feel the need. The day before I publicly announced my decision to leave Green Bay, I called my assistant coaches together. At that moment, I wasn't 100 percent certain that I would take the position at SMU, but I was pretty sure. During that short meeting none of the coaches gave me any feedback. I couldn't tell if they were angry or disappointed. Sometime later I learned that a couple members of my staff were not happy with me. Dick Modzelewski, in particular, felt betrayed by my decision. Mo and I went way back, to our days of competing against one another on the playing field, to our coaching careers—Cleveland, Cincinnati, and Green Bay. Mo had been with me every step along the way, and it saddened me that the misunderstanding marred our friendship.

———

When I was hired, President Pye told me, "You'll never be fired for not winning. You'll only be fired if you are caught cheating." I didn't necessarily like that. Of course I wanted to run a clean program, but I also wanted us to become successful on the field.

At the first press conference, I was asked, "What will you do if you catch some alum paying a player?" Without hesitation, I answered, "I'll punch him out," and I meant it.

There were some reports that the school faculty wasn't pleased with my hiring. They felt that bringing me to the Hilltop placed too much emphasis on athletics. There may have been some resentment, but I never felt any. I made it my business to get around campus and meet professors. I wanted them to know me, and I wanted to know them. They considered the football program to be a part of the university experience.

The decision for the Mustangs not to play in the fall of 1988 was made before I got to SMU. And even if we wanted, I don't think we had enough players to field a team. Three kids remained from the last SMU team and then a few walk-ons, and we only had fifteen scholarships to award for the school year. I wasn't sure if we would even be able to put together enough kids for a camp and for practice in the fall of '88.

I had to take a crash course on what we could and couldn't do. We had a gentleman, Dudley Parker, who worked as an assistant athletic director before and during the death penalty. Dudley knew the rules exceptionally well and advised us. That's not to say it was easy to navigate. The rules were vast and numerous.

In order for kids to visit SMU, they had to qualify for admission, the same as any other student. Their SATs had to be a certain minimum score before they could step foot on campus. Don't believe other schools didn't use these requirements against us. Sometimes it worked out in our favor because parents appreciated our emphasis on education. In addition, I couldn't spend any of the football program's budget to pay for recruits to visit campus.

It was tough recruiting, to put it mildly. Even after it was well known that we had quit paying, players would still ask, "What else do I get?"

Through the years I'd been back on several occasions. Both Forrest Jr. and Karen attended and graduated from SMU. During the '82 strike I visited on a scouting trip and saw the Mustangs play Arkansas and Baylor, but the opportunities to return had been few through the years. The campus remained as striking as ever, though. There was less green space and a few more buildings, but the general façade of the university remained the same. The most identifiable building on campus remained Dallas Hall, where Sleepy Morgan had taken me some forty-five years earlier and I'd fallen in love with Southern Methodist University.

One day that spring I was sitting in my office before school let out and my secretary, Rosemary Hatchman, came in and said, "I have a young man out here with his parents who would like to play football."

"Bring them in," I told her.

The young man's name was Chip Vasquez. Chip wasn't more than five feet, eight inches, 180 pounds. I looked at him and asked, "Son, what position would you like to play here at SMU?"

"I'm a guard," he confidently declared.

"Well," I asked, "are you coming to school here?"

"Yes, sir, I'm coming here to get an education, and to be a part of the Mustangs. I'll do anything to be a part of this team. I'll hold the blocking sled. I'll be a blocking dummy, anything to be a part of this team."

Hearing Chip say those words fired me up. At that moment I knew we were doing this for the right reasons.

Chip was a witty kid, and he made the team with pure determination and perseverance. I knew he wouldn't be one of our starters, but he was always there. Every game, Chip was on the sidelines, pacing up and down the line with me, always letting me know he was ready to go in the game. And when he did make it into a game...well, I don't know how many battles he won, but he was in every single one.

I think Chip was probably the only member of the team who wasn't intimidated by me, and, boy, he had a way of making me laugh. At one point in the fall of '88 the whole team was gathered around taking a break in practice. I don't recall how the conversation started, but the subject of the presidential election came up. Dukakis and Bush were running that year, and Chip spoke up.

"Coach, I'm not a Democrat or a Republican. I'm a DI."

"What in the world is a DI?" I asked.

"A damned independent!"

After Chip used up his football eligibility he asked me if there was anything he could do to help the athletic program. He still had a couple of courses to take. I took him on as an intern, and he brought to that job the same persistence and energy he'd given as a player. He was always there— ready to do anything necessary.

After graduation he was teaching in Texas. One night coming home from a school function, he was in a car accident and died from his injuries. Not long after he passed away, his parents came to see me. They wanted to know if they could put a bench in honor of Chip outside the stadium. I thought it was a wonderful idea. That bench is still there today, a reminder of Chip, his dedication and enthusiasm.

———

We offered one of our fifteen scholarships to a young man from Corpus Christi, Mike Ostos. Mike's father called me and said, "I know you're short on scholarships, and we'd like to help the program. We're all flattered and thankful that you offered the scholarship, but I'll pay his way so you can get an extra body."

I appreciated the gesture, but Mike was disappointed. He wanted to be one of the "original fifteen." And though technically he wasn't one of the first fifteen players on scholarship, we always thought of Mike as one.

During the spring of '88 we put together a list of names. Recommendations came from alumni as well as high school coaches we knew. Some locals suggested players. And we had an ear open for anyone who wanted to play. Eventually we had a bunch of kids who wanted to walk on.

We were taking all comers. Anyone who attended SMU and wanted to play, we'd find a place for him. When fall arrived we had enough to practice.

The university's marching band was on hand for our first practice—blaring out the school's fight song. It was a celebration, a new beginning, and to start I wanted the team to understand what to expect in the coming months. One hundred and twenty players were present for the first day of practice. We lost two kids. Scott Phillip, a walk-on who was slated to be a starter at linebacker, abruptly quit, as did scholarship player Phil Hazelhorst. We needed every body we could lay our hands on, so the loss of those two kids hurt, even though it wasn't completely unexpected. The attrition rate can sometimes be high. The days are hot and long, and they hurt physically. Sometimes the kids get homesick and leave school for more comfortable surroundings.

One thing I wanted to do was give them a preview of what was expected of them during the next year as we practiced. I said, "You're going to be sick of me, sick of your coaches, sick of each other. But I can't emphasize enough how important this will be. Usually when you have a football team, you have some veterans. Seniors and juniors are normally role models. When you get up in the morning and look in the mirror, you'll be looking at a role model. All you guys will be your own role models.

"Whatever you do here will be your responsibility. Whether you make it at SMU academically, whether you make it athletically…you're all over eighteen, and it's time to take responsibility for yourselves. Don't blame anyone else for your shortcomings. You'll be making decisions on how much time you'll study, and how much time you'll be spending on the streets."

And in all that time, we never had any problems. I can't emphasize enough how dedicated those kids were. They would be in the weight room at six in the morning, and then attend their classes, and then in the afternoon they'd practice in full pads. It was a grueling schedule that caused some attrition. But those who made it through were a special group of guys—*are* a special group. They've become lawyers, doctors, politicians; as a group they have done well.

I had a steadfast rule that if a player quit the team, he quit forever. One player made me reconsider that decree. Stan Thomas tried out for the team as a walk-on. He was at the university on presidential scholarship, and the demanding program was affecting his studies. Faced with the prospect of possibly losing his scholarship because of falling grades, Stan came to me and explained his situation and that he needed to leave the team. I understood. He wasn't quitting because he couldn't physically handle the demands. Rather, Stan and his family couldn't afford SMU without the scholarship.

I also understood when Stan came back to me. My inclination was to take him back. Still, I couldn't just cast aside my one firm rule, at least not without taking it to the team for a vote. As I expected, the players welcomed Stan back into the fold.

———

There was one young man on the squad who brought to mind Greg Pruitt. Michael Bowen was a mischievous kid, and like Greg he broke rules to get me to yell at him. With Michael, it was always something. He would arrive late for team meetings just to agitate me. When my players committed an infraction of some sort, I had a systematic reprimand that I termed "Mustang Reminders." One Mustang Reminder was a series of grass drills up and down the field, with the player stopping every ten yards and performing a drill. Each violation carried a varying sentence. For example, missing a class would be four or five Mustang Reminders. I couldn't catch them all the time, but I tried to enlist the professors to turn them in. With Bowen, however, I didn't need any assistance. Michael would head out to the field on his own and start doing Mustang Reminders.

I think he still owes me a few.

We talked a lot about the next year, about 1989. When you're eighteen and nineteen years old, one week seems like a long time, so it was hard for those kids to think a year ahead, but I kept referring to the first game against Rice. That's where we put our focus. I circled September 2 on the calendar. That year will pass before you know it, I told them. The date became a rallying cry for us, "9-2-89!" It was printed on T-shirts, written on the wall of the weight room. When the players were running wind sprints in the devastating Texas heat, they would chant, "9-2-89!"

How in the world will I keep these guys focused for a full year? I wondered.

Anyone who has ever played football hates to practice. They want to play a game. How could I keep them interested for a year? I wanted to start the players on a workout schedule. We had enough people, at least two deep, to hold regular scrimmages and practices. But I didn't want to scrimmage to excess because we didn't have the depth; there was too much risk of injury. So we mostly worked on the fundamentals, and that can get boring for a football player. We needed to put together our offensive and defensive systems, and we wanted to get the kids into regular routines.

I didn't want to beat them up so bad while they were playing against one another. We went through regular routines. I looked at the school schedule, and when the students took a fall break, I let the players take a break. Normally the players would stay on campus, but I wanted to give them as much time off as possible. We wouldn't work out on weekends; instead, I let the kids go home on weekends. The time off was good for them and good for the program. When the kids went home on weekends, the visits helped promote SMU football. People would say, "This guy is going to play for SMU when they start back up." It was a bit of a marketing tool. They might talk to some students from their high school and encourage them to consider SMU.

———

To ward off some of the tedium we occasionally had an intra-squad game. We were teaching the offense, defense, and special teams, but I also wanted to toughen them up for Southwest Conference football. I could talk about it all I wanted, but seeing is believing. For my players to understand the speed and ferocity of big-time college football, they needed to see a game in person.

It was my hope to take the team to a couple of SWC games. The campuses of both Baylor and TCU were relatively close, so those schools seemed like the best bet for us. One of the rules we had to adhere to: If we went to either Baylor or TCU we had to work out at their stadium. Baylor told us they didn't have the facilities to take care of us, but TCU allowed us to visit. On October 22, they welcomed us and gave us use of a dressing room. Since it was the day of a game, we had to work out early in the morning.

I called my players together and said, "You remember when we started? I told you how quickly the year would pass by. In a year you'll be playing in a Southwest Conference stadium. I want you to watch your own position; watch the guy you'll be playing against next year."

It was a great afternoon, and I always respected TCU for allowing us that privilege. For weeks my kids had been beating up on each other. I had to show these guys what they would be dealing with—how big and fast their opponents were. They all watched the game intently; they also ate a lot of hot dogs. To be honest, I didn't even know if buying the kids hot dogs was within the NCAA guidelines.

The day was a great preview of what could be expected next fall. I saw a lot of similarities in this group of kids and the replacement players I coached for three games in '87. Those guys who came to Green Bay with their belongings in a paper sack saw an opportunity to play a game they loved. Without a penny to their name, they left their families to chase a dream, however brief that chance might be. That's how my kids were at SMU. Under ordinary circumstances they never would have had the chance to play Division I, but they loved the game and just wanted a chance to play big-time college football. I admired them for their tenacity and their attitude. Still, I wished I had their confidence.

———

I told my players a year would pass quickly, and it certainly did. We began working out in the summer heat of Texas on August 7. From the beginning I told my players what to expect. "Nobody believes you can win a game," I said. "They'll start the count on you."

"What's 'the count?'" someone asked.

"Its how many games in a row you lose," I said.

Such a prospect seemed ridiculous to them. They agreed, "We're not going to lose them all."

We got a pretty good break with our schedule. There were open dates about one-third and two-thirds of the way through the season. It worked out well for us because I assumed we would have a lot of injuries due to our youth and lack of experience.

Nineteen months had passed since we began putting together the program. For nineteen months we had our eyes focused on the date, September 2, and the opponent, Rice University. SMU hadn't played a game at Ownby Stadium since Doak Walker was running the ball for the Mustangs against Texas Tech in 1948. SMU had called the Cotton Bowl and later Texas Stadium home for four decades. As an alumnus, it bothered me that people attended Mustang games without ever setting foot on SMU's beautiful campus, and I thought it was important to bring football back to the Hilltop. The cost of renovating Ownby was $1.5 million; still I thought the money well spent.

———

We wanted all the media attention we could get. Recruiting is difficult if the school's name isn't in the paper. Though we received a good deal of attention nationally, we didn't feel that we got enough publicity in our own paper, the *Dallas Morning News.*

At one time SMU was *the* game in town. Mustang football would dominate the sports page in the *Morning News* and the *Herald.* But when the Cowboys came to town in 1960 that all changed. It didn't take long before the Cowboys were the city's team. The Cowboys even won over the allegiance of my own family. While I was playing in Green Bay we played Dallas in the preseason every season. One year I got my younger brother, Boyd Jr., a sideline pass. Boyd was in his teens at the time, and he took a seat on the bench and watched the game. At one point Elijah Pitts came up to me and said, "Boy, did I catch your brother. The Cowboys had the ball and were driving, and I overheard Boyd Jr. muttering, 'C'mon Cowboys, c'mon Cowboys.'"

"Well," I said, "I guess that shows you where the loyalty lies."

Trying to carve out our own piece of the Metroplex market wouldn't be easy. The program had been dead for two years, and, if anything, the Cowboys had become even more popular. We did have something going for us, though. The novelty of bringing a football program back from the dead had sparked interest around the country. More than two hundred requests for press credentials came in from all the major news outlets. Everyone wanted to tell the story of SMU's rebirth.

———

As game day neared, I could sense it, could feel it in the air. You don't ask someone who's been farming all his life it it's going to rain. He knows when it's going to rain. Still, I couldn't help but wonder, "How good are

A pre-game moment before the SMU Mustangs take the field in 1989. We called our kick-off team "The Wrecking Crew."

we? Can we pass protect? Can our quarterback function?" We were entering the great unknown. It was exhilarating, and in its own way, frightening. I was on the Hilltop at Ownby every day of the week leading up to the contest. The weekend edition of the *Daily Campus* declared, "SMU Football Is Squeaky Clean"

If I had the choice of a team to start against it would have been Rice. Like SMU, Rice was an academic school. Their football program had struggled recently, having lost its previous eighteen contests, and I thought they would be a good gauge of our deficiencies and strengths. (Though I didn't know if we'd have any of the latter.)

The players were a little on edge as September 2 approached. I was hoping we'd get out of the game without too many injuries, that we'd still be standing at the end. Just like the kids, I had no idea what to expect. It reminded me of my first high school game. I had never played in a football game before that day, and here I was again, back at square one. I'd circled the date on the calendar more than a year earlier, and all of our efforts had been pointed toward that day. But on an afternoon when the thermometer reached ninety-five, it was a day I thought would never end.

The opening kickoff gave us a promising start; the returner for Rice sprinted up the middle of the field, and he was shellacked. Several of our blue jerseys pounced on the ball and got up from the field dancing in jubilation. Eighteen months of hard work had built up to that play, that moment, and the standing-room-only crowd at Ownby Stadium erupted when we came up with the ball.

A few moments later, a possible touchdown pass by Mike Romo was dropped in the end zone by Michael Bowen, and we had to settle on a field goal. Our 3–0 lead was brief. Less than two minutes passed before the Owls quarterback, Donald Hollas, ran for a 34-yard touchdown. We struggled to contain Hollas all day, but my kids played hard, and they executed pretty well. A 28–3 halftime deficit, ended as a 35–6 loss. But we came out of the game healthy.

———

We had an open date the next week before facing the Connecticut Huskies. If there was a team on the schedule that we could beat, it would have to be Connecticut. That's not to say the Huskies wouldn't have motivation against us. They were a 1-AA team, and we were Division 1. Beating us would be a big deal to them, but because they were 1-AA we should be competitive.

A funny thing happened: when Connecticut jumped out in front of us nearly half of the crowd at Ownby vacated the stadium. They had seen what had happened against Rice and thought this was just a repeat of that contest—we would fall behind and have no chance of coming back. Wide receiver Jason Wolf made a big third-down catch that kept a touchdown drive alive. Wolf was a character. A Michigan kid who attended Brother Rice High School in Detroit, Jason had been offered scholarships from Michigan and Michigan State as well as Clemson. Undoubtedly, Jason was a legitimate Division I player. But when Tom Rossley and I approached him about coming to SMU, he said, "What the hell, I'll pay a visit."

Before he could step foot on campus, Jason had to qualify as a student at SMU. We got his SATs and grades together, which were good enough for the school. And since we couldn't pay his way to Dallas, Jason's mother and father covered expenses. We couldn't pay for a hotel room, so we had to find someone to put him up in a dorm room. After all of that, Jason agreed to go against the grain and become a Mustang. When they heard the news, officials at Michigan State were angry.

"Those sonsofbitches are paying again," someone complained.

Jason's play against Connecticut kept us in the game. And I have to assume that a lot of students must have gone back to their dorms and turned the game on the radio, because when we got to within 9 points at 30–21, the students starting flowing back into the bleachers. Before the game was over, it looked like we had a full house.

A field goal with 3:14 remaining on the clock brought us 3 points closer. With the clock running down, we had the ball at the Connecticut 4-yard line. There was only time for 1 play. We were on the right hash and the play called was protection left, roll left. On that play, the quarterback has the option to run if his receivers are covered. Romo rolled left and didn't have a receiver, but he had some room for himself.

I thought Mike was going to run it into the end zone or get tackled at the one. He started toward the line of scrimmage, when all of a sudden he put on the brakes and placed the ball over the arms of two defenders into the arms of Michael Bowman, who caught the ball in the end zone.

That was the ball game!

The team swarmed Michael, and what seemed like half the student body joined. The other half tried to tear down the goal posts but after several unsuccessful attempts, they were chased off by security. When we finally uncovered Michael, he could barely breathe. In the locker room he told me, "When those students started jumping on me, I thought I was dead."

When I saw Michael catch the ball, I let out a yell and thanked God. The victory meant so much to the players, and it meant a lot to me, but it was hard to measure the importance the "Miracle on Mockingbird," as this victory came to be known, was to our program.

In the locker room I gathered the team around me.

"Well," I told them, "the count had stopped at one. They're going to have to start a new count now. And I'm telling you this from the bottom of my heart. I have played in Super Bowls, I have coached in Super Bowls, but I have never felt the way I did when I saw that ball in the end zone."

One victory didn't make for a season, I told reporters afterward. But it certainly made for a great Saturday night.

———

We didn't have much time to revel in our victory, not with the University of Texas waiting for us in seven days. In Texas, Longhorn football was the pinnacle, and on the face of it we didn't belong on the same field with them. But there was something in the film that not only gave me hope, but belief that we could win the game. And I told the team as much in our first meeting of the week.

"I'm going to tell you something and I want you to listen, and listen closely," I said. "We will beat the University of Texas Saturday."

I geared the entire week of practice toward that, an expectation of success.

On their first possession of the game Texas was driving, and on third down Bill Kiely broke through the Longhorn line for a sack. I could feel the kids on the sideline start to believe. "*We can do this*."

We got the ball and started a modest drive. Mike Romo took the snap and rolled left, away from our sideline. All of our receivers on that side of the field were covered, but standing all alone by our sideline was Jason Wolf, not a Longhorn in sight. "Wolf, Wolf!" our kids were yelling. Mike, of course, couldn't hear a thing, but at that instant he spun around and threw a perfect strike to Jason who ran it in for the touchdown.

A short while later an incident happened in front of the student section, which sat very close to the field at Ownby. Stan Thomas, an All-American offensive lineman for the Longhorns, blocked our Kenny Rea and kept on blocking him down the field long after the play was whistled dead. Thomas was simply embarrassing Rea, which Kenny didn't appreciate. The two players scrapped a little before being separated, but then Thomas started at Kenny again. As Thomas got near, Kenny wound up and threw a bolo punch into the Thomas family jewels. Thomas went right down, and the student section went crazy.

The referee came over to me and said, "We've got to throw the player out for a late hit."

"Well, okay," I said "but you didn't see the whole thing."

Kenny got tossed from the game, but he showed that we weren't going to *take shit from anybody*.

In the middle of the second quarter we had a 7–3 lead, and Texas had the ball. A Longhorn receiver ran an out pattern, and Cary Brabham, our cornerback, jumped the route. Nothing stood between Cary and the end zone, but he couldn't hold onto the ball. That was our last best chance in the game. The game remained close until the fourth quarter when the Longhorns pulled away for a 45–13 win.

Cary went to Hugh Spring High School in east Texas, not very far from Sulphur Springs. I went to scout Cary when his team was in the state playoffs, and on the very first play from scrimmage, a short trap on the left side, he took the ball all the way to the end zone. The opponent, Cooper High, took the ensuing kick off and drove down the field into a short yardage situation. Cary was put into the game as a strong safety and proceeded to make two tackles in a row, forcing Cooper to kick the field goal. He was fast as could be, and a great open field tackler. I had thought Cary would have made a good running back for us, but after watching him in person and seeing the film, I decided he would be a better fit for us on the defensive side of the ball.

The Texas game was followed by a loss at TCU and an embarrassing 49–3 defeat against Baylor defeat. The Baylor game stands out because of a play in the fourth quarter. The Bears had an insurmountable lead when we stopped them on third down. Rather than punt, however, Baylor coach Grant Taft decided to call a fake punt. Sportsmanship was in short supply that Saturday as well as the following week when we traveled to Houston.

The Houston Cougars had a very strong offense with a great running quarterback, Andre Ware. Understandably, I had a lot of apprehension leading up to the game. I knew with their explosive offense, they could put up a lot of points against us. And score they did, 95 points in fact. *Ninety-five points* along with a record 1,021 yards of offense including 771 yards through the air.

I had some history with the Cougars' coach, Jack Pardee. We went all the way back to college, when Jack was at A&M and I was at SMU. He was a linebacker and fullback in college. We coached against each other in the NFL, and when Jack was out of work, I hired him as a scout for the

Packers. Friendship aside, following the game I was upset with his coaching, and I spoke out to the press.

"I don't see any point in going for the home run again and again like they did in the second half. I don't think it's necessary, and I don't appreciate it. They had their second and third defense in there in the second and third quarters, but I didn't see any reason why they had to do it by sending in fresh receivers to blow by our kids, who were obviously tired. I'd never run up the score like that on a group of freshmen and sophomores. If it was an even team, that's different. It's over and I guess I should be happy they didn't get 100."

I was speaking in the heat of the moment, and my words were reprinted all over the country. But after I thought about it, I realized it wasn't Houston's responsibility to take it easy on us. We were out there representing SMU and the Southwest Conference. But this all came to me in retrospect. At the time I was worried about the kids. Boy, they were resilient, though.

Dwelling on the loss would get us nowhere, and I told the team to forget Jack Pardee and the Houston Cougars. North Texas was next, and I wanted them to focus on the Mean Green. The North Texas quarterback, Scott Davis, helped the Mustangs refocus. Davis spoke out in the press, saying that he played teams in high school that were better than SMU. I made no mention of Davis or his statements to my players, but those comments sure picked up our preparation in practice.

Come Saturday, Mike Romo threw for a school-record 427 yards and 3 touchdowns, and his counterpart had a miserable day as our defense had Scott Davis running for his life all afternoon. Our first win over Connecticut will always be special, but the 35–9 victory over North Texas was no less satisfying.

———

Because we were shorthanded throughout that season, we had a young man who played both ways for us on occasion. His name was Uzo Okeke. Scott Smith, our running backs coach, had coached Uzo in high school, and I had great respect for Scott's opinion, so we brought him in. Uzo was about 250 pounds when he came to us, and we played him at defensive tackle. On goal line situations we sometimes put him in at tight end because he was a great run blocker. He made outstanding strides on the offensive line, so much so that during his senior season Uzo became a starter. In fact, he later played for me in Shreveport of the CFL, and with the Montreal Alouettes, Uzo became an All-Pro in the Canadian Football League.

———

I wasn't too crazy about having Notre Dame on the schedule. We were definitely not in the same class with the Irish, and I wasn't sure what could be gained by our kids getting beat up by a vastly superior squad. Two years earlier Notre Dame offered to cancel the game, and I wished we would have taken them up on their offer. But Doug Single wanted to play the Irish; he thought it would be good for us and good for recruiting. When we arrived in South Bend I had the bus driver take us to the stadium so the kids could look around. Before we left, the team captains came up to me and asked, "Could we have some time to walk around and look at the campus?"

I thought that since they were already signed and enrolled at SMU, what could it hurt?

"How much time do you need?" I asked.

"An hour," they said.

"I'll hold the buses for forty-five minutes."

The walk around campus apparently took a long detour to the university bookstore. The kids came back to the bus loaded down with T-shirts, sweatshirts, banners, anything with the Notre Dame logo.

Leading up to the game I tried to prepare them mentally. During the week, Corey Beard, one of our wide receivers asked, "What would happen if we won this game?"

"It would be the biggest upset in the history of football," I said.

"What would happen to us," Beard wanted to know.

"You would all be on *Good Morning America*, the *Today Show*, ESPN…"

They actually thought they could win the game!

Though I knew it was improbable, I wished there was some way we could get a lead. However brief, I just wanted us to have the lead at some point. On our opening drive we took the ball down field and made it well within field goal range. I started thinking, "If we score, the 3–0 will flash across the country—SMU beating Notre Dame—and that will be a boon for recruiting."

Well, we missed the kick. Matt Laminick was a religious young man. I called him over to me on the sideline and asked him, "When you got up there ready to kick, what went through your mind?"

"I lined up the kick," Matt said. "I looked at where the ball would be spotted, took my steps back to get lined up. I glanced up at the goal posts, and then beyond the goal posts I saw Touchdown Jesus. Then I thought, 'Maybe I'm not supposed to make this field goal.'"

As expected, Notre Dame beat us with ease, 59–6. In the later stages of the contest, with the outcome already decided, Irish coach Lou Holtz instructed his players to fair catch punts and to take delay-of-game penalties in an attempt to not drive up the score. I thought Lou's decision was honorable. Jack Pardee had a different opinion, however. "To me," Pardee was quoted as saying, "Notre Dame should be investigated for point shaving."

Our aim at the beginning of the season was to be a better team in December than we were in September, and I think we accomplished that goal. The proof, I believe, is how well we played in our season finale against the Cotton Bowl-bound Arkansas Razorbacks. We traveled to Little Rock and gave them everything they could handle. We even scored a touchdown with five minutes to go, giving us a 24–23 lead. Though we eventually fell 38–24, I appreciated the way the kids had come together and played as a team.

"You had it within your grasp," I told them. "This is what I've been trying to tell all of you for the last year and a half. There is nothing you can't accomplish if you work hard enough."

I looked each of those young men in the eye before addressing the room. "Thank you for giving me the greatest season in my football career. I've played with and coached some of the greatest players in the game's history, and let me tell you this—none of them could hold a candle to you fellas in this locker room."

When I accepted the opportunity to come home to SMU, I had no idea what to expect. It would be a challenge; that I knew. But never could I have anticipated how rewarding the experience would be. The 1989 SMU Mustangs may not have been as physically gifted as their opponents, but they competed. The scores and the record may not represent that fact, but those who saw the games will remember. We started something from nothing, and we built a program from scratch, and we built it the right way.

———

In April of 1990, Doug Single announced that he was leaving SMU. In the short time we worked together, Doug and I had a good relationship. The only thing we differed on was that Notre Dame game. When I asked him why he didn't cancel the contest against the Irish, Doug's response was an athletic director's answer: "Great payday." And he was right. I'm glad we played Notre Dame; it was a great experience for the kids. It was good for them to see the possibilities.

Now, with Doug gone, the university offered his position to me. I knew very little about an AD's responsibilities, but I was interested.

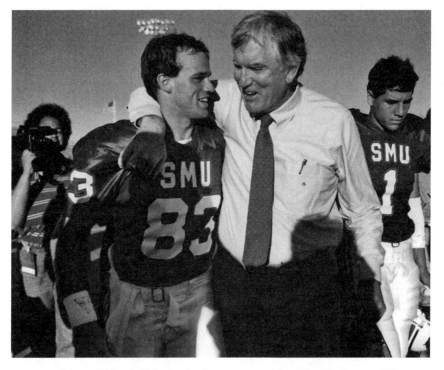

Walking off the field in my final game as coach of the Mustangs with Daniel Echols (#83) and Mark Martinez (#1).

Following some discussion with the trustees, I agreed to take the job with the caveat that I would coach the Mustangs that coming fall. I absolutely thought I'd be allowed to continue coaching beyond 1990.

Our first opponent on the 1990 schedule was Vanderbilt, an academic school with some five-year kids on their squad playing in a great conference, the SEC. We won on a day when everything seemed to go our way. That first win, however, seemed to go to our heads the next week against a Tulane team we should have competed against. The players were too loose, a fact that I noticed before the game started. As a coach, I always prided myself on believing we could beat anybody. Not necessarily that we were always the better team, but that we would compete. Losing to Tulane, losing the way we lost, angered me and still frustrates me to this day when I think about that game. But the defeat didn't stay with the kids long. And though our record for the remainder of the season didn't look like a success, I could see improvement. There was an infusion of new players, who proved to be great additions to the squad.

One of the freshmen who joined us that fall was wide receiver Brian Berry. Brian's first game as a starter came against the University of Texas. At one point in the game he went over the middle on a post pattern. Mike Romo hit Brian in stride with a perfect pass, and Brian took off down field. For a moment it looked like he might go all the way when a Longhorn linebacker clobbered him. Brian went down hard, but he held onto the ball. In a nice show of sportsmanship, the Texas player bent down and picked up Brian with one hand and set him on his feet. The Longhorn then said something to Brian and gave him a little push toward our huddle.

I don't know what was said but, boy, did Brian go berserk. Before he could reach his antagonist, a couple of our guys grabbed him and ushered him to our sideline.

"Brian," I said, "what in the world were you thinking?"

"Not only did he clobber me, knock me down, and give me a push, but he also said, 'This one's too small, I'm going to throw him back.'"

———

While I was in Green Bay I brought in Forrest Jr. as an intern. He wanted to get into coaching, and working with Mo and the defensive staff was great experience for him. Along with the defense, Forrest helped Willie Peete with the special teams. Later, when I came to SMU I was given permission to hire a few new coaches. One of those I brought aboard was Forrest Jr. as a defensive line and special teams coach. Against Rice in 1990, Forrest suggested we use an on-sides kick play that he and Willie Peete cooked up in Green Bay. The play was called "11-middle row."

We would put our two fastest guys on each side of the kicker. Those two players would take on the first opponents who arrived to contend for the ball and blast them. The kicker would barely put his foot to the ball, patiently follow the football, and then pounce on it once the ball traveled the required 10 yards. Sometimes the play would be called back because the ball wouldn't go 10 yards, and we'd just run the same play again. Against Rice we used 11-middle row several times to great effect. The rules people outlawed the play before the 1991 season. Apparently they deemed 11-middle row too risky, and they were afraid someone would get hurt. Why that particular play was more dangerous than a normal kickoff was lost on me.

We lost that game to Rice. In fact, we lost all our games after Vanderbilt. But even at 1-10, I didn't see the year as a failure. We were making strides. The kids were developing and learning the game, and I was looking forward to seeing what we could do the following fall with another year of experience under our belt.

I would be able to watch their progress. My view wouldn't be from the sideline, however. At the close of the season, I was told to make a decision: coach or athletic director? In no uncertain terms, I was informed that I couldn't continue the dual role. There was some concern that I would favor the football program over the university's other sports. That assertion was ridiculous. My intention was to hire an assistant AD, who would handle the day-to-day stuff while I was coaching, but I wasn't give the chance.

Coaching was my passion; it is what I hoped to do since my days at Sulphur Springs High School. But I had a concern. Who would the administration bring in to replace me as AD, and could I work with that person? With great hesitation I decided to continue on as the university's athletic director.

It was a bad decision.

Leaving a job unfinished is difficult, but the hardest thing was telling the kids that I had to step aside as their coach. It was an emotional moment for me. We all thought we'd be together working toward the same

Standing with SMU players Brian Berry (#81) and Mark Martinez (#1) as we give the sign of the Mustang "ears," part of a popular post-game ritual.

goal, and after promising that I'd be there with them for four years, I was leaving early.

"We faced the unknown together, and we came out wiser and stronger for having done that," I told them. "Thank you for the hard work and effort, for the dedication you displayed the year we didn't play. When all we did was practice, practice, practice, you all remained focused. I can't tell you how much I've appreciated each one of you."

I concluded with the mantra I'd been repeating since day one. "Keep your focus on education   it's important." And that they did. Everyone in that locker room left SMU with their degree, and that's the most gratifying stat of all.

The joy and satisfaction of being an athletic director is hard to measure. It's easy as a football coach—how many games did you win? As an AD, it's how much money did you raise? How are all the university's sports fairing? I was graded on that, but did I have anything to do with it? Hell, I don't know.

———

By 1990, the need for a new football stadium was obvious. Ownby just didn't work. Visiting teams had to dress across the street, and it just wasn't a good situation for a Division I school. We took our home games back to the Cotton Bowl, but that old edifice was being refurbished. Ideally, though, football games should be played on campus, and there were some alumni willing to donate money for the construction of a new stadium. But I was told by the university president to "absolutely under no circumstances mention the building of a new stadium."

I certainly didn't enjoy the job as much as coaching. I missed the competition and the challenge that came with each new game. Even more, I missed working with the young men on a day-to-day basis. It's family. The job of athletic director was a very solitary position. In my free time I found myself going to the football offices to talk with the coaches. Sometimes it would be the basketball coaches, anything to be closer to the games and speak with people to whom I could relate.

That's not to say the athletic director's job wasn't challenging. I succeeded in the mission I was given—keep the kids in school, set them on the course to graduate. We had a lot of success across the athletic department. I hired three coaches during my tenure—golf, tennis, and women's basketball—and they all went on to contribute greatly to our program.

———

**Barbara and I with the kids, sometime after their
graduation from college.**

J. I. Albright didn't drop out of my life after our 1956 meeting. He was the
first agent I ever came across, and though I didn't hire J.I. to represent me, he
stayed in contact with me through the years, especially when I was in Toronto.
Few people knew the Canadian Football League better than J.I., and if I
needed to know something about the league, or an appraisal of a player in the
CFL, he was the man I would consult. While I was at SMU, J.I. went to work
for the Ottawa Roughriders and the team's owner, Bernie Glieberman. Bernie had a construction company based in Detroit called Crosswinds, which
focused on building affordable single-family homes for young couples.

When the CFL announced its intention to expand into the States for the '93 season, Bernie wanted one of the franchises, and he was granted the Shreveport club. Through J.I., the Gliebermans contacted me about coaching their new team, the Pirates. I hadn't given much thought to leaving SMU, but my role as the athletic director just didn't match standing on the sidelines. During Super Bowl week in 1993 I was approached by the Kansas City Chiefs concerning their head coaching position. And though I gave the proposition of coaching the Chiefs and reuniting with Lamar Hunt some thought, neither Barbara nor I wanted to relocate our home. Still, I was willing to listen to what the Gliebermans had to say.

We met at the Dallas airport, and the three of us got acquainted. I was impressed with Bernie and came away from the meeting liking both him and Lonie a lot. Despite having interest in the opportunity, I felt the need to turn it down. The Southwest Conference was in the midst of disbanding, and I didn't want to walk out on SMU at the time. A year later, however, when the Gliebermans approached a second time, the university had settled into the Western Athletic Conference, and the athletic department was on solid footing.

The Pirates had entered their second training camp in the spring of 1994 when I received a phone call from Jim Garner, who worked with Lonie in marketing the Shreveport club.

"We're going to let our coach go," Jim explained. "It just isn't working out with him. Would you have an interest?"

The time was right now. "Yes, I would."

Lonie and Jim came to Dallas, and the three of us had dinner.

"We're in a bind," Lonie told me. "We'll do anything and everything we can to make this work for you. You've got carte blanche to run the team."

Before I said yes, I took Barbara to Louisiana to scout the Shreveport area. We liked what we saw. Shreveport was just three hours away from Dallas. I could go and coach, and we didn't have to stay there year round.

We went to Shreveport, where I served as the Pirates' general manager and head coach for two seasons. Unfortunately, the town just wasn't big enough to support a professional football team. Ask Lonie, and he'll tell you we drew twenty thousand a game, but in reality it was closer to fifteen thousand. Following the 1995 season, the Gliebermans tried to keep the franchise afloat by moving it to Virginia. We worked hard on finding a suitable home, but we just couldn't find a stadium to house our games. Old Dominion was the best option, but the field was Astroturf, and nearly everything inside the stadium needed to be updated. Besides, we got the distinct impression that the university wanted nothing to do with football in the fear that it might prompt calls for the school to bring back their program.

With no home for the Pirates, the CFL incursion into the United States came to a screeching halt. Playing Canadian football in the Deep South was a strange experience. The fans didn't totally understand the rules despite Lonie's valiant attempts to educate them to the nuanced differences between the NFL and the CFL. Still, I was always asked, "Why don't you run the ball more?"

"We only got one down to do it," I'd explain. But the game never caught on.

———

Ten years later the Gliebermans were back in the CFL and back in Ottawa. During that decade I remained closely tied to Bernie and Lonie. I had been working for Bernie on a number of projects, including putting together a couple of ski hills in the Upper Peninsula of Michigan—Mt. Bohemia and Porcupine Mountains. It's a pristine place on Lake Superior. They called them mountains, but they're really hills. And now that they were back in football, the Gliebermans asked if I would like to join them as the general manager of the Roughriders for the '05 season.

My second journey to Canada wasn't an enjoyable experience—for me or for the Gliebermans. The Ottawa media, mostly the local sports radio shows, criticized Bernie while he was dumping a lot of his own cash into the team. In Ottawa they don't like American ownership, and they liked me even less due to my NFL experience.

There were two writers in Ottawa, Don Brennan and Matt Sekeres, who knew football. They knew the game as well as any scribe in Green Bay or Cleveland, and I got along well with them. But I can't say the same about others in the Ottawa media. Sports talk radio had grown exponentially over the previous decade and a half and had become a fundamental part of sports coverage. During my time in Cleveland, Pete Franklin was *the* voice on the air. And while I was in Cincinnati that role was filled by Bob Trumpy. Bob had been a member of the Bengals from the team's inception in 1968 until he retired following the 1977 season. I really liked Bob. He knew the game and always had an opinion. More importantly, he was fair, as was Pete Franklin, but as sports talk radio became more commonplace on both sides of the border, fair wasn't always a prerequisite for the hosts.

Sports radio is nothing without controversy. The radio hosts in Ottawa didn't care if we did something right, or if we played a good game. All they were interested in was stirring up the muck. Most of them didn't know the first thing about football. They were complete imbeciles.

Regardless of what we did, we were always wrong. According to Ottawa's talking heads, we, me in particular, didn't know anything about Canadian football. We spent one full season there, 2005, before Bernie decided he'd had enough.

"You buy one of these teams, you're supposed to enjoy the experience," Bernie told me. "I'm not enjoying it and neither is Lonie. I'm going to get out."

I completely agreed with him.

I'm sure those critics in Ottawa wished they weren't so hard on Bernie because they might still have a team in town if they'd treated him decently.

11

IT'S JUST NOT THE SAME

WHEN I WAS A PLAYER I'D SEE OLD TIMERS COMING BACK for reunions, and I'd say, "I'm not going to do that when I get old." I thought the same thing when I was coaching. At that time I was busy with my job, so I had a viable excuse for not attending those gatherings. And I stayed away. I stayed away for years and years. Finally in the fall of 2008, I decided to go back, but it was more for Barbara than anything else. Lee Roy Caffey's widow, Dana, was going to be there, along with their daughters, Jennifer and Lee Ann, and Barbara really wanted to see them. I thought if I'm ever going to go, I might as well go now and see what I had been missing.

The Packers were playing the Cowboys at Lambeau on Sunday night, September 21. Willie Davis and I were walking along by the stands going to the field. A lot of people called out, "Hey, Coach!" some said "Forrest!" Different people remember me for different roles I've had.

Standing between two of my greatest opponents, at the Hall of Fame in 2007. That's Gino Marchetti on the left, Deacon Jones on the right.

A number of my former teammates were there. In addition to Willie there Jim Grabowski, Marv Fleming, Lew Carpenter, Donny Anderson, Jerry Kramer, and Boyd Dowler among others. Hank Bullough was there, as were some guys who played for me. I saw Walter Stanley, and I flashed back to Thanksgiving Day, 1986.

With time running out in the second half, we had a chance to beat Detroit. As the Lions were ready to punt from deep in their own territory, I knew we would have good field position, and I wanted to save time for our offense, so I told Walter to fair catch the ball. I guess I might as well have been talking to myself.

It was a high punt, and I followed the ball with my eyes, and then glanced at Walter who wasn't making any indication of calling a fair catch. He caught the ball, started to the left, and then came back around to the right near our sideline. As he passed by me I yelled out to him, "You'd better score!" and he did. Walter got the touchdown and we won, so I couldn't be mad at him.

It's memories like that—moments in time that make you smile. And I enjoyed seeing a lot of guys I hadn't seen in years. The atmosphere had changed, though. The stadium is built up higher than it used to be with additional seating and numerous luxury boxes. You used to be able to look up and identify the person in the top row of the stadium.

I walked out onto the field at Lambeau and looked around, but you can't recapture what happened there, even in your own mind. The grass is still there, but everything is different. It's just not the same.

———

At first glance, the game on the field today doesn't look all that different from the game I played fifty years ago. On the whole, though, players are bigger, stronger, and faster (notice I didn't say better). A lot of players in my day would use training camp to get in shape. The offseason was time away from the game, and most of us had to work during those months. I did my best to remain in playing condition year round. When the weather warmed up, I'd go to a local high school stadium and practice. I'd practice getting off the ball as quick as I could. I would do grass drills on my own, run sprints and some laps; as a rule I'd run a mile, sometimes two miles.

Weights, however, were never a part of my workout regiment. Today, I'm fairly certain that every player is involved with weight training, even place kickers. The NFL today is a year-round job, and staying in condition is a player's priority. In fact, they are *paid* to work out in the offseason. That is difficult for me to understand. They have a job. They're professional football players. They're asked to work out in the offseason, and to induce them to do it, they get paid! I always thought it was a player's obligation—his job, his responsibility. Teams have "voluntary" workouts, but they are voluntary in name only. If a player doesn't report to a "voluntary" workout, his absence is certainly held against him.

Through most of my playing career very few players worked out with weights. As I mentioned earlier, Jimmy Taylor was the only member of the Packers who regularly used weights. Late in my Packer career, when I was a player/coach, I overheard some talk in the weight room. Weight training had just begun to take hold in the league. As the guys were lifting a couple of players talked about some type of anabolic steroids. They discussed what this steroid did for you, how it allowed you to train longer and harder. I had no idea if anybody on the team was using them. Nor did I know as a coach, though I had my suspicions. A player would suddenly have a significant weight gain, setting off my radar.

Recently, I spoke with a former player, a man who played for a division rival in the seventies. He explained to me that he'd used steroids because it was the only way he could keep his weight up.

Lyle Alzado was the man who initially brought steroids to the attention of the public at large. At the time Lyle made his steroid use known, he was dying. His admission and subsequent death raised the awareness not only of football fans, but it forced the league to stand up and take notice of steroid abuse.

A small change in how the game is played today, but one that irks me to no end, is how players are rested at the end of a winning season. In the last week or two of the season, when a team has no incentive to win because they have already attained home field advantage or they're locked into a playoff seed, the head coach sits his quarterback or some other "key" players...but they never sit a lineman. If I were playing on that team, such a decision would tell

WINNING IN THE TRENCHES

me all I need to know about my coach and my value to the team.

Today's game also is more closely monitored. While today the players are stronger and bigger, much of the violence has been eradicated from the game. Over the last few decades there have been a number of rule changes taken for protective measures:

- Defensive players can't lead with their helmet when making a tackle.
- Defensive backs can't use what was called a "clothes line" tackle.
- The bump and run was outlawed in the seventies. Before that time, the defensive back was allowed to engage the receiver all the way down the field, as long the offensive player was in front of the defender. Now, after 5 yards, a bump is "illegal contact." The rule change was largely attributed to Steelers corner back Mel Blount, who perfected a physical style of play.
- The horse-collar tackle, when a player is taken down by the back of his jersey, was outlawed in the last couple of years. Heck, you used to be allowed to tackle by the face mask.
- The defense was allowed to tackle the quarterback in just about any way, even by the head, during my playing days. Now they can't be tackled below the knees. About the only place a defender can hit a quarterback today is around the waist. If I was coaching a defensive line today, I don't know what I'd tell my players about tackling the quarterback. I'd say, "Get him," but I don't know how.

I'm not applauding or complaining about the alterations to the game that decreased the level of violence in football, I am simply pointing out changes. As a head coach I was always involved with the Competition

Committee. Each team had a vote. Paul cast our ballot in Cincinnati, and Judge Parins did the same in Green Bay. I had a little more sway with the judge than I did with Paul, but PB listened to my opinions, and I always felt we were on the same page. Paul, like the Rooneys in Pittsburgh, believed we had a good game and didn't need drastic changes.

I got to know Tex Schramm during my one season in Dallas. Tex was the head of the committee. He was a forward-looking man. Years before anyone else was pushing for it, Tex wanted to add instant replay to the game. He would bring it up every year and finally it was passed in 1986. I wasn't a big fan of it at first, admittedly because I didn't know enough about it. I believed that officials are hired, they're trained to do a job, they're taught the rules, and they're honorable people with good judgment. By implementing the replay, I was concerned that officials would be second-guessing themselves and looking over their shoulders. It's not an electronic game; it's a football game. Additionally, they were always pushing to make games shorter and instant replay would only lengthen them. With that said, once they did the experimentation I was sold on instant replay and believe it's a good addition to the game.

But rule changes and year-round training are just part of the NFL evolution.

Nothing has altered the game or changed the landscape of the NFL more than the explosion of television and the increased revenue brought by increased popularity of the league. Everyone associated with professional football profited from the windfall—players, coaches, owners, even fans benefited from the increased exposure of the game.

I never met Bert Bell, the NFL commissioner at the time I joined the Packers, but I heard his voice once a year via speaker phone. The annual address always came at the end of training camp. "Gentlemen, just to remind you, if you can't get along with the people you're playing with, you're free to play out your option."

We would all look at one another and laugh. Nobody, but nobody played out their option back then.

The commissioner would continue, "Now, during the offseason you need to get a job so you can save part of your football earnings."

Nearly every player in those days worked in the offseason. A few guys had the opportunity to do an endorsement or two. For instance, Gary Knafelc, a Green Bay teammate, was an aspiring actor, and he was offered a role in a cigarette commercial. The problem was, Gary didn't know how to smoke so he had to learn. My few endorsements weren't complicated. One of them was with a local snowmobile dealer; all I had to do was lean against a snowmobile. That was as glamorous as my extracurricular work got. For a couple of years I worked as a car salesmen and then later with the local Budweiser distributor. Initially, my job consisted of loading and unloading cases of beer off of a truck. In later years, though, I worked in marketing for the distributor. The most I made as a pro football player was forty-five thousand dollars in 1970, not much by today's standards, but it was a good living at the time.

But things change. Television exploded the popularity of pro football, salaries increased, players were granted free agency, and some team owners took free agency for their franchises. While I was still playing, the Cardinals relocated from Chicago to St. Louis. A few decades later they moved again to Arizona. The Raiders went from Oakland to Los Angeles then back to Oakland. The NFL tried to prevent Al Davis from moving his team to L.A., only to lose in court. Davis's legal victory opened the floodgates. Any team with a stadium issue threatened to pick up and go to another city, one with a sweeter stadium deal. The Oilers took off for Nashville. The Rams filled the void left in St. Louis. I understood why the Rams left. The city of St. Louis built a stadium for the Rams that they wouldn't agree to construct for the Cardinals. The same thing happened when the Oilers bolted for Nashville. A few years later Houston captured an expansion team with a new state-of-the-art stadium. In 1984, Baltimore had its Colts taken away in the dead of night, and nine years later took the Browns from Cleveland. That was the move that surprised me the most—Cleveland without the Browns was hard to imagine.

There were other teams that used the leverage of leaving their home city, which forced the hand of local governments and taxpayers to build them new homes. Eventually the city of Cleveland built the stadium that Art Modell had wanted for years, and a new Browns team was born.

Players, too, chased the highest dollar. It's a funny thing. With free agency and salary caps, it's difficult to keep a winning ball club together for any length of time. I sometimes wonder what would have happened had free agency been available in my day. With all those Hall of Famers and All Pro players on our Green Bay teams, we would have been torn apart.

Before the merger, we had some leverage with the AFL, but our loyalties weren't always to the highest paycheck. I had my own opportunity to jump when I was told that Lamar Hunt said, "I'll pay him anything he wants." I didn't pursue the clandestine offer because we were just starting to build something in Green Bay. Being in Green Bay all those years has been so important in my life and career. Playing for Lombardi meant so much to me personally; I wouldn't have traded it for anything.

———

Playing for him greatly influenced my own coaching style, of course. Following each of my professional coaching tenures, one or two of my disgruntled former players would question my coaching style and methods in the press. The most common complaint was that I worked my team too hard. But I never wavered from my philosophy or beliefs. Still, playing was easier than coaching. All I had to do when I pulled on a uniform was worry about one guy—number 75. I had to get him ready to play Sunday, get him up for that week's opponent. And I knew his character.

So many of the Bengal players I coached went on to successful careers post-football. Everybody sees Cris Collinsworth on TV. Gary Burley is working with kids in Georgia. Max Montoya owns a chain of restaurants. At one time Reggie Williams was a city councilman in Cincinnati and today works for Disney World in Orlando. Bo Harris is in the finance business in Shreveport. Anthony Munoz has a foundation; Isaac Curtis is in the hotel business. I could go on and on. There was a common thread on those teams, and that was a quality of character in the locker room.

We set out to draft quality people with a good work ethic. The number one priority, of course, is can he play in the NFL? And then, do I want to draft him where his ability puts him in the draft? Of course some of these guys are risky. They might have football talent, but what they do off the field makes a coach nervous. Don't get me wrong—as I said earlier, you don't want choir boys on your side, but high character is imperative to a successful football team.

Before we drafted a player, we talked to the college coaches as well as the agent, but their business is to promote the kid. They want the athlete shown in the best possible light. Sometimes the problem with a player doesn't manifest itself until down the road. If you draft a player with a troubled past, you shouldn't be surprised when it surfaces again. But there have been some that I drafted with a clean background that ran into trouble.

Every fall weekend I find myself in front of a television. Saturday and Sunday, I keep up on both college and pro ball and keep an eye on my old teams. Yes, the game has changed, but it pulls me in still.

To some, my brief stint in Ottawa might appear to be an inglorious conclusion to an otherwise proud career, but I don't see it that way. If nothing else, the experience further cemented my friendship with Bernie and

Lonie Glieberman. Today, I guess you could say I'm "semi-retired." I still work with Bernie and Lonie and their Crosswinds Company, doing some consulting and public relations duties. I also do a few personal appearances and a couple of card shows a year. Other than that, Barbara and I keep pretty busy with a nice active life in Colorado Springs. My health is good, especially for an old football player.

We try to see the kids as often as we can. Karen is in Sante Fe with her husband, Jim Spehar, and Forrest is in Cincinnati with his wife, Rebecca. We get to New Mexico and Ohio as often as we can, and they all love to visit Colorado Springs.

I think back to playing catch with Forrest Jr. He got so used to having me, at six feet, four inches, as a target that when he played with his friends his throws would invariably sail over their heads.

And there was the time I took Karen for a little drive. She had always been very smart, but her grades suddenly began to slip. We drove to a nearby park, and I pulled over to a picnic area.

"Is there something going on in your life that Mom and I don't know about?" I asked.

Karen seemed a bit confused by my question. "No," she said.

A little perspective was needed.

"Karen, do you know that it hasn't been that long since women weren't allowed to vote? Things are changing quickly. Before your life is over and maybe before I'm gone, there will be a woman president. If you don't make good grades in school, it won't be you."

Well, the grades picked up, but Karen's not president, not yet at least.

There was a period of time when I thought my days with Barbara and the kids were limited. That was my fear—not being around to see Forrest and Karen grow into adulthood, not being able to grow old with Barbara. But I was given a second lease on life for which I will be eternally grateful. Since my cancer surgery, Barbara and I have become good friends with

(Right) Forrest Jr. with his wife, Rebecca. (Below) Karen and her husband, Jim Spehar.

Dr. James Sampliner and his wife, Betsy. We try to get together every St. Patrick's Day, the anniversary of my melanoma surgery, for a celebratory dinner. I remember the first time we saw James: He pulled up in an old collector's Mustang. He was younger than I was, probably in his late thirties. Barbara took one look and said, "You're not going to let that young guy operate on you, are you?"

But I intrinsically trusted him and had faith in his abilities. It is not an overstatement when I say I owe him my life. Betsy and James are not only our good friends, but we have history, and to me there's nothing better than that.

———

When people think back to their upbringing, they tend to think about the good times. The good things stand out. Personally, I never have been a person to dwell on the bad. My life was not ideal while I was growing up, but there were a lot of people who had a hard time. I don't hold grudges. Some people can never forget a slight or an offense of any nature. I don't regret my upbringing, that's just the way it was, and I have the ability to accept things as they came to me.

I went to bed hungry many nights, but I prefer not to dredge up those memories. I would rather remember the people in the Sulphur Springs community who reached out to a young man in need. Who provided me with a place to live, who gave me clothes when I had nothing to wear, and offered me a meal when I had little to eat. There is a tendency for me to think back on the good times, when looking back on my upbringing. As a teenager I picked cotton, but the money I earned didn't go in my pocket; it went to the family. There were little ones in the family who couldn't pull their load, and it was my duty to do my part to make it work. During the time I was growing up, there were things that were great. Those are the times I like to remember. But I don't dwell on the bad.

Occasionally my phone will ring and on the other end of the line will be one of my SMU kids. The message is often the same: "Coach, take care of yourself. And remember that I love you."

That will get your attention.

When I returned to SMU in '88, I knew that I wouldn't be judged solely on the number of wins we accumulated. Our success on the field would be limited, we knew that going in, but I knew we could make certain these kids got an education.

After I left the program I was sitting at home one day when the doorbell rang. On the front step was Corey Beard, a player of mine from SMU. I asked him to step inside and asked what brought him here.

"Coach, I just came to tell you that I graduated from SMU."

Corey was the last on my list. Now all of my kids had earned their degrees.

I gave him a big hug.

"That's why I came here," he said.

———

Football has played an enormous role in my life. It's brought me honors, provided lifelong friendships, gave me the satisfaction of watching so many of my players thrive, and football has afforded my family and me a comfortable life. When I was a fifteen-year-old high school student watching my first football game and playing in that same game, I would have never believed just how much football would dominate my life. But I had a determination, an inner drive to succeed. When I was coaching in Green Bay, I used to tell my players, "Every man on the street envies you and your job, but if it were easy, everybody would be out there playing on Sundays."

Every man who played the game paid a physical price along the way, and I was no different. Yes, I did have some natural athletic ability, but nothing came to me without a lot of hard work. Hard work and support—a whole lot of support.

Walking with Forrest Jr. and Karen, a long time ago....

APPENDIX

Pro Bowl Selection
1959, 1960, 1961, 1962, 1963, 1964, 1966, 1967, 1968

Associated Press/All Pro
1960, 1962, 1963, 1964, 1965, 1966, 1967

All-NFL
1960, 1961, 1962, 1963, 1964 1965, 1966, 1967
188 consecutive games played 1956-1971

All-Time Teams
• The Sporting News 100 Greatest Football Players—#28
• Silver Anniversary Super-Bowl All-Time team
• NFL's 1960's All Decade Team
• NFL's 75th Anniversary Team

• 1976 Associated Press Coach of the Year
• 1981 UPI AFC Coach of the Year
• 1982 Touchdown Club of Columbus Coach of the Year

Halls of Fame
• Sulphur Springs High School Hall of Fame   • Texas High School Football Hall of Fame
• Texas Sports Hall of Fame   • Southern Methodist University Athletic Hall of Fame
• East-West Shrine Game Hall of Fame   • Green Bay Packers Hall of Fame
• Professional Football Hall of Fame

MARIE LOMBARDI
Speech presenting Forrest Gregg to the Professional Football Hall of Fame, July 30, 1977

Last night our very distinguished commissioner spoke about Forrest Gregg's record as a player, and it is absolutely spectacular. I'm not going to try and repeat it because I'll probably forget it and won't remember half of it anyway or maybe get it all wrong. But I'd like to talk about Forrest Gregg.

I read somewhere that Vince Lombardi made football players out of men and men out of football players. But not this man. He was probably the finest all-around team player that ever played this game. Proof of the fact being that when he was an All-Pro tackle with the Packers he was willing to make the supreme sacrifice of switching from tackle to guard when he was needed. And to be able to make that switch and to be able to make All-Pro guard at that position.

When Forrest was about thirty years old, maybe he would start to look to his future. He was offered a coaching job at the University of Tennessee. After a very short time he had second thoughts about it. So the coach and I were down in Puerto Rico, and needless to say he was pretty upset about this chain of events. And one night in our room the phone rang. It was one of the assistant coaches who said, 'Vince, Forrest Gregg wants to come back and play. Do you want him?'

Well, friends, Vince yells so loud through the phone, the room shook, the building shook, and even the ground shook. He wanted Forrest back so bad, and Forrest, you might have signed the first million-dollar contract in the National Football League because he wanted you so bad. Because, how do you replace a Forrest Gregg as a player, as a coach, as a man, and as a friend? And to use the old clichés of honesty, integrity, commitment to excellence, dedication, may sound old and tired, but I don't know of any man who these apply to more than Forrest Gregg. And if you take these qualities and apply them to Forrest Gregg the coach, who will demand them of his players, how can he miss? And last year he was voted Coach of the Year.

This is very emotional for me because as I stand here today, I think of how Vince Lombardi would feel seeing three of his sons so honored. Men like Forrest Gregg, Frank Gifford, Bill Willis, Gale Sayers, Bart Starr—these men are the elite, along with the other men in this great Hall of Fame, they are the elite of the National Football League. They are the men who reached the top.

Forrest, you join this elite group, and from your friends in Green Bay, your family, your teammates, your team in Cleveland, and your boss, Art Modell, from Vince Lombardi wherever he may be, and from me—we love you, we wish you luck, congratulations.

This must be your finest hour. Thank you for letting me be a part of it.

FORREST GREGG
Hall of Fame induction speech, July 30, 1977

I knew that the time would come and I would be the one who got up here and tried to tell you people exactly how I felt about being inducted into the National Football League Hall of Fame. I could think of a lot of things to say. I could think of a lot of things I should say, but I think what happened this morning was the most emotional thing that has happened to me in my lifetime. As I went down that street in the parade, I saw friends that I knew and I saw my family sitting on the side. It made me think back to how it all started and I don't want to get too deep into this right now, and how it all started because I'm already pretty emotional about it. But as I look out and see my family, I think about how empty this would be, how little it would mean, if I did not have them to share it with.

Sometimes in the game of football, not just professional football, but in all football, the families sometimes are left a little bit to the side. But I can tell you this much right now. If it had not been for my wife, Barbara, her love and encouragement, I wouldn't be standing here right now. My two children, Karen my daughter and Forrest Jr. my son; they have known nothing in their lives except professional football.

I sit and I listen to Marie Lombardi talk about Vince Lombardi, talk about the Green Bay Packers. Marie, I would have given anything in the world to have known that Vince said that on the telephone. I would have asked for a lot more money. Vince Lombardi—I can't stand up here without mentioning his name and think about what he did for me, and I know when Bart gets up here, he's going to say the same thing. This man was the maximum, for lack of a better adjective to describe him, as a man and as a football coach. And this lady who sits back here and presented me, we have such a great love for her that it is hard to express right here.

When the time came and Earl called me and told me that I'd been selected to be in the National Football League's Hall of Fame, I could think of but one person I should immediately call and share this with, and that was Marie Lombardi.

I mentioned a couple of minutes ago about professional football and what this means. I think Frank Gifford really expressed a lot of our sentiments about this game. I spent fifteen years as a player. I don't know how many years I'll spend as a coach, but I can tell you here and now that this is the greatest business in the world. I can't think of anything in this world that I'd rather be than a head coach in the National Football League and the coach of the Cleveland Browns.

To reflect back for just one moment, I think there are some people in my past that I need to thank. I know everybody thinks first to his beginning in football. I think about those high school coaches I had, who had an interest in me, and got me started on the right track. I think about my college coaches, who were all interested in me and who did so much to further my career. I'm so pleased, since I went into professional football in 1956 with Bart Starr, who is behind me, to be inducted in that same group. This to me is an elite bunch of people, the ones who are seated behind me right here—Frank Gifford, Bart Starr, Bill Willis, and Gale Sayers. It means so much to me to go in with people of this caliber. And I just have to say, once again, that there is no thrill on earth like the one that I got when I stood up here and spoke to you people realizing that I was one of ninety-three people who ever played the game of football who will be put in that house.

ABOUT THE AUTHORS

Forrest Gregg is a member of the National Football League Hall of Fame. After playing on six world championship teams, he coached the Cleveland Browns and the Cincinnati Bengals in the NFL, as well as three teams in the Canadian Football League. A graduate of Southern Methodist University, he also served the school as its football coach and athletic director. He lives in Colorado Springs, Colorado, with his wife, Barbara.

Andrew O'Toole is the author of seven books, most recently *Paul Brown: The Rise and Fall and Rise Again of Football's Most Innovative Coach* (Clerisy Press) and *Sweet William: The Life of Billy Conn* (University of Illinois Press). He lives in Lebanon, Ohio, with his wife, Mickie.